Frontier and Pioneer Recollections of Early Days in San Antonio and West Texas

Vinton Lee James

Frontier and Pioneer Recollections of
Early Days in San Antonio and West Texas

Vinton Lee James

Originally Published by the Author
San Antonio, Texas 1938

This edition edited and re-set by Stephen A. Engelking
© 2025 Texianer Verlag
Johannesstr. 12
78609 Tuningen
Germany

www.texianer.com
ISBN: 978-3-910667-20-4

Cover Illustration:
City Hall, San Antonio, Texas (postcard, c. 1906)
Raphael Tuck & Sons – The University of Houston
Digital Library: http://digital.lib.uh.edu

Editor's Preface

I came across this book whilst carrying out genealogical research into my family history. The author of this book is related to me through the marriage of his grandmother to one of my ancestors.

In trying to locate a copy of the book for myself and our family archives, I discovered that the book was decades out of print and the only extant copy was on sale for around $800!

So I determined, coincidentally at the same age as the author, to completely reset the book so that it could be available in all current formats to a wider audience interested in Texas' fascinating history.

I hope you will enjoy reading it.

Stephen A. Engelking

Dedication
To the Memory of my father
John James
and my mother
Annie Milby James

Foreword

The material presented in this book is the result of years of experience and effort to present phases of life in early San Antonio and West Texas to the present citizens. Many of these articles have been written over a period of years and published in newspapers and magazines throughout the country.

I wish to acknowledge my thanks to the Editors of The San Antonio Express, The San Antonio Light, Sports Afield, and The Frontier Times, in which periodicals some of these chapters first appeared; and to Mr. C. A. Goethe, and Mrs. Betty Stevens Keller, for picture and photograph, and Mrs. Josephine Polley Golsen for family records.

PREFACE

My object in writing this book is, first, to perpetuate the memory of my father, who at the early age of 18 years came to Texas in 1837 from Nova Scotia and carved out of this new republic a place for himself and his posterity. My close association with him on his long surveying expeditions in locating vacant lands in West Texas, in visiting and supervising his sheep ranch in Uvalde County and his cattle ranch in Uvalde and Kinney Counties, endeared him to me. Through him I conceived a knowledge of these vast unfenced plains of Texas from the Gulf of Mexico to the Panhandle and a practical knowledge of sheep and cattle. He it was who instilled in me the finest concepts of life, and his strong, simple, rugged nature has been an inspiration and guide to me all my life. He fostered in me that natural love of the outdoors and wild life and encouraged me in the clean sports natural to a man who lives close to nature — hunting and fishing.

As I have been benefited and my vision enlarged through his generous nature, so I want my children and their children to know something of his simple greatness.

Secondly, as I have enjoyed the companionship of my father and the stories of his early life and endeavors, so I feel that my sons and daughters have enjoyed and will continue to enjoy my many interesting adventures and experiences. In my long life of eighty years, I have witnessed the great plains of West Texas thronging with thousands of cattle of many different brands; I have known the depletion of these herds through the many droughts and through the great cattle drives to Kansas; I have seen the sheep business supplant the cattle business, flourish and then decline; I have vivid recollections of conditions and hardships after the Civil War; I have seen the fencing of the vacant lands and pastures, I have seen the useless and wanton slaughter of the native wild game, and I have consistently sought the passage of game laws to protect this wild life from extinction; I have served the City of San Antonio as auditor from 1899 to 1905 and at this time had access to old records from which I derived much interesting information—much of which I used in writing these articles.

"The old order changeth yielding place to new" and the romantic days of my youth and the youth of Texas is passing and will soon be relegated to the pages of history. My children will want to know what part in the development of this great land I had and will relish the knowledge that in their veins flows the blood of the pioneer.

The love of the great outdoors, which is so strong in me, I have endeavored to transmit to my offspring, and many happy days have been spent by the whole family camping on the streams of Texas or living on the cattle ranches of the plains.

Again I hope my old friends whom I have known through the years and who have shared many of these experiences with me may relive in memory the days that are gone. May they join with me again in these youthful days of gaiety and freedom and happiness.

And finally, may the generations yet to come read these pages and rejoice that such days and experiences have been and regret that they too cannot taste the freedom and tang of the days when men drank deeply of life in this great state of Texas.

May 2/38
VINTON L. JAMES

Contents

I.	THE CROSSKILLS	11
II.	THE JAMES CONNECTIONS	15
III.	JOHN JAMES	17
IV.	JAMES' BUSINESS ACTIVITY	23
V.	THE COURT HOUSE FIGHT	29
VI.	JAMES GOES WITH HIS CATTLE ON A LONG DRIVE TO CALIFORNIA	31
VII.	PERSONALITY AND APPEARANCE OF JOHN JAMES	35
VIII.	FAMILY OF JOHN JAMES	37
IX.	ATTENDS THE FIRST PROTESTANT CHURCH SERVICE HELD IN SAN ANTONIO	41
X.	SOME RECOLLECTIONS OF THE WRITER	43
XI.	BELIEVED IN GOOD EDUCATION	45
XII.	THE DEATH OF JOHN JAMES	47
XIII.	THE ESTATE OF JOHN JAMES	49
XIV.	NOTES	51
XV.	AMNESTY PAROLE	53

PART TWO *Personal Recollections of Vinton Lee James*

I.	EARLY BOYHOOD	59
II.	RECONSTRUCTION DAYS	61
III.	PUBLIC DISASTERS	69
IV.	EARLY HUNTING EXPERIENCE	71
V.	POLECARPO RODRIGUEZ, HUNTER AND INDIAN FIGHTER	75
VI.	THE POLLEY FAMILY	77
VII.	JAMES BRITTON BAILEY	79
VIII.	J. H. POLLEY	81
IX.	MY VISITS TO THE POLLEY MANSION	85
X.	RECUPERATION	91
XI.	SCHOOL DAYS	93
XII.	RANCH LIFE	97
XIII.	BUSINESS VENTURES	99
XIV.	POLITICS	103
XV.	MY FRIENDS, THE HUNTERS	105
XVI.	WESTERN TEXAS SIXTY-FOUR YEARS AGO	109
XVII.	RECOLLECTIONS OF THE SHEEP RANGE	123

XVIII. RECOLLECTION OF A TRIP TO CALIFORNIA 55 YEARS AGO. 135

PART THREE *San Antonio*
I. SAN ANTONIO 98 YEARS AGO 145
II. OLD TIMES IN SAN ANTONIO 149
III. EARLY SCHOOLS IN SAN ANTONIO 157
IV. SAN ANTONIO AND ITS PEOPLE HISTORICAL HIGH LIGHTS 163
V. CITY OF SAN ANTONIO 167
VI. PROMINENT MEN AND WOMEN 171
VII. SOCIAL LIFE IN SAN ANTONIO 179
VIII. LIFE OF COLONEL H. B. ANDREWS 193
IX. MAYOR THIELEPAPE AND THE CITIZENS OF SAN ANTONIO 199
X. EARLY GERMAN IMMIGRATION TO TEXAS 203
XI. COMMERCE STREET 217
XII. MARKET STREET 231

PART FOUR *Western Texas*
I. THE STORY OF WEST TEXAS 243
II. THE COYOTE AND LOBO WOLF PERIL 251
III. JAMES DUNN, THE TEXAS RANGER 255
IV. ALONG THE NUECES WITH ROD AND GUN 259
V. THE DEVIL'S RIVER OF TEXAS 267
VI. A FISHING TRIP TO DEVIL'S RIVER 275
VII. MY FIRST TARPON 289
VIII. A WINTER'S HUNT IN WESTERN TEXAS 295
IX. HUNTING IN THE GUADALUPE MOUNTAINS 305
X. HUNTING DEER BY STARLIGHT 313
XI. HUNTING IN WESTERN TEXAS 319
XII. TEXAS 325

I. THE CROSSKILLS

Captain John Crosskill of the British navy, the grandfather of John James, was the founder of Bridgetown, Nova Scotia, in 1822, He was born in Norwich, England, in the year 1749. Nothing is known of his parents.

He and his brother were cared for by an aunt, who lived in Black Friars, London. After having served terms in school the two boys were able to take the required educational tests for officers in the army and navy. This aunt secured appointments for the two boys through her influence. John entered the navy and the other boy the army. This other boy was sent to India and was never heard from afterwards.

Young John Crosskill made good progress in promotion in the naval service, for in 1776 he had been advanced to the grade of captain. His ship was engaged in transporting the Hessian troops to America to fight for Great Britain in the War of the American Revolution. At the close of this war in 1781 he was ordered to the West Indies and took active part in the petty wars that took place there in the years 1784-1790. During these years he was stationed at New Providence, Bahamas, and the island of Barbados.

During his transport service between England and the revolting American Colonies he met Charlotte Fillis, the daughter of John Fillis, a successful merchant, a member of the first Legislature of Nova Scotia, and for many years a wealthy and influential man of Halifax. Charlotte Fillis became the wife of John Crosskill.

The Fillis family had come from Boston, and became very prominent in the history of Nova Scotia. Captain

Crosskill must have had rank and influence to have won the hand of the daughter of John Fillis.

Captain Crosskill took his bride to Bridgetown, Barbados, where he resided for some years and where his three sons, James, Henry, and Thomas were born.

For some reason Crosskill left his position in the West Indies quite suddenly about the year 1790, and went to Halifax, Nova Scotia. Family tradition says that he owned a large, well-equipped sugar plantation and many slaves in the Indies, and that when he left he gave his slaves their freedom and the estate. He never went back to claim his property.

Between 1794 and 1798 Captain Crosskill is mentioned in Murdock's History of Nova Scotia as "Commander of the armed 'Earl of Maria' ". This ship was owned by the Nova Scotian government and was in the service of the Province. The 'Earl of Moria' was a craft of one hundred and thirty-five tons with fourteen mounted guns, and was navigated by eighteen mariners and a squad of soldiers. In the year 1796 Crosskill was granted by the governor of Nova Scotia the office of "Vice Admiral and Surveyor General etcetera in all His Majesty's Dominions in North America."

Crosskill fell from the royal grace on account of his quarrel with the Duke of Kent. This quarrel arose over the social laxities of the Duke, Crosskill forbade Mrs, Crosskill to attend social functions at the royal residence in Halifax because of the fact that His Royal Highness' household was presided over by Madam Saint de Laurent, his mistress. Crosskill handed in his resignation and left the service. For eminent services performed, the British government granted John Crosskill fifteen hundred acres of land anywhere he might choose. He selected the present site of Bridgetown, Nova Scotia, and devoted the remainder of his life to the development of the town which he founded in 1822.

The Morning Chronicle, a newspaper of Halifax under the date of August 31, 1922, published an edition commemorating the centennial of the founding of Bridgetown. In large headlines on its front page this paper had as follows: "Romantic Career of the Naval Officer who laid the Foundations of Bridgetown: Brought Hessian Troops to America to fight in the Revolutionary War: Quelled Insurrections in the West Indies: Rebuked Duke of Kent for his Social Laxities; Built the first Vessel in Bridgetown, the 'Robert Burns,' and Established the Town". This newspaper was illuminated by large reproduction of portraits of Captain Crosskill and his wife, Charlotte Fillis.

A large bronze tablet on a granite boulder was placed in Riverside Cemetery as a memorial to him, "the first citizen of Bridgetown." John Crosskill died at the age of seventy-seven.

II. THE JAMES CONNECTIONS

Alexander James I, the great grandfather of John James the Texas pioneer on the paternal side, was born in England. He was a noncommissioned officer and served in the British army. He fought in the Battle of Quebec under Wolfe, September 13, 1759. For his bravery on this occasion he was presented with a sword by the British Parliament as a reward for gallant service. One of his descendents now living in San Antonio, Texas, has this sword. Alexander James lived to be nearly one hundred years of age. He is buried at Carlisle, Cumberland, England.

Alexander James II, the grandfather of John James, was born in 1754. He was a sergeant major in the British army, and master gunner at Great Yarmouth, England. He served in the British forces in the Battle of Bunker Hill, near Boston. He died in 1832 and is buried in Yarmouth Churchyard, Norfolk. England.

Alexander James II was the father of eleven children. One of his sons, Thomas, born in Woolwich, Kent, England, in 1791, was the father of John James. The wife of Alexander James II was named Margaret.

Thomas James was an officer in the British army stationed at Halifax, Nova Scotia. He married Ann Petty Crosskill, the daughter of John Crosskill, on December 14, 1813, when she was seventeen years of age. Four children were born of this union as follows:

Thomas, born at Halifax, 1815.

Alexander, born at Halifax, 1816; died 1889.

John, born February 13, 1819, at Gorleston, Suffolk, England, while his parents who lived in Bridgetown, Nova Scotia, were on a visit to England.

Charlotte, born at Granville, Nova Scotia, 1827; died in San Antonio, Texas, October 1895.

Thomas James became a merchant and citizen of Brooklyn- New York. Alexander James studied law and became one of the Supreme Court judges of Nova Scotia. Charlotte James married James R. Sweet, who brought his bride to San Antonio, Texas. Sweet was a successful merchant and served several terms as mayor of San Antonio in the 50'a. He resigned the office of mayor in 1863 to accept a commission as colonel in Duff's regiment during the Civil War. Sweet made a gallant officer and was one of the most popular men who ever came to San Antonio. He was the father of Alexander Sweet, the Texas humorist.

III. JOHN JAMES

John James' early youth at Bridgetown, Nova Scotia, was spent in attending school and watching the vessels and fishing boats coming into port with cargoes of merchandise and codfish. He was an ambitious lad, eager to learn, and imbued with the spirit of adventure. His ambition was to travel and seek his fortune in a strange land. In his native surroundings he saw but little opportunity for advancement. Then it was that he read accounts of the war in Texas between the American settlers and the Mexican government; he read of the fall of the Alamo on March 6, 1836, and the massacre of its defenders.

Fired with a desire to assist the Texans in their struggle for liberty, after much persuasion, young John James finally obtained his father's consent and blessing in his undertaking.

Thus it came about that John James, a lad of seventeen years, with two hundred dollars in his pocket, started on his long journey southward, the journey that was to end in far away Texas where he was to become a great pioneer in the development of that frontier state.

He traveled overland. While passing through the state of Mississippi he suffered an attack of malaria fever. A kind hearted merchant of the town of Vicksburg took pity on the helpless boy. It was due to the good care given John James by this merchant that enabled the boy to recover. The son of this merchant told the writer many years ago that hi« father thought James' case of fever was hopeless and that he would surely die. To repay the debt of kindness to his benefactor, James clerked in the merchant's store. He displayed a remarkable capacity for business and was soon manager of the store. The business prospered and grew, and the merchant proposed a partnership to James if be would stay; but the debt now being paid and young James fully recovered from the malady, be proceeded on to Texas.

John James arrived in San Antonio in 1837, and his first employment was in taking charge of the land business of Ludovic Colquhon who was desirous of making a trip east and expected to be absent from San Antonio for many months. Later James was made Assistant Surveyor of Bexar County under Bob Hays, who was a brother of Jack Hays, the renowned Ranger captain.

Bexar County then comprized the territory from San Antonio westward to the Rio Grande, and north to the Panhandle. His surveying trips took him, therefore, over the greater part of western Texas. Surveying land in the 40's was a dangerous business, for the Indians, jealous at seeing their bunting grounds being taken from them by the settlers, became desperate and made war on all surveying parties. James had many narrow escapes from death at the hands of these Indians. In the spring of 1839 his surveying party, while at work on the Frio River, was attacked by Indians. In this encounter five of James' men were killed. After this fight he was given protection by having two or three of Jack Hays' Rangers always in his company. James soon became Chief Surveyor of Bexar County.

In 1844 Henri Castro, a French nobleman, established a colony of Alsatian emigrants on the Medina River. James was engaged to survey the townsite and lay off the farm plots. The town so plotted was called Castroville. James guided Castro and his followers to the land and remained with them until they were established. James also plotted and surveyed the towns of D'Hanis, Boerne. Quihi, and Bandera.

James participated in the battle of the Salado which occurred in 1842 when General Adrian Woll, of the Mexican army, who had captured San Antonio, was defeated, Woll took many prominent citizens of San Antonio with him as prisoners on his retreat to Mexico. Among these prisoners were Samuel Maverick and Ludovic Colquhon. On this foray into Texas Woll destroyed or removed all court records and the valuable Spanish documents. One of these documents established the boundaries of the City of San Antonio.

The loss of this document and others resulted in utter confusion as to the city's right to land. Emigrants settled on any vacant land where there was no protesting owner to drive them off. San Antonio found itself helpless. One James Goodman, an alderman, fenced in land where the City Hall now stands on Military Plaza and defied the city authorities to remove him. The City of San Antonio appealed to John James to straighten out this tangled state of affairs and bring order out of chaos. James went to work and reestablished the lines and field notes, found the original corners and resurveyed the city lines. James had read the original Spanish Grant which delineated the area of the city, and knew from memory the field notes thereof. The Hon. Thomas J. Devine* was employed for the legal work and the fight against the squatters was on. The city, after a great deal of expense and litigation, through the expert testimony of James, the surveyor, was finally victorious. The squatters were ejected and the rights of the city were established. Every

---

* On account of the abuses of City Attorney Spencer, T. J. Devine was employed to prosecute suits against trespassers for $100.00 salary per year and a contingent fee of one-eighth of the appraised value of all land so recovered by him. (City Council Records, Feb. 22, 1S45.) (Case of Lewis vs. City of San Antonio, Texas.)

title to land in San Antonio today is affected by this result.

John James

Annie James

IV. JAMES' BUSINESS ACTIVITY

John James began to acquire land soon after his arrival in Texas by location of certificates on property in the wild, vacant, outlying territory. These certificates he received as pay for surveying and perfecting titles to land, and amounted to a part of all land surveyed. He soon, by great diligence coupled with a remarkable knowledge of land matters, accumulated a large number of tracts of valuable land situated on the many running streams of western Texas. The situation of a great majority of these tracts was at the confluence of running streams where there was an abundance of water as well as a quantity of fine alluvial soil fit for agricultural purposes.

On June 11, 1850, John James and James R. Sweet formed a partnership to establish a mercantile business in San Antonio under the firm name of James R. Sweet and Company. James furnished the capital and Sweet agreed to give the business his undivided attention and management. This firm did a flourishing general merchandise business until the Civil War commenced. when Sweet withdrew from business to enter the Confederate Army. James continued in the land and ranch business, surveying and locating land as far north as the Clear Fork of the Brazos River, on the Rio Grande, Colorado, San Saba, Frio, San Antonio. Nueces, and Guadalupe rivers, and as far west as what is now the town of Fort Davis, beyond the Pecos River. The fact that he accumulated so great a quantity of scattered, though valuable land is a tribute to his industry and knowledge.

In 1852 he founded, after survey, the town of Bandera in Bandera County, by giving employment to many men in a saw mill he established there. This mill was run by horse power. Its product furnished cypress lumber, shingles, and laths to the many settlers. The mill also furnished the lumber for the different United States army posts, some of which were Fort Inge in Uvalde County, Camp Wood in Nueces Canyon, Camp Verde in Bandera County, and Camp Lincoln in Medina County. In connection with this mill he established a lumber yard in San Antonio. Cypress lumber sold for thirty-five dollars per thousand, and shingles brought four dollars and fifty cents per thousand. In 1855 James brought sixteen Polish settlers and their families to Bandera. Their descendants are there to this day, happy and prosperous. James was associated in the Bandera venture with Charles de Montel, and the firm was known as the Bandera Mills of James, Montel and Company. The lumber was hauled overland by horses and oxen to San Antonio. The lumber yard was the first in San Antonio, and was located on West Commerce Street. James built a hotel in Bandera, which building is standing in good condition to this day.

James was charitable and progressive and intensely interested in the development of western Texas. He owned and operated a horse ranch in Wilson County. He had a cattle and sheep ranch in Bandera and Uvalde County.

During the Franco-Prussian War in 1873, wool sold in San Antonio for forty cents per pound. Almost every acre of land at that time in southwest Texas, except along the water courses, belonged to the public domain. Cheap Mexican labor, free range, and the high price of wool caused such a boom that there was a great rush of capital from all parts of the United States to invest in land and sheep. The cattle drives to Kansas in the

70's had almost depleted the cattle from the plains of southwest Texas. The sheep business offered greater inducements and profits than cattle as wool was in great demand. Sheep were sheared in April and October, bringing ready money twice a year. One half of the proceeds from the sale of wool paid all the expenses for the year, and the other half of the proceeds, with the increase, was dear profit. During the years between 1873 and 1883 the prosperity of the sheep business was so great that millions of pounds of wool were marketed annually in San Antonio, and during these years southwest Texas and San Antonio prospered as never before. The lowly sheep had almost driven the cow from the plains of Texas, The sheep men exterminated the lobo wolf, located the vacated lands, and the picturesque cowboy, the hero of the cattle trail in song and poetry, became a personality of the past. James may be regarded as the father of the sheep industry in Texas, for in 1860 he imported five hundred fine Merino sheep and some of the finest rams money could buy, and placed them on his Bandera County ranch. These sheep were imported from Virginia down the Ohio and Mississippi rivets, thence across the Gulf of Mexico to Galveston; from Galveston they were driven across the country to the Bandera County ranch.

He wrote many articles on sheep husbandry which were printed in the prominent newspapers of the day. In many of these articles he lauded the sheep industry as one that should prosper and grow in west Texas on account of the ready sale for wool and the fine grass and native shrubs which afforded nutritious food for the animal. He helped many young men by advice and financial assistance to engage in this business. In 1869 he moved his sheep to his Uvalde County ranch, with Henry Shane as his partner. This firm did a very prosperous business in raising sheep and selling wool. James continued in the sheep business until his death at which time he had several thousand fine sheep in his pastures. His horse brand was a "running m" (nz): his cattle brand was 210. James was a stockholder in the first woolen mills to be established in New Braunfels, Texas. These mills were called "The Comal Woolen Factory". James always wore clothes made of cloth from this factory after it was established.

So, as the years rolled by, James became owner of a vast body of land, as well as being interested in various other business enterprises. James' old land book under date of 1859 shows that he rendered for taxation 150,000 acres of land; each tract was choice land of its kind, and generally in 160, 320, or 640 acre tracts. His San Antonio property was valued at the sum of twenty-three thousand dollars in 1859. A comparison of values then and now is as follows; James' home lot on West Commerce Street cost him two hundred dollars in 1847; the same lot was sold by his heirs a few years ago for sixty-five thousand dollars.

James became the owner of Comanche Springs in 1868 on which was afterwards established the United State military post of Fort Stockton. He located the land on Limpia Creek in 1856 which is now in Jeff Davis County, on which the post of Fort Davis was located. The United States government rented this from him for twenty years at the annual rental of one thousand dollars. His heirs still own this 640 acre tract. James owned a salt lake near the Pecos River in what is now known as Crane County. This lake comprised four thousand acres. He operated the product of this lake through the firm of Peter Gallagher and Company at Fort Stockton, and shipped salt as far south as Uvalde.

John James had the distinction during his life of conveying more land to settlers and different parties than any other man in Texas. Years ago it was common talk among business men in San Antonio that James knew the location of every permanent water hole in west Texas. The name of John James affixed to a deed conveying land was in itself a guarantee that the title was perfect, and to this day of all his numerous conveyances of land his reputation for honesty and correctness has never been questioned.

He was one of the three bondsmen who guaranteed the payment of $300,000.00 to the Galveston, Harrisburg, and San Antonio Railway Company by the City of San Antonio on the completion of the first railroad into San Antonio. The road was completed on February 15, 1877.

V. THE COURT HOUSE FIGHT

In 1840 there occurred what is known as the Court House Fight on March 19, This took place on the corner of Market Street and Main Plaza between sixty-five Comanche Indians and the citizens of San Antonio. The Indians bad come into town to confer about a proposed treaty. Refusal on the part of the Comanches to bring in their captives precipitated the fight. James, then twenty-one years of age and unarmed, was attacked by a big Indian Chief who was about to plunge a knife into him when Jim Dunn, afterwards one of Jack Hay's most daring rangers, saved his life by shooting the Indian through the head, by placing his arm around James' body.*

---

* Charles Merritt Barnes.

VI. JAMES GOES WITH HIS CATTLE ON A LONG DRIVE TO CALIFORNIA

On June 4, 1854, John James, with thirty-five well-armed men in his company, started from San Antonio with over one thousand head of cattle, headed for California. The discovery of gold in that state in 1849 and the wonderful fortunes to be made there was a lure that beckoned to many men to come to that new land of wealth. The party of thirty-five herders consisted of many nationalities and included one Comanche Indian.

The country to be traversed was almost unknown and was frequented by savage tribes of Indians and wild animals. The route led over mountains, across arid plains, and through the silent, deadly Arizona desert.

One of the drives in west Texas between the Leon water hole and Presidio was nearly ninety miles without water. The route followed through Texas was as follows: San Antonio west to the Hondo; Philipe Springs (Del Rio) to Devil's River and up that stream with very numerous treacherous crossings to the Pecos basin; from the Pecos basin north to a point west from Escondido Springs and then to Escondido Springs; then to the Leon Water Hole; to Eagle Springs: to Presidio and thence up the Rio Grande to Paso del Norte (El Paso).

The herd arrived at Paso del Norte on July 25. 1854, without having had any serious encounter with Indians.

Forty miles east of the Gila River in what is now Arizona near Santa Cruz, Mexico, Indians stole one hundred and twenty head of cattle, forty head of horses and mules, and murdered Mr. Houston, one of the owners of a herd of cattle belonging to the firm of Dunlop and Houston. The Indians escaped with the stolen cattle into Mexico.* Eighteen men from James' herders volunteered, and they, together with a lieutenant from the Mexican garrison and a detachment of twenty-five Mexican soldiers who acted as guides, after a chase lasting several days, succeeded in taking the Indians by surprise and defeating them with great slaughter. Twenty-one Indians were left dead on this remote battlefield, but only one Mexican soldier was killed. The Mexican soldiers scalped all the dead Indians. All the stolen property was recovered.

After disposing of his cattle in California, James returned to Texas by way of New York. Before coming south again, however, he visited his old home in Bridgetown, Nova Scotia.

James was most favorably impressed with the great opportunities offered in California for development. After his return to Texas he often spoke of California's wonderful climate and of its growing agricultural business. He prophesied a great future for that state, and expressed the desire to return there at some future time. Mrs. James, during his absence in California, stayed with her parents in Indianola, Texas, with her little son, John H. James, who was afterwards Chief Justice of the Fourth Court of Civil Appeals for eighteen years. John James returned to San Antonio in November, 1855, after an absence of seventeen months.

John James was a friend and great admirer of Major John L. Bullis of the United States Army, the noted Indian fighter who, in command of the Seminole Indians for many years, operated against marauding bands of

---

* Information taken from "M. Erkaine Diary". 30-39-44 of Cattle Drive to California as parallel to James' drive.

wild Indians who made forays into Texas from their camps in old Mexico. Many settlers including men, women, and children were murdered during these raids, horses stolen, and the ranchmen's homes burned.

The Seminole Indians under the command of Bullis were descendants of runaway slaves from the southern states who had taken refuge with the Seminole Indians in the Everglades of Florida and who were afterwards removed by the United States government to a reservation near Fort Clark, Texas. These Seminole Indians were famous for their marksmanship, horsemanship, cunning, bravery, and knowledge of Indian ways. Their great endurance in the many fatiguing marches without rest or food under the leadership of the indomitable Bullis in trailing bands of savages is still remembered. The last Indian raid in west Texas was on April 7, 1881, and was marked by the usual cruel murders. Bullis struck their trail and followed with all the relentlessness of a hound after a wounded deer, and even crossed the Rio Grande, He never halted until his scouts reported the enemy in a mountain camp in Mexico, peacefully sleeping away the effects of their long raid. Bullis and his scouts, in the dead hour of night, quietly surrounded the Indians and in the battle that ensued at dawn, exterminated them to a man, leaving not one to tell the tale. His object accomplished, Bullis and his little band, almost ready to collapse from fatigue and loss of sleep, hurriedly retraced their steps to the Rio Grande before Mexican troops could attack them, All of this was accomplished without loss of a man or animal, and was hailed in Texas with wild joy. The newspapers of the day rang with praises of the heroic Bullis. The State of Texas and the citizens of San Antonio each presented him with a sword in appreciation of his services, and he became the idol of the people. Bullis married Josephine Withers, a San Antonio girl. He was promoted to

Brigadier General and died in San Antonio where his family still resides.

During the many years Bullis spent in Indian warfare, scouting in the wild country of west Texas, he discovered many tracts of valuable land. John James advised him to invest his savings in locating these lands. James loaned him his surveying instruments and Bullis spent his time during his leaves of absence from the army in surveying and acquiring these tracts. Bullis' field notes and other data he mailed to John James in San Antonio, who secured his patents from the State and perfected his titles. General Bullis, through the sale of these lands, became a wealthy man. General Bullis has often spoken to the writer of the great service that my father rendered him, and said that he owed his wealth to the advice and friendship of

John James. Camp Bullis, near Leon Springs, Texas, was named after General Bullis.

VII.

PERSONALITY AND APPEARANCE OF JOHN JAMES

John James was about five feet nine inches in height, clean shaven, of very erect stature, stockily built, and very strong and muscular. He was of florid complexion, had blue eyes and dark, curly hair. In the middle of life he became quite stout, attaining a weight of about two hundred and twenty-five pounds. He was of a jovial and peaceful nature, and at all times exceedingly polite to ladies, whom he regarded as superior beings. With men he was jolly and reasonable, treating them honestly and squarely and expecting them to regard and treat him in the same manner. He believed in the golden rule, "Do unto others as you would have others do unto you". He would exhaust every argument and resource to avoid trouble, but when he became convinced that he was being imposed upon, he became aggressive and never avoided an encounter. On one occasion Terry O'Neil, an old time ranchman, told the writer of an encounter between James and two men who suddenly attacked him at Leon Springs. James, with only his fists, defeated them both. Mr. Jesse Bell, father of the ex-mayor, Sam C. Bell, told the writer of a fight he saw between James and John McDonald, a prominent politician and former mayor of San Antonio. McDonald was a tall, powerful man. The fight came off on Commerce Street and lasted for some time until both combatants were completely exhausted with neither one victor. After many blows, wrestling and rolling on the ground, they ended the fight by simply walking away from each other. McDonald was afterwards shot and killed by Dr. Devine whom McDonald had attacked. Devine was acquitted by the courts.

James never sought public office, but he advised all young men to take an active interest in the political questions of the day. In the War between the States he advocated that Texas ought not secede from the Union. He endorsed the stand made by General Sam Houston against the State of Texas entering the war. During the war he served the Confederacy as a member of the Home Guards stationed at San Antonio. He was rejected for active military duty because of overweight. He went to Richmond, Virginia, at his own expense to influence Confederate authorities in regard to war measures affecting Texas.

VIII. FAMILY OF JOHN JAMES

In 1847 James erected his home at 231 West Commerce Street in San Antonio, one of the first residences of two story construction in the city. The lot on which the house was located extended from Commerce Street north to the San Antonio River, and is now one block of North Presa Street.*

His first wife was Emaline Polley, the oldest daughter of J. H. Polley. Polley was one of the first twenty-two immigrants to come to Texas in the year 1822, brought by Stephen F. Austin. The marriage of John James and Emaline Polley was celebrated at the Polley plantation near Columbia, Brazoria County, Texas. One of the persons who attended this wedding was a small barefooted boy who rode to the wedding behind one of the guests for a distance of six miles. This lad was the man who later built the first railroad into San Antonio and who became Vice-President and General Manager of the Galveston, Harrisburg, and San Antonio Railroad. This was Colonel H. B. Andrews, the daughter of whom, Sadie, became the wife of the writer.

In 1851 James married at Port Lavaca. Texas, Annie Milby, the Daughter of William Polk Milby of Maryland who had come to Texas in 1840. Milby was a member of the first Texan Congress under the Republic of Texas. He made political speeches and stumped the eastern part of the state with General Sam Houston. Afterwards he became treasurer of Calhoun County, Texas, and the owner of the only furniture store on Three Bays. At the

---

* The lot extended from Commerce Street north to the San Antonio River, and ia now North Presa Street.

time of his death he was the oldest Mason in Texas. The Port Lavaca Lodge is still named the William P. Milby Lodge: his life sized picture adorns its walls, the highest honor attained in Masonry.

Annie Milby was born in Snowhill, Maryland, on the 26th day of January, 1836, and died in San Antonio at nine o'clock on the morning of February 27, 1901.

John and Annie James had the following children:

John Herndon James, born October 13, 1852; died July 17, 1912.

Thomas Milby James, born October 21, 1854; died June 11, 1895.

Mary Josephine James, died in infancy.

Vinton Lee James, born July 3, 1858.

Annie Laura James, born January 26, 1861; died May 13, 1909.

Sidney Johnson James, born 1863; died 1916.

Lottie James, born July 18, 1866.

Agnes James, born 1867; died November 27, 1907.

Hugh Scott James, born October 13, 1868; died February 27, 1923.

Fannie James, died in childhood March 25, 1876.

Diana James, born October 29, 1875.

Annie James, the mother of the above family, was one of the most amiable and charitable of characters. She married John James when she was sixteen years old. She was of the brunette type and very pretty. A most devoted mother she was, and her beautiful character won for her the admiration of every one who knew her. When she died, her funeral was attended by Mayor Marshall Hicks and the City Council of San Antonio, who adjourned their weekly meeting to attend the last sad rites. Her death was caused by angina pectoris.

Mrs. James' sisters, Josephine, Emma, and Fannie Bell Milby. were veny beautiful women and full of charm. These sisters often visited the James family on Commerce Street. Josephine Milby married Major E. P. Langworthy of the United States Army, who was in charge of the Trans-Mississppi Department at the beginning of the Civil War. The Langworthys had two children who died at the ages of three and five years. Emma married Captain Hugh Scott, a prominent lawyer of Houston. She became a widow and afterwards married E. V. Henderson. She had one child by Henderson who was named Milby; he is now dead. Fannie Bell married Captain Frank Shoemaker who resigned from the army because of ill health and who spent most of the remainder of his life in travel abroad. Fannie Bell died in her home in Terrell Road in San Antonio on March 30, 1928. These pretty Milby girls made the old James home very attractive to the army officers stationed in San Antonio. Colonel Robert E. Lee on one occasion escorted Miss Josephine Milby from Indianola, Texas, to San Antonio.

Many of the military celebrities of the Civil War were frequent visitors at the James home on West Commerce Street. Among these were General Robert E. Lee, General Albert Sidney Johnson, General D. H. Vinton, Joseph E. Johnson, John B. Hood, General Mason. Braxton Bragg, and General Worth. The latter. General Worth, whose monument adorns Union Square in New York City, died at the James home during the cholera epidemic in 1849.

John James sold General John B. Hood a ranch on Verde Creek in Bandera County. James named one of his sons after Albert Sidney Johnson, and another after Lee and Vinton

IX. ATTENDS THE FIRST PROTESTANT CHURCH SERVICE HELD IN SAN ANTONIO

In the spring of 1844 the Reverend John McCullough and John W. DeVilis, Presbyterian and Methodist respectively, opened the first Protestant services held in San Antonio in a room of a one-story adobe house.

The house was located where the Bell Brothers Jewelry Store used to stand on West Commerce Street. There were six gentlemen and five ladies present, among them John James. James L. Trueheart, Thomas Addicks. and Mesdames Elliot, Jacques, and Bruner.

James was a member of the Episcopal Church, having been baptized May 21. 1819, at Granville, Nova Scotia. He belonged to the vestry when St. Mark's Episcopal Church was first established in San Antonio.

X. SOME RECOLLECTIONS OF THE WRITER

The writer, Vinton Lee James, when still a small boy, often accompanied his father on surveying trips in the early 70's. I often officiated as one of the chain-bearers and sometimes as axeman. My father was compass man and we had to follow him after he had taken his bearings on an object, sometimes half a mile away when the country was open. We followed him, measuring and marking trees as we advanced. We would start work early in the morning and work continuously until about four o'clock in the afternoon, without food or rest. Often when our work was finished, we would be several miles from camp, and I would be so very tired I would become disgusted with such long hours of labor. Many times I despaired of ever reaching camp again, so weary was I. But when the day's work was over. I remember how a tired and hungry boy could eat and rest. My father paid me a man's wages on these trips, and I was always glad to go again.

I was his companion on many of his land selling trips into the country. To prepare for these journeys he would order the cook at home to bake biscuits, which he then packed in his valise. The ranchmen whom he visited, thinking to please my father, usually had hot rolls or biscuits served with meals. My father would then order me to fetch him some cold biscuits from the valise. He would never eat hot bread of any sort, as such food disagreed with him.

Father took great pains to instruct the buyers of land as to the necessity of plowing deep in order to counteract the effects of possible droughts. He would furnish other information also that would be conductive to successful farming. His knowledge of husbandry was remarkable. He seemed to know something about everything concerned with stock and land. He was ever willing to impart such knowledge. I once heard a farmwife remark, "That Mr. James knows more about chicken raising than any woman." He would say to me, "My son, never look on when other people are working, but lend a hand and assist." I followed his instruction when I visited distant ranches. I was always willing to bring in wood and water, and I found out it paid, for the poor overworked housewife was always glad to have me around.

XI.

BELIEVED IN GOOD EDUCATION

John James was a firm believer in education for his children. John and Thomas were sent to Earlham College, a Quaker institution in Indiana. After attending this college, John attended Harvard College, Cambridge, Massachusetts, graduating there in the law class of 1874. Thomas finished his education for a business career in New York City. Thomas was gifted with an extraordinarily fine voice.

John H. James became a member of the law firm of Simpson and James and practiced law in San Antonio until 1893, when he was appointed by Governor Hogg as Chief Justice of the Fourth Court of Civil Appeals, which office he held until his death on July 17, 1912.

"Judge John H. James was a man of high character and splendid attainments, and whether as a citizen, as a member of the bar, or as Chief Justice of the Court of Civil Appeals, he was admired for his legal ability and for the fairness and impartiality which characterized his acts in all walks of life, and his death was sincerely mourned."

XII. THE DEATH OF JOHN JAMES

In the spring of 1877 John James' health begin to fail. He suffered considerably before he would consult a doctor or allow a physician to be summoned. His old family doctor. Dr. F. Herff, was away at the time on a trip to Europe, and he wanted to await his return. But his family urged him and his malady became more severe so Dr. Ganslen was called and examined and treated him. Then James was forced to take to his bed, which was hard for him to do as he had never suffered from any severe sickness since the serious illness in Mississippi. Dropsy developed and he was frequently tapped to get relief. He began to suffer a great deal and eventually saw that the end was near. He began to arrange his earthly affairs by having his son, John H., draw his will. He called in the Very Reverend Dean Richardson of St. Mark's Episcopal Church and asked absolution for his sins. He died on November 26, 1877, surrounded by his family. His son, Thomas, sang a hymn as his father passed away. He died in his fifty-sixth year.

So ended the career of one of the foremost pioneers who helped to carve the outline of the great State of Texas, a living example to every one of his descendents who might wish for success in life to follow in his footsteps in the path of honesty, industry, and good character.

XIII. THE ESTATE OF JOHN JAMES

John James' worldly goods at the time of his death consisted largely of west Texas land and some San Antonio property.

The able, conscientious, and conservative management of his estate by Judge John H. James and the division of the property to the children of John James was effected satisfactorily and without a complaint from any of the heirs.

Judge John H. James had the entire confidence of his brothers and sisters and their love and respect on account of the great service he rendered in his admirable and able management of their father's estate; and to this day, 1938, sixty-one years after the demise of John James, his heirs are enjoying the fruits of their ancestor's industry, made possible by the wonderful capabilities of his executor, Judge John H. James.

Copy of communication of John James to his son, John H. James written shortly before the death of John James.

San Antonio, 2nd Nov., 1877.

My dear Son John:

The chances are that before many days I shall bid good-bye to this world, and not having made any disposition of my estate I now desire you to draw up my will — Your Mother owns the house and furniture in her own right, given before marriage, and of course her half the community property acquired since marriage. I want each child to have an equal part of my estate, except yourself and Tom who have received, say $3,000. in your education which the others have not received. I want all the children educated as well as possible— I want the family kept together for several years, so the children can be provided for and educated. It falls heartily upon you. my Son, to accept more than a Father's duty to your brothers, and sisters. Your Mother I want united with you as Executor. Your position will require firmness, but you must bear and forbear with all those growing up. The income from property will partially support the expense. I want you to have full power to sell and your Mother joining with you can pass title to property. In case any of the boys and girls marry they are to be assisted if possible, on account of what they are entitled to receive. Sell the landed property (there is much that is valuable) as fast as fair prices can be got. Taxes otherwise will destroy it.

Draw up the will with care so everything possible can be kept out of probate Court.

As to the future— I do not fear it, nor do I fear death. I have nearly lived out my time anyhow. The pain is in leaving a young and dependent family upon your hands, but I do not doubt that you will do the best you can for them. If you don't— God help them.

JOHN JAMES

XIV. NOTES

The writer visited at the Sargent's Hotel in 1880 at Brackett- ville, Texas. When I registered. Mr. Sargent asked me if I was any relation of John James, and when he discovered that I was, he could not do too much for me. He told me that my father went on his bond when no one else would when he was appointed sheriff of Bexar County to succeed W. B. Knox.

Another time I went on one of the very first excursion trains operated by the San Antonio and Aransas Pass Railroad to Kerrville soon after the completion of that branch. Mr. Bundy, a prosperous sheep man of Kerr County, took me to his home, and during my stay there of several days he was a most gracious host. He said that my father had advanced him money to pay some debts when Bundy did not have a cent, and he was very grateful for the assistance John James had given him.

In conclusion I wish to say that I write this sketch of my father's life for the benefit of the grandchildren of John James, for after I am gone there will be no one left who knew him intimately. I have been very careful and have devoted much time in research to make this memorial truthful, The dates, the antecedents, and the occurrences, in fact every thing given pertaining to the life of John James, is absolutely as correct as human effort can make it.

V. L. JAMES

XV. AMNESTY PAROLE

Following is the content of amnesty granted John James:

Andrew Johnson,
President of the United States of America, to all to whom these presents may come, Greeting: Whereas John James of San Antonio, Texas, by taking part in the late rebellion against the Government of the United States, has made himself liable to heavy pains and penalties, and whereas the circumstances of his case render him a proper object of Executive clemency;

Now, therefore, be it known, that I, Andrew Johnson, President of the United States of America, in consideration of the premises, divers other good and sufficient reasons me thereto moving, do hereby grant to the said John James a full pardon and amnesty for all offenses by him committed in the said rebellion, conditioned as follows:

1st. This pardon to be of no effect until the said John James shall take the oath prescribed by the Proclamation of the President. dated May 29. 1865.

2nd. To be void and of no effect if the said John James shall hereafter, at any time, acquire any property whatever in slaves, or to make use of slave labor.

3rd. That the said John James first pay all costs which may have accrued in any proceeding instituted or pending against his person or property, before the date of the acceptance of this warrant.

4th. That the said John James shall not, by virtue of this warrant, claim any property or proceeds of any property that has been sold by the order, judgment or decree of the Court under the confiscation laws of the United States.

5th. That the said John James will notify the Secretary of State, in writing, that he has received and accepted the foregoing pardon.

In testimony whereof I have hereunto signed my name and caused the seal of the United States to be affixed, Done at the City of Washington, this eighth day of December A. D. 1866, and of the Independence of the United States the Ninetieth.

Seal of the United States

By the President   ANDREW JOHNSON

William Seward, Secretary of State.

Vinton Lee James

PART TWO
Personal Recollections of Vinton Lee James

The James Homestead

I. EARLY BOYHOOD

I was born in 1858 at 123 West Commerce Street, San Antonio, Texas, and named "Vinton" after Major David H. Vinton of the United States Army then stationed in San Antonio, and "Lee" after Col. Robert E. Lee also of the U. S. Army, who had previously escorted my aunt Josephine Milby from her home at Indianola, Texas, to San Antonio on a visit to her sister, my mother. Both of my namesakes were friends of my parents.

Our home was on West Commerce Street where North Presa Street is at present. The house was the first two-story building that had a chimney in San Antonio. The sills were hewed cedar logs, and the supports of the windows were cedar. The east wall was of hard rock and the rest of the house was adobe, except the north upper story, which was weather boarded with the six inch cedar boards. The adobe part was plastered over. The floors and window facings were of lumber hauled from the coast.

On account of the war we children were sadly in need of clothing. What wearing apparel we had came from Mexico where father had purposely made a trip and returned with new shoes and hats and other necessary things. For awhile we were the envied children of the town; but the wool hats, after being wet, flopped over our faces; and the shoes were pegged brogans, and rather than wear them, I went barefooted.

I remember when the Indians came to town dressed in their picturesque costumes of skins and head feathers. I saw the superior marksmanship of the Indian boys with bow and arrows. They could hit a small coin placed in a split stick at a distance of twenty yards.

My first impression of death was during the latter part of the late Civil War when I, a small boy, accompanied my father to a funeral of a Confederate soldier that took place in the front hall of the old Bat Cave building, situated near the northwest corner of Military Plaza. The coffin was draped with a Confederate flag. Mayor Buquor, a large fleshy, good-looking gentleman, who' was dressed in a long-tailed coat and a suit of sombre black, was master of ceremonies. He made an eloquent speech in a deep, pleasing bass voice in which he eulogized the dead as having been a brave soldier who gave his life that his country might live.

I remember when the first fire engine, which was propelled by tread-mill or man-power, was exhibited on Military Plaza. Water to extinguish the fire was passed in leather buckets by a line of men, from hand to hand from the ditch to the fire. In the dead hours of night when the fire bells gave the wild alarm, it caused great excitement. Men and boys dressed in haste and often the most impatient grabbed their clothes and completed their toilet in the street on the run to the fire.

II. RECONSTRUCTION DAYS

My earliest recollection of events in San Antonio were during the reconstruction days after the Civil War. I distinctly remember the entry of the U.S. troops under General Merrett, when he took possession of San Antonio, as they passed through Commerce Street. They certainly looked well-fed and formidable with their revolvers strapped around their waists and the short Sharp's carbines dangling noisily from their saddles. I watched them as they passed with all the hatred that a small Southern boy could feel against them for the subjection of his country.

Most of the prominent citizens of San Antonio who had taken the side of the Confederacy had gone to Mexico to escape arrest. Marital law was proclaimed and all state and county government business stopped; slaves were liberated; and a guard of San Antonio citizens was formed to protect homes at night. Gloom and uncertainty of what punishment awaited the citizens of San Antonio made life miserable.

I remember when the defeated Southern soldiers returned from the war, poverty-stricken and hungry, and how they angrily broke into the stores of Vance Brothers and those of other merchants on Alamo Plaza and helped themselves to provisions, and how we boys appropriated to our own use whatever they discarded.

The hard times were occasioned by the paralysis of all business and the lack of United States money with which to buy things to eat and wear. Father was away, and mother had one of the slaves who stayed with us to load a wagon with wood from our yard, which he sold and gave the money to mother to purchase food for us.

Christmas time was a quiet affair compared to the present times. Father and Mother on Christmas Eve attended Grenet's store, where the Crockett Hotel now stands, and bought presents for us children. We were satisfied with very little, An apple or a stick of candy and a few other trinkets were sufficient to send us into realms of joy.

I remember when only home made candles, made by hot tallow being poured into tin molds in which a cotton wick bad been placed and then allowed to cool, were in use. What a poor light they made by which to study. I remember how delighted everybody was when the coal-oil lamps were first used, They were indeed a great improvement over the tallow candles. My father, to rid our pet dog of fleas, saturated him from head to foot with coal-oil; and when the poor beast escaped, he gave the most distressing yelps, which attracted every other dog in the neighborhood. He ran into the street with the other dogs after him. They pounced on him only to get a taste of the oil. and of all the rolling and such expression of dog-misery of biting into the dust was never seen before.

The policemen in those days certainly earned their salary when they arrested drunken men for disturbing the peace or whipping their wives. I have, many a time, seen the policeman and the law violator fight until both were covered with blood. There was no hoodlum wagon, and an officer brought in his prisoner to jail by pure force, and we boys enjoyed the sight of the fight that followed the arrest until the one-room jail and the old market house was reached,

I remember the first ice-cream parlor that was established in an old adobe one-story building a few doors east of our residence on Commerce Street. I hung around the door hungry for a first taste of this delicious stuff until the proprietor asked me to go on an errand, after which he placed a saucer of cream before me; and I, a novice, attempted to swallow it at one gulp, with the result that I lost consciousness for a few moments. When I came to, I slowly devoured the remainder.

I remember when the first vaudeville or "Dingle Dangle" theater exhibited on Alamo Plaza where the Fox Kodak Store is now. J. H. Kampmann, the contractor, was employed to build the stage, and he purchased tickets for the first night's performance for all his family, but declined to go after be was informed that "nice gentlemen patronized such places, but it was no place for nice ladies."

During the prosperity of the cattle men who returned with lots of money from drives to Kansas in the seventies, the vaudeville theater and the pretty actresses did a big business and gambling and drinking were the principle diversions. The gala day was when the circus came to town. The fair lady horseback riders were fully advertised on the billboards, and we boys admired their pretty pictures. Our admiration, after seeing them dressed in their silk tights with their short skirts standing straight out from their hips, turned to love and made us wild with delight as they gracefully rode bare-back and jumped through paper hoops, at the same time throwing kisses to the audience. How we hung around the Rice Hotel, on North Flores Street, kept by Mrs. Clements, all day waiting to get a glimpse of the beautiful and adorable creatures that bad stolen our hearts away.

The principal buildings that I remember were the Menger Hotel, the French office building, situated on the southwest corner of Main Plaza, the Casino on Market Street, the Old Bat Cave, the jail, so called because of the myriads of bats which inhabited its walls and eaves and swarmed early and late in its vicinity, and last but not least the Old Market House and Bull Head Saloon on Market Street. The best people and the army officers gave their dances either at the Menger Hotel or at the Casino where what few theatrical performances were given took place.

The old Maverick home fronted on the north side of Alamo Plaza and Houston Street where the Gibbs Building is now. The lot extended along the north side of Houston Street through Jefferson Street to include the land where the Bexar Hotel is now. This large lot was fenced with up-right cedar posts seven feet high. We boys would scale this high fence and, armed with an iron ram-rod taken from an old musket, drop into this enclosure in which there were several flocks of quail. Often we would make a lucky throw among a covey and kill several quail at a whack.

I have shot rabbits in the mesquite brush where Dr. Adolph Herff's residence is on Broadway. I remember when I accompanied Willie Walton, (an older brother of our late Major

Alex Walton, prominent engineer), on a duck bunt on the Alazan Creek, now one of the most populous parts of our city. Walton's gun was a muzzle loader. He carried a powder flask and shot pouch. He was a splendid wing shot and kept me busy picking up his kill, which amounted to some fifty ducks. He gave me some of them, kept plenty for himself, and the balance he left at the Plaza Hotel, situated on the north side of Main Plaza and run by Captain William Tobin, the father of the late Mayor John Tobin.

The back part of our lot on Commerce Street bad a large front on the San Antonio River, which in those days was a bold running stream full of the finest fish life. Mr. Blankenship was the town professional fisherman, and I often watched him so as to learn bis art, for one of my great ambitions was to be an expert angler. Blankenship was an Englishman who lived in a shack in the rear of the Umsheid home on the corner of Commerce and Alamo Streets. He always carried for bait limburger cheese for catfish and a bucket of live minnows for black bass, and the number of fish be caught was surprising; but for all he caught, he found a ready sale.

Canvas bath houses resting on floating barrels adorned the river banks and were a great source of delight to the families in the summer months. I soon became an expert swimmer and diver and most of my time was spent in bathing. We boys never knew what a bathing suit looked like, and I remember a number of us swam across the river where the auditorium is now to appropriate to our use the tempting fruit that was in the Convent orchard. We, in our birthday clothes, suddenly emerged from concealment and ran directly into a group of young nuns. Shriek after shriek greeted us and consternation reigned supreme until we vigorously made our escape by plunging into the water.

One day some twenty of us boys went swimming in the Blue Hole which was in the rear of Washington Street where the river was deep and swift A tow-beaded boy named Zalmansig, who lived on North Flores Street, while in the most dangerous part of the river was attacked with cramps. He commenced to sink, continually crying for help. All the boys deserted him and climbed to the opposite bank for safety and yelled at me, who was close to the drowning boy, not to touch him for he would grab me and drown me also. I suddenly took hold of him from behind after a great effort, which came near costing me my life, got him into shallow water where all the boys then assisted.

Another time Henry Krempkau (an older brother of William Krempkau. Secretary of the Old Freighters' Association) became exhausted in the river behind Losoya

Street, and I had to rescue him after he had gone under twice. Two other boys I rescued from watery graves. I had the reputation of being a bad boy and was the despair of my teachers, but I do not remember of ever doing anything dishonorable; and when a life was in danger, I threw caution to the winds.

John James and Peter Gallagher came to San Antonio at an early date and both men by their savings and by hard work early in life became wealthy. Both had ranches in Bandera County and property at Fort Stockton, Texas. They were intimate friends and often on Sunday mornings Father, after shaving, would say to me: "Son, I have to see Don Pedro". We would go to the Menger Hotel where Mr. Gallagher, propped up in bed, received him with affection. Both Mr. and Mrs. Gallagher's faces showed great pleasure at our visit, as father's visit was a beacon of joy to the hopelessly sick man and his affectionate wife. When my father's sickness became hopeless. Mrs. Gallagher, was daily at his bedside, and her sweet, round Irish face shone with anxiety and affection at his pitiable state, she did everything in her power to alleviate his sufferings, and she mourned his death when her friend passed away.

Our friends during and after the reconstruction period were the widow of Major George Howard and his family, who lived on South Alamo Street; the Marucheau family, who lived on St. Mary's Street opposite the Catholic Church; General Wm. Steele's family, whose residence was on Market Street where the Water Supply Company Office is now; George D. Giddings, who lived on Commerce Street at the present site of the San Antonio National Bank; Sappington. whose home was on the corner of Navarro and Houston streets; the Mavericks, whose home was on the northwest corner of Alamo Plaza; Alex Sartor; Paul Wagner; the Hummel family, whose home was near our Commerce Street residence;

Nat Lewis; Leffering; Judge Thomas Stribling's family, who lived on North St. Mary's Street; the Elliots on Soledad Street; J. T. Thornton on Washington Street: W. A. Bennett; Groseback; Dwyer; and William Vance, who lived behind the County Court House; Dr. F. Herff; J. Vance on E. Houston Street; and Colonel T. G Williams on Soledad Street.

III. PUBLIC DISASTERS

On March 27th., 1865, came the great flood when the San Antonio River from the crossing of St. Mary's Street near the Catholic Convent was one continual sheet of water across Commerce, Crockett, and Market streets. All bridges went except Commerce Street bridge where old man Tanninberg was drowned and his body swept away as he tried to cross over to his home. Many persons were drowned and great suffering ensued as the sudden rise of the river came at midnight. Our family had to abandon our home on Commerce Street and take refuge in the upper story of the rock building where Calvin's Drug Store formerly was situated. The water rose several feet in the lower floor of our home, which made the house unsafe. Mr. Peter Gallagher, whose home was in the block surrounding the Alamo, made father move our family into his home, where we lived with them until our house was repaired. At the Gallagher home I met Mr. Bryan Callaghan, who had only recently returned from Fort Stockton, Texas, where he had been employed in Mr. Gallagher's store, to begin the practice of law in San Antonio. Callaghan was very intelligent and the best conversationalist I ever heard, and his youth, fine appearance, and ability to please his audience indicated that a bright future and a great success awaited him in his life work.

Cholera came to San Antonio in 1866. Father immediately ordered an ambulance from Sappington's livery stable to convey us to the J. H. Polley Mansion in Wilson County. The driver of the ambulance informed us that Mrs. Jacques, who had nursed the sick in the cholera epidemic in San Antonio in 1848, had died the previous night, after catching the disease from a cholera patient she was nursing. Mrs. Jacques was an admirable lady, famous for her charity and for nursing the sick. The Polley Mansion was thirty miles from San Antonio. It was a large commodious two-story rock house of ten large rooms and large galleries and halls above and below, built in 1846. and is today in an excellent state of preservation, I was destined in the future to spend many happy days in this delightful home. I remember the slave log houses where many of the old slaves remained with Mr. Polley. I spent many evenings listening to the negroes' ghost stories that frightened me to such an extent that I would wake up in the night screaming with fear of the "hants" that were pursuing me. My sister Lottie, Mrs. John Sehorn, was born in the Polley home during the cholera epidemic. Fortunately all our family escaped death. The death list in San Antonio numbered 293. The last case was in October, 1866.

The terrible hail storm struck San Antonio May 19th, 1868, at 7:30 P. M. and lasted two hours. I remember distinctly that event, as I was so frightened by the terrible report of thunder, the crackling and breaking of the big trees in our front yard, the lightning at intervals as bright as day, the driving rain, and the battering of the hail stones, one of which weighed two pounds, and all accompanied by a roaring hurricane wind. I crawled under a bed for protection. The Kloeppet Hotel was damaged, and the Presbyterian adobe Church, the first church built in San Antonio, was destroyed, and all the buildings next to our residence were ruined. The roof of the Alamo went. Every window glass on the north side of the city was broken. The merchants' stock of glass was soon exhausted and some time elapsed before it was replaced.

IV. EARLY HUNTING EXPERIENCE

All my life since my earliest recollection I have been imbued with the spirit and love of adventure and outdoor life. I am an ardent disciple of Isaak Walton and a hunter of wild game. Both animals and winged fowls then existed in West Texas in great numbers in the seventies in the hills and plains around San Antonio, and fish sported in the limpid streams of West Texas. My great ambition was to become an expert hunter and angler and to live a country life. I often saw in the San Antonio market, where wild game was offered for sale, numerous deer, turkey, quail, duck, and buffalo meat.

In the fall of the year I was thrilled beyond measure and delight at hearing the weird cries of countless wild ducks and geese flying high above me in the sky on their way to their feeding grounds and waters of the Texas coast. It is no exaggeration to say that almost every water hole on the outskirts of San Antonio was alive with wild life: and in the fields, prairies, and mountains were numerous deer, quail, dove, plover, and curlew. The fruit from oak trees, grape vines, insects, and wild berries afforded ample food the year round.

I present a few items about the amount of game that was published in the San Antonio Express to give the reader some idea of the great abundance of wild game that existed in the country around San Antonio:

"On December 10th, 1873, there was a sale on Military Plaza of sixty-three wagons of produce and wild game, buffalo meat, wild turkeys, and deer."

"On December 18th, 1876, A. Sartor, a jeweler; Dorsh, a saloon man; and Henry Elmendorf, a hardware merchant, returned from a hunt on the Hondo with 22 deer, one bear, and hundreds of wild turkeys."

"On December 10th, 1875, hunters returned from Nueces with 50 bucks and saw hundreds of wild turkeys that were as tame as barn yard fowls."

On January 1st, 1878, wiki turkeys sold on the streets of San Antonio for 15 and 20c a piece. Quail around the city were so numerous that the dirt roads in the afternoons were alive with the birds dusting themselves.

In 1886-7 the completion of the San Antonio 8 Aransas Pass R.R. to Rockport opened the greatest duck resort in the world. The waters of the bays and inlets to the gulf of Mexico were literally black with wild life. Often in their flight they were so numerous as to darken the sky. Texas had no laws then to protect wild life. Northern and San Antonio hunters on week ends sometimes killed 700 ducks and bragged about it. This custom spelled death to wild ducks, geese, etc. The merciless slaughter of God's most beautiful creatures began, Market hunters and game hogs also got in their work. In times of drought when ducks and geese had to have fresh water to drink, hunters guarded the water holes, and complained that their guns got so hot from constant shooting that they had to stop to let the guns cool. The poor winged fowls just simply had to come in to assuage their thirst regardless of the shooting and the death that awaited them. When I was City Auditor from 1899 to 1905, I wrote and had published many articles in local and state magazines on the necessity of a law that should be enacted to protect pur game; this law to be enforced by the employment of well paid game wardens, who would protect wild life and stop the great slaughter going on, as our wild life was fast disappearing in the way of the wild pigeon, which then was extinct.

Today, 1938, the U. S. government has taken great interest in trying to save wild life, and this is the first year that ducks and geese are more numerous than in many past years. It is hoped the good work will still go on in enforcing laws to insure more game in the future.

The first data recorded of wild life in West Texas is copied from Henry Castro's diary in 1844 when he founded Castro- ville. and is as follows: "July 16th, 1844. After leaving San Antonio with the colonists, we camped on Potranco Creek, 16 miles west of San Antonio. John James killed three bears, and James Dunn, a Jack Hays' ranger, killed a wild horse stallion and two deer. After travelling over 150 miles of territory which was so beautiful that it reminded me of an English park, and we lived off the country's hunt, and at all times had fish, game and wild honey and only coffee and sugar, brought along, was needed. We saw herds of wild horses and droves of turkey and deer."

V. POLECARPO RODRIGUEZ, HUNTER AND INDIAN FIGHTER

He often told me stories of his adventures that delighted me and were as thrilling and interesting as the stories of the life of Big Foot Wallace or Arabian Night adventures, P. Rodriguez was born on January 26. 1829. He was educated for a Catholic priest, but he came to San Antonio and was apprenticed to James Goodman, a gun and locksmith, and later an alderman of San Antonio.

When Goodman left San Antonio, Polecarpo joined the U.S. Topographical Survey, that located the site of old Fort Lancaster. In 1849, he was guide to Col. Joseph E. Johnson of the U.S. Army on a trip from San Antonio to El Paso. Polecarpo helped to lay out many of the roads to the U.S. Military forts west of San Antonio. He was guide and tent man for Col. Kirby Smith (afterwards the great general in the Confederate Army). Polecarpo Rodriguez was widely known all over the state of Texas and noted for his undaunted courage and piety. In his long life of 86 years, he had served his country well on the frontier of Texas. Later in life he joined the Methodist Church and became a preacher of the gospel in which he became as famous for the eloquence of his sermons as he was formerly nationally known as a guide and hunter. His last diocese was at Floresville, Texas. When I was in the ranch business in Kinney and Uvalde counties, he often on his religious trips visited me. I remember two stories he told when I was a small boy, they are as follows: One day Indians surprised him; he tried to escape by running, but the Indians were gaining and to escape be resorted to a stratagem. On coming to a mountain and hill, that his pursuers could not see the other side, he suddenty stopped in full view of the Indians and waved his hat and shouted: "Come on, here they are," and started his horse in the direction of the Indians, who, thinking reinforcements were coming to his assistance, took refuge in the brush; and Polecarpo escaped. Another time his dog followed a bear into a cave; the bear attacked the dog, and to save his dog Polecarpo entered the cave where he was attacked by the bear.

VI. THE POLLEY FAMILY

In 1872, when I was 14 years of age, I left home on my horse to visit the Polley family in Wilson County. I was warmly received and the most pleasant days of my life commenced at this beautiful country home. Since my last visit in 1866, during the cholera epidemic, Mr. J. H. Polly, in 1869, had passed away. Mrs. Polley had taken charge; she was assisted by her grown children as follows:

Augusta, born 1827, married Walker Baylor, brother of Gen. John R. Baylor of Confederate fame;

J. B. Polley, born 1830. married Miss Martha Le Gett of Seguin, Texas;

Emiline, born 1832, married John James in 1847, she died in 1848;

Susan, born 1835, married C. F. Henderson, killed in Civil War;

Susan 2nd., m. Mr. Brooks of Sutherland Springs;

Adelia, married A. G. Pickett of Floresville, Texas;

Catherine, born 1839, never married;

Harriet, born 1842, married Dr. Houston;

A. H, (Hub), born 1845, married Miss Beverly;

Jonathan, born 1848, never married;

W. W., born 1851, married Miss Wyatt;

All of J. H. Polley's children were born in Brazoria County except the two oldest and the two youngest.

Mrs. J. H. Polley was nine years old when her father, Brit Bailey, came to Texas from New York. When I visited the Polleys in 1872, all the married Polleys had homes of their own in different parts of Texas.

VII. JAMES BRITTON BAILEY

James Britton Bailey came to Texas from New York in 1818. He was granted a league of land lying between Angleton and W. Columbia on the Brazos River by the Mexican government and that place is still known as the "Bailey Prairie." Bailey was an educated man, noted for his honesty and integrity. He was a just master of slaves and a hunter extraordinary. He made friends with the Indians. Mary Bailey, the daughter, became the wife of J. H. Polley in 1823. They were married by a Catholic priest, to conform with the Mexican law, required at that time. Mrs. Polley made candles for the first sitting of the Texas Congress at San Felipe deAustin. Stephen F. Austin appointed J. H. Polley the first sheriff of the Texas colony. Polley moved to Wilson County in 1842 and camped on the Cibolo Creek four years, during which time he built the commodious house. The house today, 1938, is in an excellent state of preservation, and is now owned by lawyer C. A. Goeth of San Antonio. J. H. Polley came to Texas with Austin to look over the country and returned with Stephen F. Austin's first colony of 300 in 1821.

In the new Alamo Museum in San Antonio is an original order from Stephen F. Austin to Britton Bailey dated 1823 as follows;

"You are hereby notified that you cannot be received as a settler of the colony and you will not be permitted to live near the Brazos River. You are hereby allowed 60 days to move.

Signed Stephen F. Austin"

"Bailey positively refused to comply with Austin's order. Bailey later met Austin and a fight ensued. Bailey had a beautiful daughter of whom he was very jealous and whom he guarded. Bailey one day on his return from Brazoria found Austin calling on his daughter and seizing his rifle ordered Austin to dance. Austin complied." All the above and more too of the quarrel between Bailey and Austin is now on exhibition at the Alamo Museum, San Antonio. In Bailey's last will he says: "All my life I have gone West and lived an upright life and I desire to be buried ERECT, (standing up) facing WEST with my rifle by my side." His grave today is marked on Bailey Prairie by a pecan and an oak tree. Bailey came to Texas and settled on land three years before Stephen F. Austin's colony arrived in Texas.

VIII. J. H. POLLEY

Mr. J. H. Polley owned in 1859 and 1860 more cattle than any man in Texas with the exception of the owner of the King ranch. His brand was J-P. Herewith is an affidavit, copied from the Polley papers from Ed. Tewes:

"Before me K. H. Wiseman the undersigned on this day personally appeared Ed. Tewes Bexar Co. Texas who is known to me to be a creditable person and who after duly sworn did depose and say (among other things) I know Mr. J. H. Polley who lived at Sutherland Springs, Texas, in Guadalupe and Wilson. I went on several cattle hunts with sons of J. H. Polley. Mr. Polley owned more than 150,000 cattle when I knew him, they ran at random from the San Antonio river to the Rio Grande, a distance of 150 miles. In 1859 and 1860 I personally assisted in branding 3500 calves in Guadalupe Co. and the same number in Bexar Co. in 1858."

The above information is copied from Britton Bailey and J. H. Polley's papers received from Mrs. Josephine Polley Gol- son, 915 Howard St., San Antonio, a grand daughter of J, H. Polley.

Mr. J. H. Polley's memorandum book, dated from 1826 recites historical incidents of his business for the different years from 1826 to almost the time of his death, in 1869. Besides his cattle. Policy owned and killed many hogs for his own use, as follows, in pounds, in Wilson Co.:

1849— 3872 lbs.	1854— 7266 lbs.
1852— 5409 lbs.	1855—12621 lbs.
1853— 7049 lbs.	1856—22776 lbs.

Dr. G. B. Houston, at an early date, also built a beautiful two-story house very much like the Polley residence on the opposite side of the Cibolo Creek. Dr. Houston was the father of the Honorable Augustus and Reagan Houston, two of San Antonio's most able and influential lawyers. The Houston house was badly constructed and unsafe; the walls cracked and the Houston family moved to San Antonio.

The Polley Mansion

IX. MY VISITS TO THE POLLEY MANSION

In 1874, when I was 16 years of age, I again visited the Polleys on the Cibolo. Mr. Polley, having died in 1869, Mrs. Polley was then in complete charge of affairs, being assisted by Miss Adelia, the housekeeper, and Walter Polley, who with Hub had charge of the cattle and hogs. General Joseph B. Polley was executor of his father's estate. He walked with a peg leg, as his foot had been shot off in a battle of the Civil War. Joe had entered the Southern Army at the very beginning of the war and he took part in all the big battles around Richmond, Virginia.

Mrs. Polley was a rather small sized lady, gifted with unbounded energy. She was the first one up in the morning and the last one to go to bed at night. She personally oversaw the dairy, kitchen, and household work, and I never saw her idle. She excelled in preserving the great amount of fruit her orchard produced and her branded peaches and cream for dessert was the joy of my life; and her buttermilk biscuits, baked hams, fried chicken and game dinners I will never forget. Mrs. Polley had a lovable disposition. I never saw her angry, or heard her speak ill of any one. Every one who came under her influence loved her for the kind interest she took in all persons.

I daily began the life that I enjoyed so much, hunting wild game and riding horses. In the post oak sandy lands east of the house were many deer and in the Cibolo bottoms were some wild turkeys. My father gave me his rifle, an English finely made gun with a hair trigger that shot an ounce ball; that gun formerly belonged to my unde, Major Langworthy of the U.S. army who had married my aunt Josephine Milby. I took great interest in moulding the bullets for that rifle, which was a powder and cap arm of very light weight. In the morning I hunted game, but on account of my extreme youth and ignorance of game habits, I did not have much success; but I experienced many thrills in seeing wild game in their natural haunts and sometimes I got a shot, but I always missed. I was often jollied by the ladies on my poor success in hunting. One day I surprised a herd of deer that were lying in the sand, and after a bad attack of buck ague, I succeeded in killing a spotted fawn. Words cannot express my happiness at that auspicious event. I will never forget the pleasure it gave me to ride directly with the deer behind my saddle among the ladies who had jollied me.

The following winter I induced my dear friend J. M. Vance to go with me. I got 10c a day for going to market and was paid for watering the pecan trees father had planted. We bad considerable money to buy ammunition; and, like boys, bought an abundance of shot, 25 pounds, and 10 pounds of black loose powder, at George Dullnig's grocery store. The clerk secured it for us, and when we got it, we had a grocery boxful, which we buried in our back yard. When we arrived at the Polley home, they made us store our ammunition in one of the vacant outhouses. Well we had a grand time but were unable to use up all of our ammunition.

The next summer I succeeded in killing a large deer, which excited me to such an extent that after loading the deer on my horse, I forgot my rifle. I discovered the loss before I got out of the black jack sandy country, where I tied my handkerchief to a tree. I accompanied Egbert Polley the day after and showed him the handkerchief;

he then followed my horse's tracks and to my great delight found my gun.

The winter following, I had great sport hunting green headed mallard ducks that were numerous in the ponds along the Cibolo Creek where they fed on acorns. The wild pigeons, which are now extinct, were feeding also on acorns by the thousands among the post oak trees; in fact they were so numerous that in their roosts they broke down limbs. An incident occurred then that I will never forget. After shooting some pigeons, I was in the act of finishing loading my shot gun by ramming the paper wad on the shot when suddenly before me, not 50 feet away, appeared a large 10 point buck deer intently regarding me. I immediately fired the gun at the deer without removing the ramrod. I never recovered chat ramrod or got that deer.

One day the dogs got into a flock of young turkeys. Their loud barking caused the turkeys to take refuge in the trees, and I killed two of the turkeys by shooting from my saddle.

Mrs. Polley must have liked me, for she allowed me to bring Jim Thornton, son of Col. J. T. Thornton, the San Antonio banker, with me. We had a wonderful time. Mrs, Polley sat at the head of the table during meal times and served three delicious meals daily. The large table seated many guests. Oh! how I enjoyed those meals. Every day the wagon returned from the field with a load of watermelons and cantaloups that were served at 10 A.M.

The afternoon was spent in riding parties with the girls and young ladies, whom I accompanied as escort to the Sulphur and Cleyabeate Springs. As we had splendid riding ponies, we sometimes ran races on the good roads. The ladies all used side saddles. I was a very active and an important boy in those days, as 1 got up the riding horses and saddled them and was a willing slave to answer every one of the ladies' fancies.

I was then at a romantic age, and pretty girls were an inspiration never to be forgotten. In fact I was in love, head and heels, though I was too young for any serious affection, as the ladies were older than I. Sometimes my partner and I, with our heads together, would read Walter Scott's beautiful poem The Lady of the Lake ' and I would shyly put my arm around her waist. Oh! the happy days of one's youth! Among the many girls that visited the Polleys were two from San Antonio, Miss Lady Napier, whose family lived on the west side of Travis Park, a beautiful blonde, and Miss Bettie Bennett, her companion, a strikingly pretty brunette, a daughter of W. A. Bennett, the wealthy San Antonio banker. Miss Napier later married Dr. Frank Paschal of San Antonio, and Miss Bennett married Frank Yoakum, the railroad magnate.

In the evening Mrs. Polley and the guests repaired to the parlor to enjoy the accomplishments of the ladies' singing and playing on the most beautiful piano that had mother-of-pearl keys. A relative of the Polleys was a very pretty young lady from Wharton, Texas, gifted with a beautiful voice who sang the "Whippoorwill' song; another red-headed girl from East Texas also took part in the entertainments. When the time came for me to leave this paradise of hunting and pretty girls, I certainly was an unhappy boy, who hated school with all the strength I possessed.

The only objection to Wilson County was that it was in a malarial district. The faces of the inhabitants seemed to have a yellow look. In the Cibolo bottoms, the live oak trees all have great bunches of hanging moss, a sure sign of an unhealthful district.

One night I suddenly became infected with a terrible malady, so much so that I became delirious and this condition caused great excitement and alarm. A rider was immediately dispatched to Sutherland Springs for a doctor. How long I remained unconscious, I do not know, but I was told afterwards that for some days my life was almost despaired of. None of my family was nearer than San Antonio. I must have been a most pitiable object, and if it had not been for the careful nursing by the young ladies, who I was told took full charge of me and in turns were always by my side, I may not have recovered. I distinctly remember one incident, when I emerged from my stupor and was conscious. One summer midnight the full moon flooded the room and besides me in the bed in her night dress was one of the girls whom I had often escorted sound asleep. Do you blame me if I regarded that girl beside me fast asleep as only one degree removed from being an angel from heaven?

As soon as I was able to travel, I returned to San Antonio, but the chills and fever stayed with me for over a year, and all Doctor Herff's ability and medicine failed to cure me, as I was a complete wreck. After this experience my parents refused to let me return to the Polleys.

X. RECUPERATION

The chills and fever I had contracted in Wilson County made my life so miserable that I quit school. Father at last told me to go to Narceso Leal's horse yard at the corner of Flores and Dolorosa Street and buy a pony. He purchased a new Winchester 44 centre fire carbine from Norton 0 Deutz' Hardware store, and I departed west. The second day I arrived at Henry Shane's ranch, who was my father's partner in the sheep business. Mr. Shane gave me a dose of medicine of his own concoction, which I have described in one of my articles in this book.

After my health was further restored, I thanked Mr. Shane for the success of his medicine and hospitality and departed further west some 50 miles to visit Mr. Henry Ramsey's ranch on Turkey Creek in Kinney County. Mr. Ramsey was my father's partner in the cattle business. Ramsey's son Tom was of my age; he and I became fast friends; I had one of the best times of my life with Tom as we enjoyed fishing and hunting together. I went on several cow hunts and became useful as a cowboy, keeping together cattle. I succeeded in getting Mr. Ramsey's consent to accompany him and Mr. Pete Bowles of Uvalde in a prolonged cow hunt on the divide between the head waters of the Nueces and Llano rivers, to gather a herd of cattle to be driven to Kansas, all of which I have recorded in my following articles. After that delightful trip, I returned home.

XI. SCHOOL DAYS

I first attended the German-English School on South Alamo St. where I went for several years. I had a better reputation among my teachers and my boy companions as a fighter than as a student. The biblical rule was observed "Spare the rod and spoil the child." No child was spared and the teacher practised over time, not only in the classes but sometimes teachers used the rod during recess. I stood the punishment a long time until forbearance ceased to be a virtue, and one day I rebelled when a certain American teacher started to thrash me unmercifully without just cause. I resisted him, until he got furious; and then we had it out back and forth. He afterwards told some of my friends that was the hardest fight he ever had; though I was only in my teens. I gave him as good as he gave me. I was sent home. My father was mortified and threatened to send me to the negro public school, but he relented and sent me to Mr. Martin's school. Mr. Martin, a Presbyterian minister, conducted a school in the basement of the old Presbyterian Church on North Flores St. He gave a boy a square deal and I attended his school afterwards for several years when he was principal of the first public school located in the old Kloepper Hotel on West Commerce Street.

My brother John H. James returned to San Antonio after graduating from Harvard law school in Cambridge, Mass. He examined me and found my education sadly neglected and advised me to quit school and that he would hear my lessons so as to enable me to acquire a foundation to enter college advantageously and he also advised me to abandon my trifling habits and get down to hard work. After three months of constant daily study among the trees in our backyard, he discovered that I had become a good student, and took great interest in the studies that be had proposed to cover my deficiency.

In company with my boyhood friend, J. M. Vance, who had the previous year attended The University of the South, an Episcopal Military College located at Sewanee, Tenn., I left San Antonio after New Year, 1875, when the winter term began, and on arrival at Sewanee I was enrolled in the freshman grammar class. I did not like the sudden change of the pleasant Texas weather to the snow and the icy temperature of that mountain air. I had the most terrible case of homesickness come over me suddenly. I wrote father the most pitiful letter asking to be allowed to return home as I was sure I would sicken and die if I had to remain at Sewanee. I also promised him I would gladly go on any one of his ranches if he would only send me the money to come home. Fortunately for me my request was ignored. The only thing I could do was to busy myself in my studies to keep from going crazy, I succeeded during my first term, which ended in August, in passing in all my examinations and in standing at the head of all my classes and in making such a wonderful record that it was as great a surprise to me as it was a joy to my parents. I brought home the prizes I had won at Sewanee. I did not do so well the following term, and at Christmas I was home again for good. The Sewanee College professors were nearly all former very prominent noted officers of the late Civil War. At the head of mathematics was Major Gen. Kirby Smith; Col. Shaller and Col. Sevier were prominent also, and General Gorgas was head of the Ordinance Department in the Jeff Davis government. Prof. Dabney of the English and history department was author of the "Life of Stonewall Jackson". On account of my good record at the University, the faculty promised to make me a senior if I returned. J. M, Vance wore an officer's uniform and I had a sergeant stripe on our return from Sewanee.

XII. RANCH LIFE

In my ranch life, I had several miraculous escapes from serious consequences. In the seventies, Indians from Mexico often on moonlight nights made raids in West Texas to steal horses and kill people. Mr. Henry Shane, the most noted Indian fighter of his day, had killed two Indians in two fights after he was surrounded and attacked, but Shane was a dead shot and knew how to defend himself and always escaped. I was surprised and attacked by an Indian near the place previously where one of Shane's Mexican herders had been killed by Indians. The Indian that attacked me thought I was unarmed, as I was driving my wagon and my carbine was lying in the wagon bed under me. After being attacked and wounded by bis lance thrust, I sprang from the wagon with my rifle in hand. The Indian took refuge in the surrounding woods. It was broad daylight, and I was for a few seconds face to face with the Indian whose painted face and Indian rig was an awful sight. He let out a blood curdling yell that frightened my team. I managed to reach unaided Mr. Shane's ranch, where I collapsed from loss of blood. Mr. Shane and his wife examined the wound, which was in the region of the kidneys. Shane placed me on a mattress in his wagon bed and took me to Joe Ney's Hotel in D'Hanis, where I remained two weeks under the doctor's care until I recovered.

Another time when I was unarmed I was attacked in Uvalde by a gun man who called me a vile name and struck me. I retaliated by quickly striking a hard blow in the face, which so surprised and disconcerted him that his 45 caliber pistol, which he had loosely placed in his shirt-band, fell to the floor, and before he could regain it I was onto him. That was one time a gun man had to stand up in a fist fight. That fight is still remembered by those who witnessed the affair. 1 used only the weapons that nature gave me. My opponent and I afterwards became friends.

I have been associated in my ranch life with some famous characters of West Texas, whose lives make interesting reading for posterity. I refer to King Fisher, Judge Roy Bean, and Henry Shane, all prominent for the part they took in the development of our great West Texas.

XIII. BUSINESS VENTURES

After my father's death, Mr. Henry Shane, his partner in the sheep business, had an unfortunate affair with a San Antonio negro barber, who demanded 75c for a shave. Shane was drinking at the time and got his gun and killed the man. It cost Mr. Shane his fortune to pay his lawyers. His wonderful record in protecting the Texas frontier from Indian raids saved his life, and he was acquitted by the jury. Shane was compelled to sell his sheep, and I was employed by the purchasers to lamb and shear the flocks, which I did, and I afterwards bought an interest in the business, which I pursued for five years on Rio Frio. Finally I sold my interest in the sheep and invested my savings in the land surrounding the Frio Ranch. Land at that time was very cheap, and Mr, J. J. Stevens of San Antonio became my partner. Stevens left all land purchases to me. Mr. Stevens never saw any of the land I bought. He furnished his one-half of the money after I closed the deals. I bought many sections of state land and many old headrights that joined our land on the Frio River. A choice tract of ten thousand acres lying between the Frio ranch and the Leona River owned by a resident of New York City, was offered to me for $1.50 per acre cash. John Stevens, who was secretary to Col. H. B. Andrews and President T. W, Pierce of the G H. 8 S.A.R.R, who were then building the S.P.R.R. west of San Antonio to connect with the California road, was on a business trip in San Francisco for the railroad, but he had left his check for $7500.00 with me for his part of the expense. I had $5000.00 cash, but lacked $2500.00 to close the deal. I applied to F. Groos &

Co,, bankers, for a loan of $2500.00. Groos asked for an endorsement, which I was unable to furnish as my brother, Judge John H. James, was away in Nova Scotia visiting relatives. I told Mr. T. C. Frost (then a merchant), who had sold my wool the previous year, of my predicament. Mr. Frost advised me to see Mr. Groos again, and tell him that "if he did not let me have the $2500.00, he would," Mr. Groos then let me have the money and I closed the deal for $15,000.00 cash. In the following six months, cattle prices advanced and the 28,500 acres we had secured together in a single body, that had a large front on the Frio and also a small front on the Leona rivers, we sold to Nat and Dan Lewis of San Antonio for $65,000.00. The land I sold is now the Uvalde Kincade Ranch. I cleaned up with $35,000.00 for myself, and then I got married when 24 years of age. After disposing of land on the Frio, I went into the cattle business on Turkey and Muerlo creeks in Uvalde and Kinney counties. Cattle prices had slumped and between the decline in prices and the droughts the business suffered greatly.

I discovered a rich asphalt deposit on some 4000 acres of land lying near Muerlo Creek that I had leased from the New York and Texas Land Co. Ira H. Evans of Austin. Texas, was the agent, who asked me $2.50 an acre. Although I did not have the $10,000.00, John J. Stevens and my brother Judge John James, furnished the money, and I closed the deal with Evans and bad the deed conveyed directly to me, (as James and Stevens advised). By deed I afterwards transferred the land to James and Stevens. The asphalt mine was leased to a company, who built a railroad to the mine and leased the mine for a monthly payment of $800.00 of which Mrs. John H. James received one-third monthly; and the Stevens heirs received two-thirds monthly, which the company paid for many years until the depression came. I never had a better friend and partner than John J.

Stevens and his good wife, who had entire confidence in me and in time of stress and sickness always helped me. 1 sincerely mourned their death. John Stevens loved his friends and often assisted them financially by furnishing them money or by going on their bonds, etc., which often he was forced to pay. He told me in confidence that altogether he had lost many large sums of money from friends who never paid him.

My aunt, Mrs. F. B. Shoemaker, who lived on Terrell Road, Alamo Heights, died intestate in 1928. I was appointed administrator by Judge Augustus McClosky. Her property consisted of New York stocks, real estate, and personal property. I collected $120,000.00 from sales and divided the money among the heirs. My final report was delivered to the Judge and County Court of Bexar County. They reported it was the best and most complete of any that was ever turned in.

XIV. POLITICS

When President Diaz of Mexico expelled Francisco Madero from Mexico for aspiring to the office of president, Madero came to San Antonio and resided with a friend of mine, through whom I met him. Madero informed me of his ambition and desired me to assist him in certain matters that I will not disclose. I consented to only in certain things. He informed me he had plenty of money and wanted me to purchase his arms, etc., which commission I refused. Madero made an attempt by force of arms to enter Mexico by way of Eagle Pass. He was badly defeated and was also reported wounded and captured by Diaz' troops, all of which caused great excitement in the United States and Mexico and San Antonio. Madero's family at that time were guests at the Presnall House on St. Mary's Street and, of course, they were almost frantic from reports of his defeat and arrest and death. I received a telegram addressed to me, which on opening I found was in code. I immediately presented it to the Madero sisters at the Presnall House. As I was a stranger to them, they received me cooly; but after they read and deciphered the code, they almost overwhelmed me with thanks at the good news my telegram had conveyed, which changed their despair to joy and happiness.

A large reward was offered for Madero's arrest. He had suddenly disappeared and the mystery was. what had become of him? I knew all the time where he was. I had never in my life been guilty of a dishonest act, and I certainly would not betray the confidence of a friend for a money consideration.

Francisco Madero made another armed attempt to enter Mexico, in which he was entirely successful and soon became President of Mexico; and Diaz fled to Spain. Unsolicited by me, President Madero sent me a letter delivered to me by one of his ministers to a Central American Republic, in which he acknowledged his indebtedness and offered me certain assistance which I had never asked for. Some day I may tell all of this story and in the language of Jimmy Fiddler, "Believe me. it will be an interesting story," I have President Madero's letter to me at 303 King Williams Street, my residence.

XV. MY FRIENDS, THE HUNTERS

Among the many successful hunters of San Antonio, who are now sleeping across the dark river in the shady lands of the Happy Hunting Grounds, were the following sportsmen: J. O. Sullivan, who was the owner of several double nose liver colored pointer dogs, that were wonderful hunters and retrievers: W. B. McMillan,* with whom J, O. Sullivan and I enjoyed many happy days quail hunting when the birds were plentiful around San Antonio; J. M. Vance, who was a good hunter; James V. Dignowitty, who was among the best all around rifle and shotgun experts and to whom the writer is indebted for most of his knowledge of hunting; T. H. Micklejohn, who was the most accomplished angler and hunter in the city; Peter Sheilds, who always had his hunting dogs following him on the streets of San Antonio and who was an ardent hunter of birds: Harry Moore, who succeeded Charles Hummel in the gun business and who hunted both quail and ducks; Papa Page, who was a fisherman of the first water and the most amusing teller of stories and the boon companion of Mayor Callaghan on his fishing trips: R. A. Arthur, who considered himself the best shotgun expert in Texas, and when beaten, always had an excuse of some sort; General Geo. W. Russ, who was the handsomest man in Texas, and a wonderful shot with both the shotgun and rifle, and whose fine presence and companionship was eagerly sought after; Oscar Gussaz, Gus Critzer, Joe George and T H. Micklejohn who were the crack shots of the city and

---

* W. B. McMillan was the father of the present D, S. Judge Robert M. McMillan.

who represented San Antonio in all State and National shoots, often carrying off the prizes.

My hunting friends among the living are T. W. Campbell, Judge Duval West, C, A. Goeth, Sam C. Bell, Aaron Pancoast, Palmer Giles, John A. James, Harvey Baer, Wm. Wurzbach, Chas. and Herman Simmang and many others.

Vinton Lee James at the age of 16

XVI. WESTERN TEXAS SIXTY-FOUR YEARS AGO

Wool sold on the San Antonio market in 1873 for 40 cents per pound. Every acre of land in Western Texas at that time, except along the water courses belonged to the public domain of the State of Texas. Free range and the high price of wool caused such a boom that there was a great rush of capital from all parts of the United States to invest in land and sheep in West Texas. This period marked the advent of the sheep industry, which for ten years was very prosperous, and at the same time marked the decline of the cattle industry. The high price received from wool soon made the sheep owners independent, who bought the land upon which their flocks grazed, and thus forced the cattlemen to move their herds to the unoccupied lands farther west.

In the summer of 1874, during a visit to Wilson County, I contracted a bad case of malaria which would not yield to treatment, and from which I suffered for more than a year. My father concluded that a trip to two ranches in which he was interested west of San Antonio, where the climate was dryer, might help me. So he bought me a twenty-dollar pony and a Winchester carbine and with plenty of advice about the care of my pony, Indians, etc., he sent me on my way.

One bright summer morning I turned my pony's head westward on the Castroville road, and two days later I arrived at Henry Shane's sheep ranch on the Sabinal, where I was again made miserable by an attack of chills and fever. Mr. Shane said he could cure me even if Dr.

Herff had failed. I promised to inform him the next time I felt the attack. As usual, a few days elapsed, when I again felt that I was going to be sick. Shane advised me to go to bed and he immediately got busy pounding and crushing some material, which he afterwards carefully strained several times through a glass of pure whiskey. He now approached my bed and told me to shut my eyes and not to stop to taste the "stuff," but to swallow it. I was desperate for relief, and I drained the glass of its contents and fell back to await developments. I did not wait long. Never will I forget the intense burning pain in my stomach. Shane afterwards informed me that 100 pods of mashed small chili petins, peppers, were strained through that glass of whiskey; I was drunk as a lord. For several days afterwards I was very weak, but the chills and fever were gone. In fact, as it afterwards proved, I was completely cured.

The Sabinal was then a most beautiful running stream of water, with great cypress trees overhanging its banks. The pioneers of West Texas 64 years past were fearful examples of ignorance. Though I was only a lad, just in my teens, yet I was amused and surprised at their questions. One man informed me that "about three-thirds of all the fish in a certain water hole were suckers." A neighbor of Shane, who was a man of wealth, spoke of a certain rocky mound in a prairie that was conspicuous for many miles. He said it "was caused or created by volcanic corruption," He also asked me if Rome was in Jerusalem. The early settlers in those days were fighters not scholars. Their entire time was occupied in tending their herds and defending their precious families from the murderous attacks of savage Indians, who committed many crimes of theft and murder and often left the poor ranchmen financially ruined, and sometimes even worse, his wife and children butchered during his absence. Shane was renowned over the West as a dangerous man in a personal encounter. He had had numerous fights with the red men. He was surprised and surrounded on two different occasions, and each time single-handed, he had slain an Indian and escaped. He was of athletic build, with restless eagle eyes, and when armed and astride of his beautiful bay horse, he was the most superb figure I have ever seen.

Wild turkeys in those days were so numerous in the Sabinal bottoms that the cattle actually refused to graze in the valleys where the turkeys ranged.

My health, after a couple of weeks' stay on the Sabinal, was greatly improved, and after I had thanked Mr. Shane for his kindness, I departed west, and late that same day a very tired boy and pony arrived at Henry Ramsey's cattle ranch, situated in the foothills on the north side of the Anacatchio Mountains on Turkey Creek. Here my boyhood's fondest dreams of a hunter's paradise were at last realized. The country was open and almost free from brush; the mountains and valleys alive with all kinds of game and the crystal streams full of fish. Antelope by the thousands swarmed on the plains south of the Anacatchio Mountains toward the Rio Grande, and it was a beautiful sight to see a bunch of them gracefully funning around in a circle, with their white rumps glistening in the sunshine, There were also many bunches of wild mustang horses, with beautiful manes and long, sweeping tails, that roamed the prairies, all of which lent a wildness and charm to this interesting country which has long since disappeared.

Tom, the son of Ramsey, was about my age and we soon became comrades, and many were the days we spent hunting and fishing together. The canyons were redolent with the sweet incense from wild flowers of every color that profusely decorated the valley and hillsides. The humming of wild bees was ever in the air, and during our daily excursions we never failed to startle deer, javalinas, and turkeys. I now received my first lessons in cowboy life, and afterwards often assisted in the roundup. I became expert in heading wild cattle, and for a boy, was considered a good hand. Sometimes the cattle would run into a bunch of deer or wild turkeys, and then I never failed to entirely neglect my duties as a vaquero, and shoot as long as the game was in sight. I always got a scolding from Mr. Ramsey on my return, for the cattle took advantage of my absence and escaped from the side I was guarding. I committed this offense so often that I was finally barred out from helping to drive cattle.

On account of the danger from Indians we were not allowed to hunt far from the ranch, and we were instructed never to leave our horses; but we managed to slip off to our most favored place about five miles south of the ranch, called Wood Slough, where we could depend on seeing great numbers of deer in the middle of the day resting under the shade of the scrub mesquite trees. The deer always managed somehow to discover our approach first, and our shots at them running never took effect. One day we cautiously approached on our ponies, and imagine our disappointment on seeing, about 400 yards away, about twenty-five deer standing perfectly still, intently watching us. I told Tom to remain quiet, as I was going to try a new scheme. My pony was a fast quarter-horse, and the country, with the exception of a few mesquite trees, comparatively open. I suddenly pushed the spurs into my horse's sides and gave him a free rein ahead, with my carbine in my right hand. I was off like an arrow, headed straight for the dear. The deer were so surprised by my rush that they actually bunched closer together, until I dashed among them, shooting. I have never been so close to so many wild deer since. I followed two large bucks that ran together. I was very close and sent shot after shot, finally hitting one in the throat, severing the jugular vein, and, with the blood streaming from its wound, he ran about a hundred yards and fell; and when Tom arrived on the scene, I was so out of wind and excited that I could hardly talk. I certainly was the proudest boy alive. I would not have exchanged places then with a king.

Wild honey, fresh butter and buttermilk, clabber, hot corn-bread, and fresh beef constituted our daily bill of fare, and the appetites Tom and I presented at meal time, after our daily rounds, certainly did justice to the good things put on the table.

We always had fresh meat hanging up. A fat yearling was usually selected. The ribs, tenderloins, hams, and tallow were taken; the balance, fully half, was left on the ground for the buzzards and wolves. The hide was cut up to make hobbles' for the cow ponies.

I followed my father's advice and often assisted in ranch duties. I would bring in wood for the kitchen, go to the spring for water, and the result was that I was always welcome whenever I went, though I admit it was much pleasanter to see others work, and it was sometimes with great reluctance that I assisted.

On one occasion I noticed an activity by one of my hosts and the Mexican hands, to wit; saddles were inspected and a great number of rawhide hobbles were made. A messenger was dispatched to the remuda (pony herd), which, on account of the Indian raids, was sent miles away from the ranch, where there was good pasture and concealment, and where a reliable man constantly watched them. I was informed, subrosa, that the outfit was going to start in a few days for the headwaters of the Nueces River. Now, here was my chance for adventure, and I determined if possible to accompany this expedition. I broached the subject to the rancher, who refused me. He said there was great danger for a boy of my age who would go hunting alone, and that Indians would get me. I pleaded with him again the next day and promised to obey him in all things, and he finally agreed to take me: and then I was the happiest boy alive.

One afternoon, the rancher, myself, and several Mexican vaqueros drove about thirty saddle ponies, each with a rawhide hobble around its neck, across the high grass in the direction of the Nueces Canyon, the mountains of which we could see dimly in the distance. That night we arrived at Chalk Bluff on the Nueces River, where we met a party of three men from Uvalde. Pete Bowles and son, John Bowles, and Newman McCarthy, and some Mexican vaqueros. 1 became the target for ridicule from one of them, who was very much amused at the style of my saddle and hat, and he was so persistent that I could bear his taunts no longer and we quarreled. He reached for his pistol and I grabbed my carbine. My host and friend interfered and made us shake hands, and we became warm friends; and indeed, I was sorry afterwards when the time came for us to part. It is the unexpected that always happens, and the cowboys were always armed with pistol or gun, which, day and night, was always close at hand, ready for any emergency.

The next day the outfit headed up the meanderings of the beautiful Nueces River. Its water was as clear as crystal; on the banks were tall pecan, stately sycamore and elm trees when I first saw it in all its virgin wildness. I remember seeing only two occupied cabins on our entire trip. The occupants were generally outlaws from other parts of the State, and they were not molested by the local authorities as long as they behaved themselves and helped protect the settlements from Indian raids. Every day a fat beef was killed by our party for fresh meat. The carcass, with the exception of the ribs, tallow, and tenderloins was left on the ground.

At night we gathered around the camp fire to watch the fat ribs broil before the hot coals. After our wolfish appetites were satisfied, Pete Bowles would tell stories. The father of my chum on this occasion, who was one of the first settlers of Uvalde County, surprised three Indians one bright moonlight night who attempted to steal his horses, and with one shot from a double-barrel shot gun he killed two outright and finished the other with the remaining barrel. The Indians afterwards captured him when he was unarmed, and in revenge, deliberately skinned him alive.

I can see myself now in the recollections of long ago when we gathered around him as he sat cowboy fashion on the ground smoking his pipe in the glare of the campfire, telling tales of hunting or of Indians. We listened intently to these stories, for he was full of humor, but he could be pathetic or tragic, as the situation or the trend of his story demanded. His country twang, kindly manner, and his aptitude for the dramatic lent an indescribable charm to his narratives, and he never failed to absorb our entire attention.

Tired nature would at last assert her rights, and, with my saddle for my pillow, I rolled up in my blanket on the ground and went quickly to sleep with the purling sound in my ears of the Nueces water as it rippled among the rocks in the river.

I often went fishing with my gun. During the middle of the day the large bass would hunt the shallow water to feed on minnows in the shade of the sycamore trees, and with a few shots I generally could secure enough of them for a meal for the entire camp.

The road up the canyon crossed the river many times, and after the second day the Nueces River had dwindled to a small stream, where we pitched our camp near a hut occupied by a solitary young man. What his business was in this wild country I never discovered. I regarded him as one of those unfortunate individuals who was forced to flee from justice.

The members of our party each took turns on visiting this interesting man, for he evidently possessed some information that our leaders were desirous of obtaining. I surmised from their disappointed appearance after each visit that things were not going to suit them. After several days everything was satisfactorily arranged and the following morning, guided by this stranger, who led the way through a dense cedar brake, we proceeded on our journey, driving the cow ponies.

We ascended the divide and entered a rugged, rocky country. Our altitude made the panoramic view of the valleys below us and the hills around us very beautiful.

We saw numerous bear signs and actually two bears in plain view on a distant mountain side. The country was too rough to approach them on horseback. The country became more picturesque as we ascended, and we traveled among pine trees that extended for miles and miles, and finally late in the afternoon, we emerged from the forest of pines to a plateau that extended, almost level and open, northward, broken here and there by a few small cedar brakes. As we advanced, we found very little water; and after a great deal of trouble and delay we finally succeeded in finding a small water hole. Here we pitched our camp, not a very great distance from the head water of the south fork of Llano River, or about where the town of Rock Springs in Edwards County is now situated.

I discovered now for the first time the object of the expedition, which was to gather a herd of cattle.

Next morning at daylight we started on our first roundup. We succeeded after a great deal of trouble, as the cattle were very wild, in gathering quite a bunch of all kinds of cattle, the larger part consisting of bulls and cows, but no calves. There were quite a number of four-year-old bulls without a mark or brand, and a great many mavericks. The bulls absolutely refused to be driven or to leave the herd; and though we would try to cut them out, they fought so viciously that the cowboys drew their pistols and guns and after a bombardment of the bulls in which some of them were killed, we succeeded finally in getting rid of them. Mr. Ramsey and a few Mexicans succeeded in building a corral out of cedar, into which we drove the captured cattle. That night, and every night afterwards, we kept large fires burning around the corral to keep the cattle from stampeding.

Early one morning we rode past, within a few hundred yards of a bunch of 50 lobo wolves that stood quietly and watched us pass. Each of those wolves drawn up in a compact circle was as large and powerful as a police dog. They regarded us with more curiosity than fear, and they so remained an unbroken circle with every head pointed directly towards us until we passed out of sight, I regarded these killers as the wildest and most interesting sight I ever beheld. Mr. Bowles informed me that the wolves ate all the calves, and sometimes even attacked large cattle. That day we found a three-year old steer with his thigh badly torn and bleeding from the fangs of the lobo wolves. After several days' work from daylight to late afternoon without dinner, the trial began to tell on me; and one morning I refused to accompany the outfit, pleading the want of rest, and that day I lounged around camp. I tried to talk to the Mexican cook, but failed to make myself understood. They say idleness is the father of vice, and my lounging around camp that day was the cause that brought this cattle roundup expedition to an abrupt close just when their fondest hopes of gathering a large herd were about to be consummated.

I realized that I was very dirty, and the inspiration struck me that I was sadly in need of a bath. I disrobed and thoughtlessly waded into our only water supply, and with a bar of homemade lye soap, lathered myself from head to foot and afterwards proceeded to roll around in the shallow water. I was having a great time when suddenly the outfit rode into camp. Picture their anger and disgust as they hurled epithets of unprintable names at me. the innocent cause of all the trouble. I protested that I never thought of any wrongdoing. The cook luckily had his bucket full of water, which the thirsty outfit drained. After a hasty supper they concluded that there was nothing else to do but break camp, as even the Mexicans absolutely refused to drink water from the pool. Never as long as I live will I forget the misery of that bright moonlight night. We suffered from thirst as we drove the tired cattle southward toward Uvalde County; then there was no sleep for any of us until nearly daylight, when we found barely sufficient water after our thirst was satisfied for our cattle, I was in such disgrace that even the Mexican cook refused to speak to me. After the weary men's thirst was satisfied, they regarded my bath in their only drinking water in a humorous light. I could hear them describing my naked appearance with laughter and shouts.

We had succeeded in gathering about 300 head of all kinds of cattle. I afterwards heard that these captured cattle were sold by the bosses to a buyer who was gathering a herd to take to the Kansas market. The real owners of these cattle, which had drifted from the lower Llano country, never heard of them. This dishonest practice that was allowed in those days by common consent among the stockmen of Texas came back in a few years with a fearful vengeance to the originators. Their cattle, which had drifted from the home range, were gathered and sold likewise. Mr. Pete Bowles, who was considered wealthy and who estimated the number of his cattle on open range at twenty thousand head, was dumbfounded to find that his herd had dwindled to a few hundred head, which he succeeded in gathering and moving to Wilderness Lake, in Zavala County. Henry Ramsey was more fortunate. He succeeded in moving nearly one thousand head to Beaver Lake, the headwaters of Devil's River,

The former has passed away long since in the town of Uvalde. The latter was cowardly assassinated, shot in the back, near Devil's River many years ago. His death is to this day unavenged, as his murderer was never caught.

In the early 70's a ranchman generally owned only enough land on which to build a house and have a horse pasture. His cattle ranged in the public domain, and he bad his brand on them to distinguish them from other men's cattle. There were few fences. There was no cattlemen's protective association, and few inspectors. There were in fact, no limitations or restrictions as to the number of his cattle or the extent of his range. He was "lord of all he surveyed," provided he did not resort to downright dishonesty and theft: and if he was guilty of these offences, it had to be proved, which was a hard thing to do.

To a great extent he was a carnivorous animal and lived off the "fat of the land": his principal article of food being beef, which he always selected from the youngest and fattest animals regardless of the brand it bore. He did this to protect himself, as he knew other stockmen killed his cattle for meat, He used only the choicest cuts; the rest of the carcass was left for the buzzards and wolves. The hide sometimes was cut up and used to make hobbles, quirts, and lariats. This custom was generally indulged in by all cattlemen and was made right by common usage. Cattle that had strayed from the home range were often gathered and sold to the owner of a herd going to Kansas. A report to the real owner was supposed to be made, but sometimes this formality was neglected. This atmosphere of crime had a most demoralizing effect upon the younger generation, who went a step further to make easy money and commenced rustling cattle and horses. Some of the most desperate characters of this period sprang from this criminal atmosphere. Among these were John Hanahan, King Fisher of West Texas, and Billy the Kid, of Arizona, all of whom died violent deaths in the days of reconstruction. King Fisher, a man of strong personality and winning social ways, gave himself up and the courts acquitted him. He reformed and became a renowned peace officer. He gave promise of a wonderful future when he was cruelly murdered. Billy the Kid was offered pardon even if he were convicted by the courts, if he would promise to reform and go straight, but he refused the Governor's offer. Twenty-one men died by his pistol, one man for every year of his life, before Pat Garrett killed him.

I always felt sorry for the wives of the ranchmen who became prematurely old from hard work and lack of diversion. They deserve gold medals and soft places in heaven. At daylight they milked the cows, cooked the meals, washed the dishes and clothes, and carried water from the spring or well, besides sewing and caring for the children. In fact their life was an eternal grind from morning until bed time. There were no neighbors. The children to be schooled had to be boarded in the distant town, and their husbands would be absent several days at a time on cattle roundups. During this absence the wives had to be on guard against surprise attacks from Indians, who murdered many unprotected women and children. But this was not all the poor wives were up against; the husband, to get supplies, had to go to the town many miles away where he would relax and "tank up" on liquor, and for a time forget about the loved ones at home.

The stockmen's wives of Frio County fared better, Cav Woodward, Lu O'Shea. Blackalley, Slaughters, and B. L and Joe Crouch, all of whom drove vast herds of cattle to Kansas, saved the profits, which they invested in lands which they fenced; but best of all they gave their good wives help by building comfortable homes. Joe Crouch, a fine business man. died and left his wealth to his brother, B. L. Crouch, who was of a most benevolent disposition; he gave his fortune away in assisting every friend in need. When old age and sickness stared him in the face and his money was all gone, the boys who had worked for him and whom he had assisted to become successful business men, came to his relief, and laid him away in a style befitting his Christian character of benevolence and good works, but what a memory of love and affection he left behind him!

XVII. RECOLLECTIONS OF THE SHEEP RANGE

In the winter of 1876, when I returned from college, my father desired me to go into the sheep business. He was suffering from a malady from which he died a few months after my return from Sewanee, Tennessee. Mr. Henry Shane, my father's partner in the sheep business, killed a negro barber in an affray on West Commerce Street, in San Antonio. Bail being refused, he was indicted and jailed for murder. All this happened during my father's last illness; and after his death, Mr. Shane being still in jail, I went west to look after things and take charge. I was eighteen years of age, and the former spring I had attended the ewe flock during lambing time, and had assisted Mr. Shane by serving as a herder. I had, therefore, a quite familiar idea of conducting the lambing, shearing, and tying the fleeces, and packing the wool in long bags. I had also learned to speak the Mexican language, and all of these experiences stood me in good shape when the time arrived for me to take charge of some five thousand fine Merino sheep. Mr. Shane, to pay his lawyer to defend him, was compelled to sell his one-half of the sheep. Judge Thomas J. Devine of San Antonio and General Larkin Smith of Georgia became the purchasers. The lawyers desired to start their sons, Joe Devine and Will Smith, in the sheep business. As young Smith had no practical knowledge of the business, I was employed by Judge Devine and General Smith to look after the lambing and shearing, after which the sheep were to be divided. Will Smith was with me during lambing and shearing, and then the flock was divided and the Devine and Smith sheep were driven to the Devine ranch in Bexar County, then called the "Redlands," some twenty miles north of San Antonio to what is now the Claussin ranch. The James sheep I moved to the old Code Adams ranch on the Frio River in Uvalde County. Code Adams bad, the year before, driven a vast herd of cattle to Kansas. Adams owed almost every cow man in Uvalde County and had promised to pay up on his return from the sale of the cattle. But instead of returning he went to California and never paid his debts. The Code Adams ranch house was a picket plastered affair of two rooms. He had built an immense cattle pen, made of upright pickets sufficiently large to hold three thousand cattle. The horse pen was built of upright pickets bolted together in the ground so as to make it impossible for Indians to dig up the posts to steal the cow ponies. Old Man Moore, who was formerly a member of the Texas Navy when Texas was a republic, was care-taker of the Adams ranch. He had a Mexican wife, and a step-son named Buck. Moore, finally realizing that Adams was not coming back, had to seek employment elsewhere and left with his family.

I had been camping with my sheep herders; and, as my father was the owner of the Capron survey on which the Adams ranch house was located, I immediately made the place my headquarters. The surrounding country at that time was almost devoid of cattle, which had been driven in herds to Kansas. The range was beautiful, covered with grass knee high, and stocked with an abundance of game of every description— deer, wild turkey, javalinas, and quail of two varieties. The Frio stream was full of black bass and cat fish; in fact it was a veritable paradise for me, as I always have been a lover of the country and consider that the happiest time of my life was in pursuit of game and fishing. Deer in those days went in droves, and many times I have seen, during a dry spell, as many as one hundred turkeys drinking water. However, I was kept so busy looking after the Mexican shepherd, counting the different flocks, and hunting lost sheep, that I did not have much time for hunting. The lobo wolves and coyotes were numerous and did great damage in killing lost sheep. One lobo wolf killed fifteen mutton sheep, which I found after trailing them. 1 bought strychnine poison by the dozen bottles, and always carried in a buckskin pouch a bottle of the poison, and wherever I found a dead lamb or sheep I poisoned the carcass. Often at sundown I would drag the paunch of a dead animal for a mile by my stake rope and scatter baits along the trail. Next day, by watching buzzards. I located many dead coyotes and lobo wolves. At night the howl of the big lobos and the yelping of the coyotes made the air ring with their voices. By persistent poisoning I finally came out victorious, and often a bunch of lost sheep would be gone for several days without any of them being killed. After killing out the varmints, the game became more abundant than ever and turkeys were so numerous that one riding the range would never be out of sight of a flock of these birds. I remember one morning I killed a turkey in camp. The turkeys had roosted in the trees over my head.

I certainly led a happy life when I had time to hunt and fish. I can truthfully say that I never killed any more game than I and the Mexican herders could consume, and all of my life I have made that my rule, and I never had any game to spoil on my hands.

After several months of work with the sheep I visited my mother and brother in San Antonio, and became civilized, but was always glad to return to the country.

I met several interesting characters while out west. I got my mail and did some trading at the Bill Smith farm on the Leona, about six miles west of my camp. Here I met a boy about my own age, named John Hanahan, who lived on the Leona, a few miles north of the Smith farm, with his mother, a widow, and a one-eyed brother named Jim. John was good looking, pleasant and intelligent, and I liked him. Through some unfortunate reason he did not get along well with his neighbors, who accused him of some rascality and went before an Uvalde County grand jury and had him indicted. Hanahan became furious and vowed vengeance, and actually threatened his accusers. He hid out to avoid arrest, and often afterwards visited me. I treated him as though I had never heard of his trouble, but I noticed he was always armed. Franck Stockton, a friend whose health was failing, left his position in Washington, D.C., and came to visit me with the expectation of going into the sheep business. Stockton met Hanahan and on a trip to Uvalde he told the sheriff that Hanahan was camped near my ranch. Frank informed me that Meek, the sheriff of Uvalde, had deputized me to arrest Hanahan on sight. I was alarmed at Frank's indiscreet action in informing the Uvalde authorities of Hanahan's location, as by this time I knew he was rustling horses from Uvalde and Frio County ranches and driving them to the border and disposing of them, and he had always been friendly by leaving me out of his unlawful pursuits. Hanahan's friends informed him of his danger of arrest and he quit visiting me. One morning I found my favorite saddle horse, which was belled, killed. The bullet that killed him was from a rim-fire cartridge shell I found, fired from a brass mounted winchester. The fence had been let down, and from the tracks I was convinced that an attempt had been made to drive all of my horses out, but I had two wild mules that refused to be driven and ran back into the brushy pasture, followed by the rest of my horses and it being night, with no horse bell to guide the thieves, the attempt proved a failure. Hanahan was soon afterwards killed while resisting arrest, near Laredo, by King Fisher, who was deputy sheriff of Uvalde County.

King Fisher was an interesting character, and one of whom I saw a great deal. Old Man Taylor, who had a ranch on the Leona below Uvalde, bought the NO brand of Nat Lewis horses and employed King Fisher to dispose of them. The horses were wild stock and ranged in the vicinity of my ranch. I often watched Fisher roping and taming the wild brutes. His work in the pen was wonderful. He would toss the lariat among a bunch of running horses and catch the wanted one, sometimes by the head, and often by roping the running animal's two front feet, which immediately threw the horse to the ground, and before he could arise Fisher had him tied down. He was as strong as a bull, and had an eagle eye. He was not a large man. but tall: he was sparsely built, with a handsome face, and his movements were rapid and graceful. It was reported that in a duel to the death, with five men all shooting at him, he escaped unhurt, after killing all of his adversaries. Fisher often took his meals with me, and proposed that he and I go into business together, the proposition being for him to run horse stock and for me to continue in the sheep business. As he was such good company and possessed an engaging personality, I was tempted by his offer; but his former reputation was bad, so I declined. He never referred to his past life, and we became fast friends. I admired him when he spoke of the bright future in store for him. as the best element of Uvalde citizens had favored to elect him sheriff of Uvalde County. The last time I saw King Fisher was at the corner of Commerce Street and Main Plaza in San Antonio, He informed me that he was on his way to Austin to interview the Governor of the State in regard to the fence cutting law and the manner in which to proceed to stop the unlawfulness, as he was to be the next sheriff of Uvalde County. He returned from Austin to San Antonio with bad company, Ben Thompson, who was drinking, and a most dangerous companion, who persuaded Fisher to go with him to Jack Harris's saloon. Fisher, from the evidence afterwards taken, had not taken a drink of liquor, and had tried all of the time to quiet Thompson and avoid trouble. He had, during the shooting, made no attempt to draw his pistol. He was cowardly murdered in the spring of his life when the future seemed so bright for him who had reformed and left behind him all his bad reputation.

In the spring of 1880, I sent word to F. A. Piper Co., of Uvalde, to send me down some teamsters to haul my wool to San Antonio. Who should appear on the scene but Roy Bean, who afterwards became famous as "The Law West of the Pecos." He had several wagons with Mexican teamsters, Roy Bean's freight outfit to haul my wool was the sorriest I have ever beheld. The six wagons were rickety. The teams to draw same were an equal number of jackasses and emaciated horses, that had seen better days. The harness consisted of ropes, leather and raw hide thongs, chains, and ill fitted collars for the jackasses. In case of rain there was not a wagon sheet. As the weather was rainy, I refused to allow him to leave. He had turned his teams into my horse pasture where the grass was fine. He stayed with me almost a week to allow his teams to recuperate. It surely was a comical sight to see the little jacks hitched up with horses, with my wool aboard on the way to San Antonio.

A funny incident occurred that gave Bean a great deal of pain. I had fenced a one-room house with barbed wire, and to make the gate firm I had placed a crooked cat-claw limb, that had the shape of an arch, over the entrance. But I made the arch too low. and Frank Stockton and I nearly killed ourselves bumping our heads on the obstruction until we finally got used to it. Roy Bean entered all right, but next morning to go out he lowered his head but came up too soon with such great force with the weight of his body to help the blow that he struck the cat-claw wood with the top of his head, It nearly paralyzed him with pain; and when he came to himself, he made the air blue with profanity. He cursed the man who made the gate and all of his people. I was not present; and as I was the guilty party, it was a good thing, but Frank Stockton told me about it.

In the seventies the Indians from Mexico were greatly feared, for they made raids on the settlers during moonlight nights to steal horses and often murdered defenseless people, including women and children. Everybody went armed, as there was no telling when one would be attacked. Henry Shane, my father's partner in the sheep business, had many encounters with Indians. In fact he had killed two redskins. He was perfectly fearless, a dead shot, and rode a fast horse. He often told me of his different fights with Indians and his narrow escapes; he seemed to bear a charmed life. He was acquitted in his trial for the murder of the San Antonio negro, mainly by his wonderful record on the frontier of Texas as a successful Indian fighter. Columbus Upson, the greatest and most successful criminal lawyer that Texas ever had, defended Shane and made the old court house on Soledad Street, in San Antonio, ring with his eloquence in describing Shane's bravery in defending the women and children of West Texas from the savages. Shane always told me to pursue his method if I was attacked. The main thing was not to shoot until I was sure of hitting, and not to waste my ammunition, nor to get excited.

One morning I was returning from D'Hanis, in Medina County, driving a two horse wagon, loaded with provisions for my shepherds. I was singing loudly while going through a thickly wooded hackberry bottom near the Sabinal River in Uvalde County, where, the spring before, one of Shane's herders had been captured by Indians, and his companion some distance away had heard his screams of agony as an Indian pushed an arrow into his heart and left him dead, tied to a tree. Suddenly from behind I heard the rush of a horse; and as I turned in my seat, an Indian only a few feet away wounded me in the back with a lance. It was a glancing wound made so by my turning as he passed me swiftly. He gave a most unearthly warwhoop almost in my face. He was hideously painted and was riding without a saddle. I got a near view of him, and he was the most terrible apparition I ever beheld. To say I was frightened is to express it mildly, but I did not lose my presence of mind. In less time than I can tell it I reached for my rifle and jumped to the ground, all of the time holding the reins in my hand. The sudden rush and that awful yell of the Indian stampeded my team, but I finally stopped the horses by directing the pole of the wagon between two trees. I was determined that the bunch of Indians should not get my team, and I dropped into knee high grass, expecting them to attack me. After waiting for some time, and nothing more occurring, and realizing that I was wounded, though at the time I did not feel any severe pain, I decided to move on. I put my hand to my back and found my clothing saturated with blood. I made my way to the nearest ranch of Henry Shane where I became so stiff and weak from loss of blood that I could not stand. I was placed on a mattress by Henry Shane and taken to D'Hanis, to Joe Ney's hotel. The wound, though dangerous, had missed the kidneys, but paralyzed the muscles of my back. Under the care of the doctors, I recovered in a couple of weeks and went back to my camp, ready for another adventure.

    My ranch was about half way between Frio Town, the county seat of Frio County, and Uvalde. When there was a dance at either place, I attended, if possible. Need Pulliam, a friend from Uvalde, would stop at my camp and say, "Vint, there is going to be a dance in Frio Town. Don't you want to go?" In a few minutes I had donned a white shirt and clean clothes, and hopped into his buggy for the dance some twenty miles away. We would dance all night. Gabe Hans would furnish liquid refreshments. What happy times we had in those days of long ago, when youth and pretty girls were the attraction. Fond memory recalls the belles of the ball: Mary Little and Sallie Blackally of Frio Town, Ella and Lilly Nunn, Mary Bowles from Uvalde, and Maggie Clark from Nueces Canyon, all lovely and accomplished, great friends of mine. I remember in those days of Indians and my encounters with rough men I could always depend on my lady friends of Uvalde to take my part, and they were true friends indeed.

Smith Ditch, on the Leona where I received my mail, was an irrigation project of several hundred acres. The labor was Mexican, whose jacals adorned the side of the main ditch of running water. I often attended the "bailes" or Mexican dances. The music was an accordion and the floor was the ground, hardened by sprinkling water thereon. One did not have to be introduced but selected the senorita, who was sitting by her watchful mother. You were not supposed to talk to your fair partner, and after the dance you could escort her to her mother. This procedure became monotonous, and we boys, to have some fun, put up a game on the old lady chaperones. Two of us became involved in an imaginary quarrel; hot words were passed, and we clinched, drew our revolver and fired (in the air). Immediately the dance became a riot. The old Mexican women grabbed their girls and disappeared in the darkness.

Will Blair, the son of a San Antonio dentist, quit his position as a clerk in T. C. Frost's store in San Antonio, to visit me. Will was good company, always full of fun, and enjoyed the novelty of ranch life, A stray dog had taken up with us and Will and the dog put in time hunting wild cats. The dog proved a wonder in trailing and treeing the varmints, and Will soon had a number of wild cat hides to sell. He also brought in kittens alive, which he tried to raise, but always failed. He assisted me during shearing time, after which we made a trip in a wagon to the border.

The first night we stopped at Sargent's Hotel in Brackettville, Kinney County. After we had registered, Mr. Sargent inquired if I was any relation of the late John James of San Antonio; and when he discovered I was his son, he could not do too much for us. He said my father went on his bond when he was appointed sheriff of Bexar County to succeed W. B. Knox. The good meals he served us of hot waffles and butter was a great change from our camp fare.

We visited the town after supper, and you may imagine our surprise to find ourselves in the liveliest burg in West Texas, where the night life could only be compared to the saloons and gambling places that existed in the early days of the gold excitement of California and the Klondike. It was pay day at Fort Clark, adjacent to the town, where thousands of United States soldiers were stationed, and such an assortment of humans I never saw before. There were painted Indians with feathered head-dress, Lipan and Seminole scouts, and members of the famous Bullis band that was the terror to marauding Indians, with Mexicans, white and negro soldiers, desperadoes, and other characters, all armed and ready for a fight or a frolic, with a sprinkling of fair females, soliciting for the bar, where several bar-tenders were as busy as ants serving liquid refreshments, Gambling devices of every description lined the floors of the saloon. Gold, silver, and greenbacks were in plain view on the tables, and the dealer shuffled cards for the many betters who either lost or won, as lady luck would have it. String bands made music, while everybody was busy dancing, drinking or gambling. Will was a natural born gambler, and immediately got in the game, only to lose several dollars before I could stop him. There were several of these sociable places and we visited all of them. One hall was owned by an old friend of mine, a bearded Irishman, who spoke with a distinct brogue, by the name of Tom Maloney, who formerly was a cowman. I knew him in 1874 when I went on a cattle gathering expedition to the Edwards Plateau beyond the head of the Nueces River. Maloney had charge of the remuda of cow ponies which were hidden away in the hills far from the ranch to be safe from Indian raids, as the Indians always raided the settlements, Maloney made me stop gambling, saying that was his business, and advised me not to commence that bad habit. I knew his advice was good, but I had hard work to make my friend, Will, quit.

Next morning after a hearty breakfast of hot cakes and coffee we told our genial host, Mr. Sargent, goodbye and started on our way to Eagle Pass. The country we passed over was a flat open prairie, we saw many a herd of antelope as they circled around us.

At Eagle Pass I met an old school mate by the name of Zoller, who introduced us to the river guard, who allowed us to bring over from Piedras Negras cigars and liquid refreshments.

Will Blair accepted a clerkship in F. A. Piper's store in Uvalde and became a great favorite with the Uvalde people. During a religious revival he joined the church, but he did not stay good for long, for in a few months he was back in his old ways. In 1884, I again met him in Los Angeles, California, where he was running a shoe store. Once more I had the time of my life with him. He knew everybody, and I saw everything in Los Angeles, which at that time was a town about the size of the present San Antonio. I often wonder what became of him. I envied his winning ways and his charming personality.

XVIII. RECOLLECTION OF A TRIP TO CALIFORNIA 55 YEARS AGO.

In 1882 I sold my land and sheep at a handsome profit and quit the business. In the spring of 1883 my mind gently turned to thoughts of love and after a swift courtship I married a seventeen year-old girl of my choice. We had a decorated church wedding, followed by a grand reception at the home of the bride's parents, which was attended by Mayor French and the elite society of San Antonio, and the next day we left for a trip to California.

The Southern Pacific Railroad, and the G.H. S.A. Railroad were joined by driving the golden spike some 200 miles west of San Antonio on January 12th, 1883. On the following February 6th the first through freight train to New Orleans from California passed San Antonio. The morning after our departure we had breakfast in a box car, and afterwards almost all our meals through Texas and Arizona were either in lumber shacks or box cars standing on the railroad track. After we passed Devil's River we saw no trees until we arrived in the beautiful San Bernardino Valley in California. After we passed El Paso, Texas, we saw no water until we arrived at the Colorado River at Fort Yuma, Arizona, except a small stream called the Gila. The country we passed through was mainly a desert of wind blown sifting sands, bordered by high distant mountains with not a tree to break the monotony of the scene. We suffered greatly from the stifling heat in the only one Wagner Sleeping Car, which was a poor excuse for the splendid modern vestibule

Pullman cars now used. At Langtry I met my old friend Roy Bean then the "Law West of the Pecos" (He had hauled my wool to San Antonio in former years). He named his place "Vinagoroon" (the name of a deadly poisonous insect peculiar to that locality). In 1881 the world famous beauty, Lily Langtry, got the conductor of the S. P. train to stop so as to allow her to interview Roy Bean, who fell in love with the Jersey Lily and immediately renamed his town Langtry.

In 1883 the eyes of the people of the United States were focused on the States of New Mexico and Arizona. Billy the Kid and Geronimo, the Apache Indian chief, were giving the government both state and National a good deal of trouble. Billy the Kid, that most wonderful misguided picturesque desperado that the southwest ever produced, had killed twenty-one men: all of whom were desperate two-gun characters, one man for every one of his years. The Kid had many good qualities inasmuch as he never forgot a favor, and never forgave an injury. His friends were legion and they protected him when pursued by the legal authorities by absolute silence as to his whereabouts. His superb bravery, his daring, his love affairs (the women fell for him), his wonderful escapes from death are to this day recounted at the hearthsides and camp fires of Lincoln County, New Mexico. The Kid never saw Pat Garrett, the man who laid in wait in the house of his sweetheart and killed him. Kipp McKinney was deputy sheriff to Pat Garrett and was present when Garrett killed "Billy the Kid". McKinney afterwards worked for the writer on his Muerlo Ranch in Uvalde and Kinney counties, Texas. The United States sent the renowned General Lew Wallace, the author of BEN HUR, to New Mexico to straighten out the feud existing there. General Wallace sent for the Kid and personally offered him amnesty and pardon, even if he were convicted by the courts, if he would give himself up and stand trial, or leave the country. The Kid refused, saying "that was his country and he would take the consequences". Geronimo, that old Indian murderer, and his band of cut-throats succeeded in defying the United States army for several years. The army however, followed him across the Sierra Madre Mountain into Old Mexico almost to the Pacific Ocean until he was almost worn out. He returned to the United States fighting with all the desperate valor that savagery knows. He finally surrendered to General Nelson A. Miles of the U.S. Army.

I remember seeing from the train in 1883 several detachments of the United States Cavalry trailing Geronimo. The dust they raised could be seen for miles. They looked fatigued and suffered from the intense mid-day sun. 1 viewed this Arizona country we were passing, with a great deal of interest, for in June, 1854, my father, John James, with 35 armed men, drove a thousand head of cattle from San Antonio, Texas, to California along the same trail that the S-P. railroad now runs. The cattle and men arrived at El Paso July 31st, 1854, without any conflict with Indians. On September 13th, 1854, near the Mexican town of Santa Cruz, the Apache chief "Mangus Colorado", killed James Houston and a Mr. Franchild, two Texans, and stole more than a hundred head of cattle. "Captain Collahan of Seguin, Texas, was in charge of the Erskine herd of cattle, got sixteen men from the John James outfit and with a lieutenant and a company of twelve Mexican soldiers followed the red skins; and in an encounter killed twenty-three Indians, all of whom the Mexican soldiers scalped with the loss of only one Mexican soldier and recovered all the stolen cattle". (The above was copied from the "Erskine diary" of the Erskine cattle drive to California, that proceeded John James' herd.) One of the John James herders was an educated young man from Tennessee who was working his way to California, and who kept a diary which was filled with graphic description of the daily events of this memorable trip, as follows:

September 13th, 1854—"Passed a ranch, owned by a wealthy Mexican who is the lordly possessor of eighty leagues of land with some dozen ranches thereon. We passed a very good looking house, very extensive, probably large enough for thirty families. I learn the owner is the Governor of Sonora, Mexico, the mission of San Gabriel (the oldest mission now in the United States) is in fine preservation. It shows two fine octagon towers in front, a dome in the rear, the face is handsomely ornamented with moldings and, etc."

September 20th, 1854—"Mr. James is endeavoring to trade for eight mules with the commandante of Tucson. Nearly one- half of our mules and horses have died of a disease of the lungs. It is difficult to distinguish the Mexican soldiers from the citizens, they are in fact a set of ragamuffins. The padre (the priest) is rather the best specimen of manhood I have seen, and from the (solemn duty of his corporation). although the thought is impious, I suspected his indulgence in unspiritual things. The priest came into our camp with the commandante. Mr. James suggested that a bottle of champagne would not be unpalatable. When we went to get the wine the commandante sent word not to get too much for the padre would get drunk."

"The Jesuits must have been far ahead to have established this mission in this wild country." All this country, including the town of Tucson, at that time belonged to the State of Sonora, Mexico. The ratification of the treaty of Hidalgo gave the above country to the United States.

The train stopped at Fort Yuma. The Yuma buck Indians clad only in a waistband and a breech cloth with an ornament either on the nose, wrist, or neck, met us, and offered for sale, trinkets, bow and arrow, etc. After suffering intolerable misery through the desert next day, we entered the beautiful San Bernardino Valley in California, and here we felt that we were in paradise. Beautiful residences terraced among the many hills, which were covered with stately trees, the surrounding farms and orchards, loaded with ripening grain and luscious fruits, all showed what wonders irrigation could produce.

Los Angeles was soon reached. The street from the depot to the city was lined on both sides with Mexican jacals, which reminded me very much of San Antonio. We became guests of the only prominent hotel called the Pico Hotel, named after one of the former Mexican governors, and which was a two story Mexican affair, built around a patio which was filled with the most beautiful flowers and roses. The city population then was about forty thousand, and the buildings were small and confined entirely to the valley. The surrounding hills were only a barren waste of earth and sand, and the town itself was only a business center for the surrounding agricultural country, famous for its fruits and grain. We visited in Los Angeles every place of any consequence, and I remember seeing nothing of interest except vast hogsheads of native wine stored in the cellars.

On our way to San Francisco we passed through another desert (Mojave). We arrived in Oakland where we took the ferry across the bay to San Francisco, the metropolis and most beautiful city on the Pacific Coast and also the gateway to the Orient.

The cosmopolitan population was composed of many different nations, caused by the rush of humanity to California in 1849 on the discovery of gold. Americans from the different states predominated, but there were also Mexicans. Chinese, and Japs by the thousands. The Chinese to this day have a business part of the city that is occupied wholly by them with their stores, apartments and living quarters called ' China Town," and a trip through China Town in former years was a great attraction as it is today.

The location of San Francisco is one of the most beautiful in the world. Golden Gate is the entrance to the bay from the Pacific, and its superb harbor is deep and protected by the surrounding hills. In the bay are several rocky islands which give it the most picturesque appearance. Across the bay are the cities of Oakland, Berkeley, and Alameda, where the climate is much warmer than San Francisco, though only a few miles distant. San Francisco is cold, windy, and often foggy and disagreeable. The cold water of the Pacific is not pleasant to bathe in, and I often went across the bay to Alameda to bathe, where the waters were warm and pleasant. The apartment houses in San Francisco are equipped for fires the year round.

In 1883 San Francisco had the best and cheapest restaurants in the world; for the small sum of fifty cents one could feast on an elegant dinner served in courses consisting of several different kinds of meats and vegetables, with a quart bottle of claret wine, followed by a dessert and coffee. Meat and fish could be left out in the open for several days without spoiling.

We stopped at the Palace Hotel, corner of Montgomery and Market streets, one of the finest hotels in the United States. It was built of California redwood and was only a few blocks from the Market Street ferry which was then, as it is today, the center whirlwind of travel, with people coming and going to and from trains, street-cars, and boats.

Colonel Andrews, the man who built the first railroad into San Antonio, my father-in-law, now arrived from Texas, and we departed for the Hotel Del Monte, near the old Mexican town of Monterrey, on the Pacific Coast, where we met the prominent and wealthy people of San Francisco and California, the Crokers, Huntingtons, Hopkins, and Fargoes, who had acquired great wealth by building the Central Pacific Railroad across the Rocky Mountains under great handicaps, until it was joined at Salt Lake City with the railroad which the U. S. Government constructed from the East. The Central Pacific was afterwards merged into the Southern Pacific, now one of the wealthiest corporations in the United States, rated at seven hundred million dollars. Hotel Del Monte was owned by the Southern Pacific Company, and worlds of money was spent to make it beautiful: rare flowers and roses of every description adorned its walks and giant trees made shade. The bathing pavillon was filled with great tanks of heated water from the ocean. The beautiful scenic seventeen mile drive along the Pacific Ocean was known to every traveler on the Pacific Coast, Every summer evening the dancing hall was filled with happy couples dancing to the music of the finest orchestra. Here the guests enjoyed life to its fullest extent by driving along the coast, bathing, and picnicking under the big trees, going on excursions to adjoining pleasure resorts, spending the day along the many beautiful resorts, and dancing to an orchestra on a tarpaulin under the checkered shade of the big trees with wine and all the good things to eat and drink to while away the time.

Miss Hattie Croker, the red-headed daughter of Charles Croker, was a very attractive young lady, gifted with a wonderful personality, and was the life of every party she attended. My wife had many accomplishments; she was a good musician and gifted with a sweet voice; she was quick at repartee, a born mimic, and an elocutionist of dramatic ability; with these accomplishments, together with her youth and charm, she could favorably entertain the most cultured audiences. She became a great favorite and was often called upon to display her talents at entertainments. She would play her own accompaniment and sing a comic song which would get the audience laughing at her wonderful mimicry, and at the encore that always followed, she would let down her long hair over her face and shoulders and recite the "Maniac" with dramatic ability, and she looked the part. We were entertained at the palatial residence of Charles Croker on Knob Hill, San Francisco, the president of the Southern Pacific Railroad. It is beyond my ability to describe the grandeur of that home, suffice to say that the appointments were regal, and I never before saw such a magnificent display of wealth; even the dinner plates we ate from were solid gold A banker and his wife entertained us at his beautiful home in Stockton, California, where we spent many happy days. Colonel Grey, chief engineer of the Southern Pacific Railroad, also invited us to visit him in his San Francisco home. During our entire stay in California of over three months we were guests at the Palace Hotel in San Francisco and Hotel Del Monte on the Pacific Coast. My wife had a serious attack of pneumonia, and on her convalescence. Col. Andrews secured the private car of the General Manager of the Southern Pacific Railroad in which we returned from San Francisco to San Antonio.

PART THREE
San Antonio

I. SAN ANTONIO 98 YEARS AGO

The records in the city clerk's office of the council proceedings, during the turbulent period of the early days of the Republic, present interesting reading characteristic of the disturbed condition of society then existing in the frontier town on the border of the great West. The only inhabitants west of San Antonio were wild Indians who roamed unmolested over the boundless prairies covered with high grass, on which grazed countless bands of wild horses, antelope, deer, buffalo and other animals.

After the battle of San Jacinto, the feeling of security consequent to the retirement of the Mexican troops across the Rio Grande was rudely shattered by the sudden appearance of a formidable Mexican army advancing on San Antonio. The inhabitants fled in terror, neglecting to conceal the archives of the council, which were either destroyed or carried away by the invaders. The valuable Spanish documents which established the validity of the Spanish grant were lost during former Mexican occupation and the field notes defining the boundaries of the town tract were in utter confusion. The influx of immigration subsequent to the establishment of Texas independence was great, and the immigrants settled wherever there was unoccupied land and no protesting owner on hand to run them off.

The corporation of San Antonio found themselves helpless and it was only after great expense, litigation and time, that the rights of the city were firmly established, and squatters finally ejected. The records of the city council on February 20th, 1840, furnish an interesting case, which portrays vividly the condition then existing, which is replete with facts that are humorous, as well as tragic. The following is an exact copy taken from an old volume now on file in the city clerk's office:

"J. M. Smith, mayor, read the following petition of James Goodman to the council: To the mayor and corporation of this City: I deem it proper to lay before your honorable body the many causes that induced me to act as I have done and undertake to put up a fence, repair the roof of these premises, etc.

1. When I came to San Antonio I requested the then corporation permission to work in the place where I now occupy. Their reply was, that the corporation had no quorum and nothing could be said or done by them.

2. I understand from persons well informed (they appeared so to me) that it was doubtful whether the premises belonged to the corporation, or to the public, in a short time after those premises was inhabited by a hoard of runagates from the Rio Grande, some of whom broke into my place and stole a pair of pistols and double gun. I could guess very close who^the persons were who committed the theft, I cautioned them to keep at a civil distance for the future, their next proceeding was to fire at me in the night when in my bed according to the old saying an inch is as good as a mile, I then applied to Mr. Maverick and told him that they should be turned out of the place that that band of Rio Grande runagates were the persons that was robbing and committing depredations in town, after that they stole my sign board whilst I was sick, that was taken down to one of the missions and something made of it. Therefore as there was no corporation or no authority, I myself undertook to clear them out and succeeded. Since there was no whooping nor hallowing at nights, nor robberies committed, I began to form a corporation within myself by making a fence in front of said premises to secure my

life and property and be prepared for the attack of HOGS, DOGS, COWS, and THIEVES, buc now there is an incorporated corporation that promises to secure life and property, consequently I hope there is no need for my preparatory proceedings against the above mentioned nuisance but I will be on the lookout for the latter.

3. I considered what I was doing towards the premises would be an improvement and would be looked upon as such by the corporation or the Republic of Texas when either would claim it,

4. And finally I wish to make myself permanent in some healthy part of Texas and there make myself at home, or in other words, make myself a home, for it is not an easy matter to be moving from place to place, the quantity of tools and machinery that I have got. Mr, Patterson is gone to New Orleans, he promised to bring me a large pair of bellows as I intended to do smith work in general wagons, carts, etc. Now gentlemen with all dues respect I wish to hear from you as soon as possible and state what encouragement you would be pleased to give to a person of my capacity and ability so that I may have time if it be necessary to countermand some arrangements I have made that will be expensive.

Yours always obedient to justice.
"San Antonio, Thursday, February 1840.
(Signed)   JAMESGOODMAN".
(Remained on table until a full meeting.)

The location of the land squatted on by James Goodman was directly opposite Kalteyer's old drug store on Military Plaza, near where our city hall now stands. Goodman held possession for many years and defied the city authorities to move him.

The following is taken from the records of the council:

"On April 26, 1841 the council acted on J. Goodman's petition as follows: That Goodman pay the corporation 25 per cent from January until such time until he proves he can hold possession of premises.

October 28, 1841, James Goodman's case decided in favor of the City.

July 16, 1842, James Goodman defeated for alderman by Van Ness.

March 3, 1841, Ed. Dwyer elected mayor and J. Goodman elected an alderman in the new council.

May 25, 1841, Goodman tenders his resignation and gave the following reasons: That it has been proposed by Alderman Garza to give instructions to City Attorney Spencer to take an appeal from the judgment of the district court of the county of Gonzales to the supreme court of the republic in the case of the City of San Antonio vs. James Goodman and order him to prosecute the same to final judgment. Mr. Goodman therefore thought it incumbent on himself to resign his seat at the board, as he might become interested against the corporation as defendant in said suit. Mr. Goodman's resignation was accepted.

February 22, 1845. On account of the abuses of City Attorney Spencer, T. J. Devine was employed to prosecute suits against trespassers for the salary of $100 per year and a contingent fee of one-eighth of appraised value of all land so recovered by him".

It is a matter of history that after a great deal of expense and time the city of San Antonio was finally successful and succeeded in ejecting all trespassers from the plazas.

II. OLD TIMES IN SAN ANTONIO

JAMES R. SWEET was mayor of San Antonio many times His first term was in January, 1855, and after that he served four other terms, at intervals, the last being to January, 1863. Mr. Sweet was the most progressive and highly educated mayor up to his time and was in every sense a leading citizen. There was more improvement during his term of office in new buildings than ever before, and the evidence of the public trust reposed in him and his efficiency as a public servant and a man of high character was recognized. He came to San Antonio from St. Johns, New Brunswick. He married Charlotte James, who eloped with him when she was a pupil in a convent in Nova Scotia. Charlotte James was a sister of John James, the pioneer. Mr. Sweet was connected with the old Daily Herald as editor, and afterwards, in 1850, he became a prominent merchant in San Antonio, at the same time he was elected mayor. He became wealthy, was a large land-owner, and his home at the head of the San Antonio River, was one of the most beautiful spots in the South, and included what is now Brackenridge Park and the Incarnate Word College grounds.

When the Civil War came Mr. Sweet resigned as mayor and quit his large mercantile business to become a colonel in the Confederate army. Colonel Sweet made a gallant and brave officer and his name is indelibly written in the history of San Antonio.

Alexander Sweet was a son of J. R. Sweet, and afterwards became famous as the editor of THE TEXAS SIFTINGS, published in Austin and New York. He was a graduate of Heidelberg University in Germany, and surprised his parents on his return to San Antonio by introducing bis wife, a pretty German girl, Miss Zittell, who could not speak a word of English.

Before the Civil War San Antonio was fast becoming a prosperous city, which was supported by a rapidly developing country that was stocked with vast herds of cattle and many sheep. Along the many beautiful streams settlers from other states were settling to engage in farming and stock-raising, Protection from Indian raids by the United States troops, who occupied the many frontier posts in Western Texas, promised security and confidence for the future.

Among the prosperous merchants of ante helium days were James R. Sweet, Nat Lewis, who came to Texas in 1842, the Vance Brothers, Samuel Bell 6 Sons, Groesbeck ft French, and Wilson Riddle.

In 1859 the San Antonio Gas Works, located on West Houston Street, was inaugurated by Mr, Torrey. The Casino German Club had a grand opening on Market Street on its completion in 1858. The Menger Hotel, on Alamo Plaza, did a flourishing business and was enlarged in 1859. The U.S. Arsenal, on South Flores Street, was completed and in operation in 1859. The Episcopal rock church, on Travis Street, was half completed at the beginning of the Civil War. All of the above improvements occurred during the mayoralty of James R. Sweet.

Suddenly, like a bolt of lightning from a clear sky, came the firing on Fort Sumter, which shattered all the bright prospects of San Antonio. Everything was changed to ruin and despair and the most dreadful calamity that ever cursed the human race descended, causing such bitter feelings even brothers were arrayed against each other in the fight to death. Old Sam Houston, the father of Texas, tried bis best to keep Texas from seceding. After four long years of strife, although victory sometimes perched on the Southern banner, the end was defeat for the South. All of the glorious expectations of wealth, happiness and future greatness were shattered in San Antonio, for the South was broken and poverty-stricken. All evidences of wealth, property and slaves vanished, Everyone had to commence life over again, but San Antonio citizens after a time, recovered and went to work to rebuild their fortunes. Among the heroes who returned from the war, started anew and succeeded beyond their expectations were Major J. H. Kampmann, G. A. Duerler, Dan and Barney Oppenheimer, Manuel Yturri, Col. M. Pryor, Gen. William Steel, Col. T, G. Williams, H. B. Andrews, J. R. Sweet and Gen. George Howard.

A new set of merchants after the war conducted the mercantile business in San Antonio, among whom were several Jewish firms who, by strict attention to business and fair dealings, built up great business houses, and today are among the wealthy and respected citizens of San Antonio. After the Civil War business was at its lowest ebb, there being no money to make improvements or to keep the city clean. Real estate was a drag, its value destroyed by taxes. The gas works, completed in 1859, was idle, there being no funds to run it. The streets at night were dark. The plazas during the rainy weather were quagmires; people who went abroad at night carried lanterns to avoid mud puddles. Paschal Square, on the west side, had a deep gully, where dead dogs and cats were thrown; and the stench was something awful. The trash and garbage was thrown into the back yards. Drinking water was obtained from shallow wells and irrigation ditches, and this water became contaminated from outhouses, and typhoid fever and malaria was always prevalent. Livery stables did a big business, while the grain waste and garbage harbored thousands of rats and millions of flies, which were the principal inhabitants of San Antonio in those gloomy days. Where there is one rat in San Antonio now there were thousands then; they "fought the dogs and killed the cats". We boys had a great time hunting rats at night with the help of a little wire haired reddish dog called a rat terrier. We killed them by the hundreds.

In 1866 the cholera epidemic came to town, and the total fatalities were two hundred and ninety-two. Our city fathers then got busy and cleanliness got a start.

One of the greatest assistants financially was the U.S. Government headquarters in San Antonio, which gave protection from the Indians by resuming command at the different posts in Western Texas. During the Civil War the Indians became a great menace, as there were no soldiers to keep them in bounds. By re-occupation of the different forts by the U.S. soldiers the ranchmen and farmers again became prosperous. The settlers in West Texas, who returned to their ranches, found their herds of cattle had immensely increased during their absence, and then commenced the great cattle drives to Kansas, where good prices were obtained. During the Franco-Prussian War in 1874 wool sold in San Antonio for fifty cents per pound. The vacant lands in West Texas at once became valuable, all of which caused a great rush of immigrants to engage in the sheep and cattle business, and San Antonio reaped a harvest and soon became famous as the greatest cattle and sheep market in the South. San Antonio, to complete its prosperity, only awaited the advent of the railroad, which had been promised so many times, but these promises never had materialized.

In 1857 the United States Army had its headquarters in the Vance House, at the corner of Houston and St. Mary's streets with General Albert Sidney Johnson commanding. In 1860 General Robert E. Lee was in command. In the seventies the U.S. Infantry soldiers' quarters were housed in the Vance block on Travis Street, and the parade grounds were in the enclosure between Navarro and St. Mary's streets. Capt. William Tobin's hotel opened at the corner of St. Mary's and Houston streets in 1872. A band of Indian squaws, with one Indian buck named Castalito, was guarded on those grounds in 1873; they had been brought in by General Mackenzie, and were visited by the citizens. There was one pretty young squaw who attracted a great deal of attention.

Houston Street in the early days was called by the Mexicans and Americans "Paseo Hondo," or Deep Gully, because it was almost impassable in wet weather and drained all the land lying east of Travis Park and north of the Alamo, and across Houston Street where the Washer Store is now, extending south across the Maverick building lot to where it entered the San Antonio River, and where the North Presa Street bridge is now.

The most valuable property today is on Houston Street, of which I will try to give a short history. On account of the periodical floods there was only Commerce Street bridge which was permanent. On March 22, 1865, Houston Street bridge was washed away and seven people in the city were drowned. The foot bridges connecting Houston Street with Commerce Street at Navarro and St. Mary's streets were only temporary affairs that went out with every flood, all of which caused Houston Street to be neglected for business reasons, on account of its inaccessibility. The Vance Brothers and Samuel Maverick, in 1866, owned all the north side of Houston Street, extending from Alamo Plaza to St. Mary's Street. In those days there was no Avenue C, or Jefferson Street. The only residences on the north side were the Maverick, at Alamo Plaza, Sappington and Lingsweiller's at the corners of Houston and Navarro. On the south side was the James Vance, the Dr. Herff, the Dittmar, and Professor Plaeggue's. Afterwards Mr. Crider had his carpenter shop where the Central Trust Co. Bank is now.

Wagner Bros, had a planing mill and carpenter shop where the Majestic Theater is now. The first real estate improvement on Houston Street was in 1872. The Samuel Maverick Estate generously gave a large lot situated at the corner of Jefferson and Houston streets to the "Alamo Literary Society", a club composed of San Antonio young business men who desired to erect a building suitable for their needs. The officers of the club at once entered into a contract with J. H. Kampmann, who agreed to erect a building according to plans, etc. Mr. Kampmann erected an ugly soft rock one-story building, which enclosed a large room with a stage that was to be used for theatrical performances, for dancing parties and for political gatherings; but the building was never finished according to the plans, and Mr. Kampmann, to get his money expended for the ugly building, became the owner of the building for a song on account of non-payment. In 1890 he built four large stores and a hotel, and today that property is worth around a million dollars.

J. M, Vance, was the first merchant who opened up a grocery store at the corner of Avenue C and Houston Street, in the late seventies. Afterwards W. G. Edwards became his partner, and the business was moved to the northeast corner of Navarro and Houston streets. Houston Street began to improve in 1890. The U. S. Military headquarters were located in the Maverick Building, on the south side of Houston Street January 1, 1887. The U.S. Cavalry had their stables at the corner of Losoya and Houston streets, which extended south along Losoya to the Losoya residence, where the cavalry officers had their quarters. Scouting parties of U. S. cavalry were here started to pursue Indians after raids in West Texas were reported. I soon forgot my hatred of the Yankee soldiers, and we boys spent many happy hours consorting with them. The Infantry soldiers taught us to play cards and the cavalry soldiers instructed us in the care of our ponies. We often felt sorry for our friends when they violated the rules by getting drunk and the sergeant would drill them in their drunken condition unmercifully and compel the poor fellows to carry a heavy log of wood on their shoulders until they would almost collapse from fatigue.

Sappington's Livery Stable was located on the north side of Houston Street next to the bridge. Where the Texas Theatre building is now, in former days, was a large vacant lot, and afterwards, in 1885, F. F. Collins had his machine and windmill shop there. The Maverick Bank Building, at the corner of Alamo Plaza and Houston Street, was completed in 1884. Sam Maverick had previously a lumber yard on this site.

III. EARLY SCHOOLS IN SAN ANTONIO

The German-English School was established in San Antonio principally by members of the German Casino Association in the latter part of the year 1858. Julius Berends, who kept a book store in San Antonio, was the principal. He also taught a c*ass one hour each day. The school was located on the north side of Commerce Street, where Newton £1 Weller's crockery store later stood. The two story house with galleries, upstairs and down, sat back from the street some forty feet; a wide hall up and down stairs divided four large rooms connected by an ell with a very large room twenty by forty feet, and another large room further down which was afterwards used as a kitchen, A large cellar was under the last three rooms. There was no Crockett Street in those days, and all lots fronting on Commerce Street extended to the San Antonio River. This commodious structure was afterwards used as a hotel by Mr. and Mrs. Kloepper from 1860 until 1875.

In the seventies the first San Antonio public school was inaugurated in the Kloepper Hotel with Mr. Martin, a former Presbyterian minister, as principal. Mr, Martin resigned his pulpit in San Antonio to take charge of the first public school. He discarded whipping and to take its place he appealed to the boys' honor and pride. He was a man of the highest education and his school was very successful. The school was afterwards moved to the Martin Muench Building on the corner of South Alamo and South streets. The city of San Antonio in 1882 erected its first public school building of three stories on Main Avenue.

Pastor Mueller, William Schuwirth, and Pat Troy were the first teachers employed by the German-English School in 1858. and taught in the old Kloepper Hotel Building on West Commerce Street.

Among the students in 1858 and 1859 were Dave Alexander, John Fraser, F. A. Piper, Andrew Wren, John H, James, and Nic Tengg. Nic Tengg became Berends' clerk, and after Berends' death he succeeded him in the book store business in San Antonio. All of the above named students are now dead except Dave Alexander,

In 1860 the German-English School was removed to its site on South Alamo Street. Mr. Duvinick, Mr. Probandt, Mr. Bookout, Mr, Pollmer. Mr. Briedenbach, and a lady, Mrs. Milner, were added to the faculty. Mr. Schuwirth, who was a most efficient teacher, taught German, writing, arithmetic, and singing. He was admirably adapted to his profession by having a positive and interesting personality. He used the rod less and kept better order in his classes than the other teachers, and consequently he was better liked and more respected than the others I remember his leading his class in the singing of the old German song "Lauf Yager Lauf." Even at that early age I had the hunter's instinct within me, and consequently this was my favorite song. Mr. Schuwirth lived to a good old age and died at his residence in San Antonio at 433 Madison Street. Pat Troy and Mr. Duvinick taught the senior class. Probandt and Mrs. Milner taught the elementary classes. The other teachers had the intermediate classes. The motto, "Spare the rod and spoil the child," was religiously lived up to. The Lord only knows how many whippings I received during the years of my attendance from 1865 to 1873. IF we pupils unfortunately informed our parents of these beatings, we got no sympathy but immediately got another for good measure. It is no wonder the teachers sometimes passed the limits of justness and whipped the pupils without good cause. Even during recess the teachers were armed with rulers and used them repeatedly upon the slightest provocation. The scholars sometimes rebelled and resisted to such an extent that a fight ensued. A small boy named Burns got a terrible flogging from Pat Troy, a redheaded, crippled teacher of slight build. Burns informed his grown brother Dick, who was one "tough guy," of the whaling he had received. During recess when the teachers were on the grounds, Dick Burns appeared and cursed Troy for whipping his little brother. Schuwirth's heroism in protecting Troy prevented a tragedy, and it became a fight between Burns and Schuwirth. When Burns drew a revolver and attempted to shoot Troy, he was disarmed by Schuwirth. Burns, nothing daunted, then drew a knife and was again conquered by Schuwirth who used Burns' own pistol to subdue him.

Belger Baylor, a cowboy from the wide open spaces and a nephew of General John R. Baylor of Confederate fame, attended the school and sat next to me in the third class room. One day Mrs. Milner whacked him across the head with a ruler. Baylor was innocent of any disturbance and became furious. He immediately quit his seat, disarmed her of the ruler, and left the school for good,

Charles Herff and Professor Bookout had it out after Bookout had mistreated a friend of Herff's. Fred Newman, who attended the school from 1869 to 1873, informed the writer on January, 1932, that Bookout once whipped him on the school grounds during recess without cause. I was viciously whipped by Bookout for some trivial act which I have forgotten. I resisted him to the best of my strength, for which act I was sent home.

In 1870 the German-English school had 265 pupils and had new additions built to accomodate 500 pupils.

Probandt was a very determined character, and the old pupils remember the stubborn fight between him and a pupil named Oscar Lefering, who is now a resident of El Paso, Texas. Probandt outlived all the other German-English teachers. He was a confirmed bachelor and lived in a small house which he owned opposite what is now the Crockett Hotel. He saved his money and bought real estate, and at his death was worth some $50,000.

Briedenbach was the best liked of all the teachers. He taught geography and history, and woe to the student who failed in recitations. He often used a rod instead of a ruler, and no student ever dared to resist him because of his great size and strength. He was a very nervous individual and had a habit of constantly gnawing and biting his finger nails. He always used the expression "Not so, not so," when he whipped his pupils. He endeared himself to his students by bis wonderful gift of story telling. He was intensely interesting and very sympathetic in delineating the suffering of children in distress. He always had the undivided attention of his pupils, and silence reigned supreme during his lectures. I have a composition I wrote in 1869 based upon one of Mr. Briedenbach's stories. After leaving the German-English School, Mr. Briedenbach taught school in Monterrey, Mexico, for the children of the German-American colony there. He afterwards returned to Texas and taught school in Loyal Valley, situated between the towns of Fredericksburg and Mason. Old age and infirmities found him destitute, and he became an inmate of the San Antonio City Hospital, where he passed his declining years. His only solace was his pipe. He was buried in a pauper's grave during the Marshal Hicks administration. "Peace be to his ashes." He will always be remembered by his pupils for his sympathetic kindness and his beautiful historical stories.

Mrs. Milner came to San Antonio from the North and created a great deal of amusement in her classes by using the expression "Hark" when someone disturbed the class.

Bookout was a teacher who had the highest education. He resigned as a teacher and became a lawyer and partner of Mr. Lawhorn in South Texas. His sign board reading "Bookout and Lawhorn" created considerable amusement. He afterwards located in Dallas and became very prominent in his profession.

Mr. Duvinick, after his teaching days, operated a lumber yard and boarding house in the town of Boerne, Texas.

This account of San Antonio schools would be incomplete without mentioning another private school, that of Professor Plaugge, which rivaled the German-English School. Mr, Plaugge was a very large and dignified man of military bearing and wore a long grey beard. He was an accomplished musician and performed creditably on any musical instrument. He was very rough and a pastmaster in the art of flogging his pupils. When his anger was aroused, he looked dangerous. During the Civil War he cast bis lot with the South and became band master of the famous Hood's Texas Brigade.

Professor Plaugge was a wonderful teacher, and by having small classes, he gave his undivided attention to his pupils and individually imparted his knowledge by constant repetitions until his scholars became imbued with his spirit. Professor Schu- wirth left the German-English School and became a co-worker of Mr. Plaugge. A large following of pupils of the German- English School went with Mr. Schuwirth to Mr. Plaugge's school. This school was situated on the southeast corner of the Navarro and Houston streets intersection, and in the summer for coolness the front doors, which opened directly on the sidewalk, were left open. This offered passersby a full view of his classes. He married a widow, Mrs. Baur, who had two sons. They lived in the rear of his school. He will always be remembered by his pupils who, though disliking his rough methods, blessed him in later life for the good results they received from his teachings.

IV. SAN ANTONIO AND ITS PEOPLE
HISTORICAL HIGH LIGHTS

The colony of Spaniards came to San Antonio from the Canary Islands in 1731. The Spanish Crown gave them liberal grants of land, and their descendants today are prominent in the history of San Antonio.

On March 26, 1836, occurred the Fall of the Alamo. Santa Anna ordered two immense pyres on the Alameda-East Commerce Street. The first pyre was on the north side where the Ludlow Building is now located. The second was on the south side of the old Post Yard where the home of F. Gross was located. The bodies were first stripped then burned; it took two days of fire to consume them.. This was a more humane way to dispose of great numbers of human bodies than the fate meted out to the Mexican soldiers. The Mexican dead were so numerous that Santa Anna ordered Francisco Ruiz, the Alcalde of San Antonio, to bury his soldiers. There was insufficient room in the cemeteries, and thus many bodies were thrown in the San Antonio River, where they lodged against obstructions and checked the flow of the current. Great flocks of vultures hovered over the city for weeks afterwards. Due to the stench of decaying bodies and the unsanitary conditions, many people fell sick, including General Santa Anna,

In 1840 the Court House fight took place on Main Plaza and Market Street, in which 35 Indians and 7 Texans were killed.

Henry and Ben McCullough went first as rangers under the famous leader, Jack Hays, in his many encounters with wild Indians in West Texas. Henry McCullough afterwards went with Colonel Hays in his Texas regiment to the City of Mexico in the war between the United States and Mexico. He was in command of the Confederate forces in San Antonio and it was to him that U. S. General Twiggs surrendered his troops, receiving liberal terms by the Confederate Commissioners — Samuel Maverick, Thomas J. Devine, and Luckett, being permitted to march to the coast with their arms and horses.

The first military company was organized in San Antonio in 1857 with John Wilcox as its first commander. The Alamo Guards was the second company, formed in 1859 with William H. Eager as captain, who performed many other duties in San Antonio for the Confederacy. The San Antonio Rifles was organized in 1884 with C. M. Granger, captain. Henry E. Vernor and Duval West were its first and second lieutenants. Frank Badger succeeded Granger, and Perry Lewis became second lieutenant. The Belknap Rifles was organized with Captain Robert Green as captain; its lieutenants were E. W. Richardson, W. B. Hamilton, W. G. Tobin, and J. F. Green. The San Antonio Zouaves was organized in 1896; Eugene Hernandez was captain.

San Antonio in the early seventies of the last century was the largest wool market in the United States. The wool was hauled in two-wheel ox carts, the bodies resembling immense crates, in which the freight was placed and covered with heavy canvas on circular bows, to shield it from rain and sun. The yoke was fastened to the horns with raw hide thongs, leaving very little movement to the oxen's heads.

In 1875 Charles Cotten, Charles Seabaugh, and John Martin started the San Antonio Express.

Don Narcisso Leal's horse market was at the corner of Dolorosa and South Flores in 1880.

The old Ben Ficklin's Stage Office occupied the building next to the present Dreiss Drug Store on Alamo Plaza. Mr. Muncey was the first agent.

South West Texas in the early days was inhabited mainly by cattle-men who, by great industry and perseverance, became wealthy owners of vast herds that roamed the Texas plains. The cattle drives to Kansas in the later sixties and seventies brought their owners great wealth. The cattle barons were a great meat-eating people, and generally hard liquor drinkers. Inured to the rough life of the frontier, they spent their time fighting Indians, rounding up and branding their increase. This sudden accumulation of wealth made them great spenders when they visited San Antonio. They came to have a good time, and they had it, regardless of cost. They and their friends visited every amusement in the city, both good and bad. and generally ended all by having a great time eating and drinking. During these festivities, sometimes quarrels and disagreements occurred, and homicide took place.

V. CITY OF SAN ANTONIO

San Antonio was settled in the year 1714. It was incorporated as a city in June 1837. The population in 1850 was 3,480; in 1860, 8,235; in 1870, 12,266; in 1890, 37,673; in 1903, 58,016. On November 1, 1904, the bonded indebtedness was $2,151,000. Cash on hand in the sinking fund was $149,344.21. Real Estate improvements and other assets were $3,033,790. Assessed valuation was about 60% of the cash value. There was no default in the payment of principle on interest on the bonded debt, or any other obligation that has ever been made by the city. The first $50,000-at-6%-interest bond was issued by the Callaghan Administration for the purpose of Public Improvements, on July 1, 1887. The second $150.000-at-5%-interest bonds were issued August 1, 1887, for the purpose of building a City Hall. Bryan Callaghan was elected Mayor in 1883, and held office in the Old Bat Cave on Military Plaza. Gas for lighting streets was inaugurated in 1860. Electric lights came in 1883. The first street cars were mule-drawn in 1875. Electric cars came in 1890. The first Volunteer Fire Department started in 1866 with G. A. Duerler as Chief. In 1845 Texas was annexed to the United States[*].

The oldest German newspaper was The Freie Presse Für Texas by A. Simering and G. Pollmer. It was founded in San Antonio in 1869, and afterwards was conducted by Robert Hanschke and Dr. Rochs.

W. C. A. Theilepape, former mayor of San Antonio during the reconstruction period, was an artist and

---

[*] V. L. James was auditor of the city of San Antonio from 1899 to 1905 and secured this information for city records.

bookkeeper for Theodore Schleuning, the grocery merchant.

In 1852 the voters of San Antonio rejected an act to incorporate the city.

On January 29, 1877, the city of San Antonio voted to pay $300,000 for a subsidy for the entrance of the G. H. & S. A. Railway.

In 1878 San Antonio commenced to build.

King Fisher and Ben Thomson were killed in the Jack Harris Saloon and Theatre on March 11, 1884.

The first newspaper was issued in San Antonio in 1848 by Henry Lewis, editor.

The Weekly San Antonio Herald, John A. Logan, editor, was issued March 23, 1854. The Daily Herald was issued on March 23, 1857. Afterwards, Logan was succeeded by Colonel J. Y. Dashiell with Alex Sweet, the humorist, as city editor.

The Old Bat Cave was the first City Hall, and was built in 1850.

The convent foot bridge (floated on empty barrels) was built on November 27, 1868.

The Camels came to San Antonio on November 9, 1859. The Ice Factory opened up for business in 1866. Formerly when the ice wagon came to town, the advertisement said "Arrival of the Ice Wagon from the Bay".

General Ronald Mackensie commanded the U.S. Texas forces from November 11, 1883 to December 1883, when he lost his mind and was succeeded temporarily by General Gearson, who at that time was commander of the U.S. forces at Fort Davis.

The first water pipes were laid in 1878.

The first railway freight train of the G. H. & S. A. R. R. entered San Antonio on February 7, 1877.

During J. M. Devine's administration as mayor in 1856, stock of the Mexican Gulf R. R. was issued for $50,000, but the sale fell through.

Nathan O. Green

VI. PROMINENT MEN AND WOMEN

LAWYERS

A half century ago was the day of harvest for the successful criminal lawyer in San Antonio, who demanded large fees to represent the defendant. I will say, unreservedly, that after the Civil War there was an array of criminal and civil lawyers in San Antonio, whose legal ability and eloquence has never been surpassed.

The criminal lawyer of that day was not like the criminal lawyer of the present time whose employment nowadays points the finger of guilt on the defendant even before the trial takes place. The old lawyers were men of the highest class with splendid war records. They distinguished themselves by bravery and gallantry, and were loved and respected by their fellow citizens.

Among these intellectual giants were Columbus Upson, N. O. Green, T. T. Teel, and Mac Anderson.

Nathan O. Green was one of the most brilliant and able lawyers in the south. He was District Attorney for many years, when the district court was held on Soledad Street. He was endowed with the most remarkable memory—he never forgot a name or face. He was by nature very sociable, which faculty endeared him to every man, woman, and child in the city. He was a prominent officer of the Confederacy in San Antonio.

T. T. Teel was another noted criminal lawyer and distinguished officer in the Confederate Army during the Civil War.

Russell Howard was a brilliant lawyer; his wife was a Miss Elliot, daughter of the owner of the Plaza Hotel on Main Plaza.

Judge Thomas Stribling was a prominent attorney and district judge of Bexar County.

Columbus Upson, the most brilliant and able criminal lawyer San Antonio ever had, was noted for his fine presence and eloquence of speech. He was a brave Confederate soldier, and distinguished himself in the terrible battles in Virginia during the Civil War, Upson held the rank as Colonel in the Confederate Army, and served in the Seven Days Battle before

Richmond, Virginia. He became a member of U. S. Congress. He was the most brilliant in mind, the bravest in action, and the most lovable of men.

Mac Anderson was another criminal lawyer, who, it was said, had no law books in his office. He possessed the most remarkable natural ability, and was a great advocate and successful lawyer.

Colonel Henry Brewster was a prominent attorney: he excelled in his knowledge of military law, and was civilian counsel of many U. S. Military Court-martial cases. He was Commissioner of Insurance, Statistics, and History of Texas at the time of his death in Austin, Texas.

Five brothers named Devine figured prominently in the history of San Antonio. Doctor James Devine was mayor in 1859. In a difficulty with John McDonald, also a former mayor of San Antonio, McDonald was killed by Devine on the northeast corner of Commerce Street and Main Plaza, where Devine had a drug store. Devine was acquitted by the court. Thomas J. Devine was District Attorney from 1842 to 1856, He was appointed Associate Justice of the Texas Supreme Court, and he afterwards became Chief Justice. He was prominent during the Confederacy, and was charged with treason and arrested after the war by the U. S. authorities and confined with Jefferson Davis at Fort Jackson, Mississippi: he was later released. He was considered as a very able and talented lawyer, and often was mentioned and advanced by West Texas politicians as highly qualified for the office of Governor of Texas.

The above criminal lawyers were masters in the art of using invective, ridicule, mimicry, and satire. Their speeches during the murder trial for the defendant were heard by crowded audiences who flocked to the Court House to be entertained by the wonderful forensic ability of the intellectual giants who swayed the jury and audience to tears one moment, and the next amused them by the witticism followed by representation of the innocence of the defendant who, if his past record had been good as an Indian fighter in defense of the frontier or as a soldier, was generally acquitted.

DOCTORS

Dr. John Ganslen was a prominent physician and successfully treated the cholera patients in the 1866 epidemic.

Dr. Ferdinand Herff was the Nestor of San Antonio physicians. He was noted for his many successful major operations. He was universally beloved, as he performed and practiced among the poor, to whom he never sent a bill. His son, Dr. Adolph Herff, also became famous as a great surgeon: and his grandson, Dr. Ferdinand Herff, still keeps up the famous reputation of his illustrous forebears.

Dr. Schleyman also was a prominent physician and administered to the afflicted in the cholera epidemic in 1848. He took Dr. Ferdinand Herff's place during Herff's absence in Europe.

August Nette had the most prominent drug store on Commerce Street in 1865. Nette always wore carpet slippers in his store.

MERCHANTS

Bryan Callaghan, Sr., Nat Lewis, and John D. Groesbeck were prominent merchants, who had their stores in the center of Main Plaza.

Edward Dwyer owned the corner where the present County Court House stands.

A. Dreiss was another prominent druggist whose place of business was at the southwest corner of Alamo and Commerce Streets.

Carl Hilmer Guenther came to Fredericksburg in 1848 and built a grist mill there. When the water gave out, he came to San Antonio and founded, on the San Antonio River, the upper and lower mills, which his descendants own at the present time.

William A. Menger built the Menger Hotel and the first brewery within a radius of many miles. Menger's beer became famous.

Charles Degen was his brewer, and afterwards moved to Blum Street, where he made the purest beer in the United States, so declared by the U. S. authorities, who proclaimed the fact to the world.

William Chrysler was a prominent furniture merchant whose store was located in the French Building on the southeast corner of Main Plaza. He became a confirmed drunkard and lost his business. He spent the balance of his life, when full of liquor, in making speeches to street crowds; he had a splendid voice: and his sharp cracks of witticism always attracted a crowd of amused listeners.

Melfott Norten came to San Antonio in 1838; he was the father of four sons who, in 1857, dealt extensively in hardware in San Antonio. In 1869 the firm became

Norten and Deutz, which continued until 1879, when they dissolved. Deutz left San Antonio and became a banker at Laredo, Texas.

Three brothers, William, James, and John Vance, came to San Antonio from Arkansas. James and William had a store on Alamo Plaza, where they accumulated a fortune. John became a merchant at Castroville, where he built a grist mill; he also was successful.

Peter Gallagher by trade was a rock mason. He became wealthy and owned at one time all the block on which the Alamo now stands, and on which he built a beautiful home. He was also a merchant at Fort Stockton, Texas.

Sam C. Bennett, a brother of the banker, W. A. Bennett, was a prominent merchant in the 60's and 70's of the firm of Bennett and Minter and Cockran. Their store was on the corner of Main Plaza and Market Street.

OTHER PROMINENT CITIZENS

Mrs. Jacques was a heroine during the two cholera epidemics in 1849 and 1866. She nursed the stricken Lawyer Russell Howard in 1866, from whom she contracted the disease and died. Her death was sincerely mourned.

P. L. Buquor was one of the mayors of San Antonio during the Civil War.

James L. Trueheart was taken to Mexico, a prisoner of the Mexican General Woll. Trueheart was District Clerk of Bexar County. John James was appointed District Clerk during Trueheart's absence.

Sam S. Smith was County Clerk for many years. Smith owned the famous Jack Harris Saloon corner of Main Plaza and Commerce Street where Ben Thomas, King Fisher, and Jack Harris were killed, and many other prominent characters met their sudden deaths.

Captain Phil Shardein was City Marshal for twenty-five years.

George H. Noonan came from Castroville, where he had a fine horse ranch, to San Antonio in 1868. He was elected District Judge of Bexar County and served as judge for 25 years, as Bexar County's only District Judge. Afterwards he was elected to the U. S, Congress.

Ed Braden, proprietor of the Braden Hotel on Market Street, was fire chief in the early days of volunteer firemen, and also a Confederate Army Captain during the Civil War.

Senora Candelaria, who died in San Antonio at the great age of one hundred and ten years and who was present in the siege of the Alamo, was granted a pension by the State of Texas on account of her great life work in behalf of Texas.

Jose Penaloza was a butcher and deputy sheriff and had great influence, politically, with the Mexican population of San Antonio.

Thomas Whitehead, an Englishman, married the widow Yturri, who at one time was the owner of the entire block from Yturri Street west along Commerce Street to Main Plaza.

John C. French built the first large office building in the South on the southeast corner of Main Plaza and Dolorosa Street, where many Federal, state, county and city offices for the last fifty years had their different departments.

James H. French was mayor of San Antonio many times. He was distinguished by his fine personal appearance. He made many improvements, built bridges with no bond issue, and was so popular that reelection to the mayor's office often found him with no opponent.

Harden B. Adams was Captain of the Alamo Rifles, organized in 1859; he afterwards became a Confederate officer and subsequently a partner of E. D. L. Wicks. They made a fortune as U. S. Government Contractors by supplying the many different U. S. Army posts in West Texas.

William B. Knox, a former Bexar County sheriff, became a very influential politician in the early days of San Antonio history.

Joseph Schmidt built many prominent homes and business houses, including the old John James residence and the first St. Mary's Catholic Church on St. Mary's Street.

A. A. Wolff, whose beautiful home was at the corner of Garden and King William Street, became alderman and was San Antonio's first Commissioner of Parks.

Max Nuendorf was a justice of the peace; he married a daughter of Don Antonio Menchaca, who was a San Jacinto veteran. J. B. Lacost was also a son-in-law of Menchaca.

J. B. Lacoste was a progressive citizen and organized the present system of San Antonio Waterworks.

Thomas P. McCall was sheriff of Bexar County many years.

John Dobbin was also sheriff and city marshall.

Jose Antonio Navarro was one of three Spanish signers of the Texas Declaration of Independence. He was also a member of the unfortunate Santa Fe expedition and was imprisoned for a great number of years in Mexico.

Colonel Thomas G. Williams was a former U. S. Army officer. He allied himself with the South and became very prominent on Jefferson Davis' staff in Richmond, Virginia, during the Civil War.

Captain Ed Dorsh was famous as a great hunter of wild game. He was also a former Texas Ranger. His collection of deer antlers was the finest in Texas.

L. Uhjassi, Hungarian patriot and exile and former great cavalry leader under Kosuth in the Battle of Sandowa in Poland, came to San Antonio. Uhjassi committed suicide at the age of eighty. He was the father of Mrs. Madrasz, who owned the Madrasz Park.

(The information in the above article was secured from proceedings of City of San Antonio Council records; "Wm. Corner's San Antonio de Bexar" and Charles M. Barnes' "Combat and Conquest of Immortal Heroes", and personal recollection of Vinton L. James.)

VII. SOCIAL LIFE IN SAN ANTONIO

Fifty years ago the two outstanding leaders of the elite society of San Antonio were Mrs. J. H. Kampmann and Mrs. J. J. Stevens, who for many years exercised their power and dominion over the festivities and gala events and all celebrations in the history of the city.

Mrs. Kampmann's antecedents were very prominent in the state of Kentucky. Her father, I. P. Simpson, was one of the most learned and efficient lawyers in San Antonio. The beauty and the lovely disposition of Mrs. Kampmann endeared her to every one both of high and low degree. Mrs. Kampmann once truthfully said: "The richest people are not by any means the nicest people".

Mrs. Kampmann, who was elected chairman of the ladies' committee in 1891, the year the Battle of Flowers celebration of the San Jacinto victory was organized, mothered the association by active leadership. When advanced age and illness disabled her from active participation, she had the parade form in front of her residence, where from the upper balcony she reviewed the procession and gave the signal for the parade to commence the journey through the San Antonio streets.

Mrs. J. J. Stevens for many years was one of the most influential leaders in both charitable and social organizations in the city. She possessed great practical administrative ability, and any work she undertook for the improvement of conditions both civic and social was sure to be successful.

Mrs. J. J. Stevens was chosen the first president of the Battle of Flowers celebration in 1892*.

* "The year after the organization for the celebration of the

Her long life was filled with good works, and her influence was always used for the benefit of humanity.

Anniversary of the Battle of San Jacinto was formed, its management was placed in the hands of the ladies of San Antonio. Mrs. J. J. Stevens was chosen its first president"
*See page 124. Charles M. Barnes "Combats and Conquests of Immortal Heroes."

Mrs. John J. Stevens

SOCIAL EVENTS

THE SUNDAY SCHOOL PICNIC

Among the many annual social events in San Antonio, the St. Mark's Sunday School Picnic was eagerly looked forward to by both old and young. These picnics were held at San Pedro Park, Riverside Park, or later at Sutherland Springs, under the supervision of General Young, the Sunday school superintendent. The younger members played such games as "Ring around the Rosey" or "Pleased and Displeased" while the mothers and fathers sat around and thoroughly enjoyed the "forfeits"; especially when the privilege of kissing the girls was allowed under the rules of the game. The older members of the classes strolled about in groups of twos or threes, went boating, or danced in the pavilion. Of course the greatest moment of all was when the basket lunches were spread beneath the old live oak trees, and great platters heaped with fried chicken, baked ham, homemade potato chips, stuffed eggs, pickles, preserves, and other homemade delicacies were produced to the delectation of all. After the short, but ever too long grace by Dean Richardson, if he happened to honor your particular family group, everyone "fell to" and ate until he could eat no more, but still the table was full of good things which the women would carefully put away until later in the afternoon when "coffee" would be served.

DANCES

At the dancing school we learned the social graces, such as how to approach the young lady of our choice and ask her for the pleasure of the next dance, how to "trip the light fantastic toe" to the accompaniment of music in such dances as the landers, the polka, the quadrille, and the waltz.

Later came the time when we had the pleasure of escorting the young ladies to parties held at the Casino Hall on Market Street, the old Literary Hall on Houston Street, or Turner Hall (Turn Verein) on Nacogdoches Street and the grand balls at the Menger Hotel and the San Antonio Club above the Grand Opera House on Alamo Plaza,

The Ladies Dancing Club was organized by the young married women and they sponsored the debut of the young misses to society.

THE OYSTER ROAST

On March 15, 1891, the San Antonio Express contained the following item:

"Wynne Andrews issued invitations to, and his father gave a charming entertainment last week in the shape of an oyster roast. This was, no doubt, the happiest combination possible. Every one who read the invitation recognized in it the pleasing literary style of the seductive railway folder, and any one who has seen Colonel Andrews preside at a feast knows that the important feature of the oyster roast was better off in his hands. The all-embracing hours mentioned in the invitation gave the guests the privilege of going as early and staying as late as they pleased. Most of them pleased to go early and they all got home too late for supper.

"The view from the ranch is superb; the miniature mountains up at Boerne could be seen trying to raise their heads to the cloudless blue of the sky, and the city nestled in the valley, etc., etc., but an old boiler head, relic of Colonel Andrews' railroad days, was a far more interesting object to that hungry company than any quantity of blue sky and scenery. The boiler head mounted on four stout legs was the "roaster" and around that the crowd lingered from early morn to dewy, or rather frosty eve.

"The Colonel with five able assistants made fish chowder, and took all the praise that it received to himself with the greatest complacency and never mentioned the assistants. Mr. Ed. Andrews excelled all the other gentlemen present in the skill with which he opened oysters, and some of the company really ate a shocking number of them. Reagan Houston, for instance —but it isn't quite fair to tell on him, and want of space forbids the mention of all those who distinguished themselves in the same way. Colonel Andrews' hospitality was really put to a severe test, and he has been heard to say since that the next time he gave an oyster roast he would know who not to invite.

"It was such a really charming party that the society editor feels truly sorry for those who will not be asked to the next one. Fortunately she feels perfectly certain of her own invitation to all Colonel Andrews' parties, because on this occasion he himself presented her in a touching speech with a large bottle of green pickles as the first prize for good behavior".

I have in my possession a group picture taken of this event. The women, with their beribboned, be-feathered bonnets, their pinched in waists, leg-o-mutton sleeves, watches pinned on breasts, are still charming and delightfully feminine; the gentlemen in their derbies, high white stiff collars, four-in-hand ties, and stick pins look quite formal; and the little girls in long ankle length dresses are like pictures from a Kate Grenaway picture book.

Among this group 3re Arthur Seeligson, Mr. and Mrs. H. B. Andrews, Mrs. J. Slayden, Albert Wooley, Miss Pressnal, Mollie Smith, Barclay Andrews, Jim Simpson,

Ned Winstead, Billy, John, and Charles Tobin, Mrs. Areon, Sarah and Lizzie Reed, R. W. Andrews, Ed. Andrews, Mr. and Mrs, V. L. James, Camp Robards, Reagan Houston.

THE FIRST BATTLE OF FLOWERS

An item from the Daily Light of Tuesday, April 14, 1891, gives the following information about the organization of the San Jacinto Day annual Battle of Flowers celebration.

"A largely attended meeting of ladies and gentlemen was held in the club rooms of the San Antonio Club yesterday afternoon. Action was taken to inaugurate an annual celebration of San Jacinto Day, in commemoration of the battle that gained for Texas her liberty from Mexico. Colonel Andrews occupied the chair. The meeting was held to arrange a flower festival and have a battle of flowers in the afternoon. As President Harrison will be in San Antonio on the 20th, it was decided to hold the festival this year on the 20th, instead of the 21st, in his honor.

"In each succeeding year, however, the 21st. will be the day celebrated in this manner. The celebration will take place on Alamo Plaza about 5 o'clock.

"The following Committees have the matter in charge: Financial and program—W. B. Wright, R. W. Andrews, C. W. Ogden, W. C. Robards, W. W. King, E. B. Chandler, J. L. S. Hunt, H. D. Kampmann, J. S. Alexander, G. G. Watts, Major Burbank, Major Morris, and J. H. McLeary.

"Committee on flowers—Mesdames H. D. Kampmann, C. W. Ogden, W. B. Wright, J. H. McLeary, Slayden, H. B. Andrews, W. W. King, S. M. Johnson, Fry, Burbank, Darragh, Stevens, Schramm, and Drought.

Oyster Roast at the Andrews Ranch, March 15, 1891

"Any member of this Committee can receive donations for flowers.

"Everyone who will decorate a carriage or horse, is invited to join in the parade that will be given.

"The following have signified their willingness to decorate carriages and join in the parade:

"Mesdames King, C. P. Smith, Drought, Herman Kampmann, G. G. Watts, S. G. Newton, A. C. Robards, Darragh, Sullivan, E. A, Fry, Michelson, Stevens, McLeary, Wooley, Wash, Fry, Beaumont, Slayden, W. W. King, A. Maverick, E. B. Chandler, Waelder, J. M. Johnson, Burbank, C, P. Smith, Dickman, Morris, C. W. Ogden, A. C. Schrogner, Merriam, Moore, Booth, W. B. Wright, and J. J. Stevens, and Misses Smith, Rummel, and Harnish",

Monday, April 20, 1891, saw a rain soaked citizenry greeting the Chief Executive joyfully and the splendid rain thankfully.

The San Antonio Light of Saturday, April 25th, 1891, gives an account of this first parade:

"The long talked of battle of flowers in celebration of San Jacinto Day occurred yesterday afternoon on Alamo Plaza. The grand street parade was given first and then the battle. By five o'clock nearly every store on Commerce Street was closed and a great many on Alamo Plaza and Houston Street also closed. Street cars and carriages poured their thousands in these streets and on the plaza, and around the Alamo Plaza every balcony and housetop, every door and window and other points of vantage were packed and covered with people. The plaza was one dense mass of humanity and a close estimate made places the number of sight-seers and participants at 15,000. The parade started about 5:30 o'clock on East Houston Street and then moved down to Jefferson through Jefferson to Martin, then to Navarro, and from Navarro to St. Mary's to Commerce Street, to Main

Plaza, and back through Commerce Street, to Alamo Street and Alamo Plaza.

"The procession contained over 100 carriages and other vehicles all gaily decorated and many containing decorations of real artistic merit. Mrs. Madarasaza's carriage, decked in pure while lilies and variegated grasses, with honeysuckle was plain, pretty, and neat. Colonel H. B. Andrews' pony phaeton, with four Shetlands drawing it, was exquisite, and J. J. Stevens' children in a four-in-hand Shetland surrey representing a yacht, was also very pretty.

"A bower of beauty on a heavy float contained about 8 young ladies, all dressed gaily and looking as pretty as possible. Still another float contained about 20 little girls in white, protected in the battle by bulwarks of white frieze and flowers".

Captain Duerler was the chief marshall of the parade and Capt. Geo. T, Chase the chief of staff with a number of army officers as his aids.

BEAUX AND BELLES OF THE ELEGANT EIGHTIES:

H. P. Drought	Charles Tobin
S. G. Newton	Albert Steves
Ira Hewitt	Ernest Steve
Thomas James	Sadie Newton
V. L. James	Adele Redaz
John James	Zulime Tobin
Gus Houston	Lula Frost
J. M. Vance	Annie Tobin
Sam C. Bell	Caro Simpson
Bob Fly	Mary Tobin
Nat Fly	Agnes Tobin
Madison Foster	Ella Tobin
Herman Kampmann	Nellie Norton

Johnson Minter	Lottie James
Bob Lay	Bessie Bell
Ned Ord	Lizzie Stribling
Jimmino Ord	Lizzie Simpson
John Pyron	Fannie Simpson
Mat Pyron	Ethel Tunstall
Sid Shepherd	Sallie Tunstall
Ed. Steves	Bettie Holcomb
Harry Norton	Katie Hewitt
Reagan Houston	Ida Hewitt
Erastus Reed	Sallie Andrews
Charles Florian	Bertie Ord
J. J. Stevens	Julia Ord
Jim Thornton	Belle Howard
John Sehorn	Agnes Howard
Ben Andrews	Emiline Wagner
Wynne Andrews	Bettie Thornton
Reiley Gordon	Amanda Guenther
Arthur Seeligson	Ollie French
James Simpson	Kate Devine
Garracheu Ord	Cora Ogden
Frank Yoakam	Sallie Nagel
Frank Grice	Smithie Graves
Adolph Wagner	Belle Martin
Joe Devine	Nellie Sullivan
Neteville Devine	Charlotte Thornton
Charles Hummel	Lydia Muncy
Albert Wooley	Lizzie Reed
John Laffin	Myra Reed
Will Smith	Celeste Gaylord
J. Woodhull	Lola Gaylord
Hal Howard	Minnie Russ
James French	Mollie Smith
Will Weiss	May Williams
N. T. Wilson	Maria Williams

Harry Fowler
Jesse Oppenheimer
Duval West
Fred Cook
W. C. Rigsby
Hilmer Guenther
Arthur Guenther
S. P. Maury
Joe Chew
Sam Bennett
George Eichleitz
Frank Badger
Louis Lindheim
Albert Maverick
Adolph Herff
John Tobin
Will Tobin
Charles Tobin
Albert Steves
Ernest Steves

Matilda Guenther
Minnie Kalteyer
Mamie Florian
Irene Florian
Kate Foster
Blanche Frank
Bertha Frank
Mollie Norton
Routez Houston
Laura James
Agnes James
Lillie Meyer
Minnie Halff
Camille Howard
Marie Guenther
Jessie Newton
Flo Eager
Blanche Eager
Charlotte Newton
Ella Jones

VIII. LIFE OF COLONEL H. B. ANDREWS

Soldier, Statesman, and Builder of the First Railroad into San Antonio

Colonel H. B. Andrews was born of English parentage, on the Island of St. Thomas, in the West Indies, September 21, 1828. He was the youngest of three children, whose names were Edmund, Isabelle, and Henry. His father died a short time after the birth of his son Henry.

In 1830, Colonel Andrews' mother removed to Texas and settled in Columbia, Brazoria County, Texas, where she married Judge Edmund Andrews, a distinguished lawyer. Colonel Andrews' father was named Barclay and when his mother married Judge Andrews, the latter adopted his stepson and gave him the name of Andrews. When about fifteen years of age, Colonel Andrews was sent to Yale College to complete his education, but after a short stay at college was suddenly summoned home by the death of his adopted father.

In 1844 he removed to Galveston to engage in the mercantile business. Not finding it congenial to his tastes, he began the study of law under Governor Pease. He was admitted to the bar, and soon won distinction as an able lawyer; and in 1846 to 1848 he served one term as district attorney of the Galveston District Court. In 1845 Colonel Andrews was married to Miss Martha Wynne of Galveston, Texas.

Colonel Andrews was postmaster at Galveston from 1857 to 1861.

On the breaking out of the Civil War he organized a company, comprising many of the foremost citizens of

Galveston, and was elected its first captain, commanding Cavalry Company Coast Rangers. Later, on January 12, 1863, he was assigned Chief of the Labor Bureau, with the rank and pay of colonel, with headquarters at Houston, Texas. He resigned as Chief of the Labor Bureau on April 13. 1864, to represent Galveston County in the Legislature that convened at Austin, Texas, on May 9, 1864. His record as a soldier is brilliant, with many deeds of courage and heroism.

In 1868 Colonel Andrews turned his attention to railroad matters, and induced Bacon and Pierce, then large merchants of Baltimore, to become interested in the Galveston, Houston, and Henderson Railroad, at that time the only road connecting the cities of Galveston and Houston. Bacon and Pierce, under the name of Cowdry and James, controlled the road, and Colonel Andrews was made general freight and passenger agent. About 1870 Colonel Andrews, noting the rapid development of the State, induced Colonel Thomas W. Pierce to buy the Buffalo Bayou, Brazos, and Colorado Railroad, at that time extending from the town of Harrisburg (seven miles below Houston on Buffalo Bayou) to Alleytown. Upon acquiring this property, a charter was obtained for the Galveston, Harrisburg, and San Antonio Railroad, and Colonel Andrews was made vice-president and general manager. The president, Thomas W. Pierce, being a resident of Baltimore, Md., Colonel Andrews was almost in complete charge of the road, and under his wise management the road was completed to San Antonio, and the first passenger train was run into the city on February 19, 1877. This road stands as a monument to the ability and perseverance of Colonel Andrews. When he took charge of the old company, difficulties arose before him at every turn; but with his indomitable energy and signal ability, he surmounted them all, and completed the road. He filled the office of vice-president and general manager for several years, and afterwards served as land commissioner for the same company. He resigned the office in 1884, but not until the road had been extended from San Antonio to El Paso, completing what is now known as the Southern Pacific Route. Upon the completion of the Galveston, Harrisburg, and San Antonio Railroad into San Antonio in 1877, Colonel Andrews removed with his family to San Antonio, where he resided until his death.

In politics, Colonel Andrews was a staunch democrat. As representative from Galveston, he served in the House and the Senate; in both positions he acquitted himself with honor and distinction. He ranked high in the councils of his party and was a political speaker of rare ability.

He was appointed one of the commissioners of three from the State of Texas by Governor R. B. Hubbard, in December 1877, to represent Texas at the World's Fair Exposition at Paris, France.

Colonel Andrews was a member of the Christian Church and was widely known for his many deeds of charity and benevolence. He was a Royal Arch Mason, Past Grand Master of Odd Fellows, and Past Exalted Ruler of the Benevolent Protective Order of Elks.

Colonel Andrews had nine children by his marriage with Miss Martha Wynne of Galveston, as follows; Emma. Cynthia, Harry, Lilly. Ed, Wynne. Ben. Sadie and William; the only one living at this date is R. W. Andrews. Several years after the death of his wife. Colonel Andrews married at Tuscumbia, Alabama, Mrs. Frank Smith of New York, formerly Miss Mol- lie Huston of Alabama. To this marriage one boy was born, Harry Barclay Andrews.

Colonel Andrews was a man of medium height, weight, and build; his carriage was very erect and dignified. He had clear cut cameo-like features, with a slight cast in one eye, that improved rather than detracted from his personal appearance. He was a deep thinker, a skilled parliamentarian, a student of political economy and literature, quick at repartee, a master in the use of invective and ridicule, with great natural ability and powers of expression, all of which qualities naturally fitted him to fill the distinguished positions he held during his life. He loved to travel, and was favorably known to many prominent people in the great cities of the United States, both on the Atlantic and Pacific Coast. It was generally up to Colonel Andrews to head the citizen committees to welcome prominent celebrities of our country who visited San Antonio, and he individually entertained them at his palatial home; and, as he was a man of considerable wealth, he spared neither time nor expense to make their stay agreeable. He was essentially a man of the people. He loved his fellow man. He participated with the people in their joys and assisted them in their misfortunes. Nothing pleased him better than to make a patriotic Fourth of July speech, and the same evening attend their celebrations by opening the entertainment as the leading man in the grand march.

Colonel Andrews was an actor; on one occasion, when he was called upon to address the Confederate Veterans in San Antonio, soon after his removal here from Galveston, he being at that time almost a stranger to most of his audience, he began reading from manuscript and then—with dramatic suddenness—he threw the paper violently from him and said, "Speaking to Confederates, I need no written words, but would speak as my heart feels", and then from his lips flowed such impassioned and fascinating oratory that swept his audience from their feet, and at the conclusion of his address, the storm of applause and the ovation he received created such a scene that will never be forgotten.

Among Colonel Andrews' personal effects were many old letters addressed to him, marked "Private and Confidential"; these are in the hand writing of the great men who made Texas history famous, as Sam Houston, David Kaufman, Governor P. Murrah, General S. P. Scurry (the victor of the battlefields of Val Verde, Gloriette, and Galveston Harbor), also Major- General Beauregard, Governor Sul Ross and Governor R. B. Hubbard. The contents of these letters make very interesting reading and go to prove that Colonel Andrews during his life was a man of great influence and power in the councils of the distinguished men of his country, and he was sometimes "The silent power behind the Throne".

The end of his long and useful life came on April 14th, 1895; he had been in bad health for some time and had entirely retired from business affairs; he was a sufferer from Bright's disease and his death was not unexpected to his family and friends. He was in full possession of his mental faculties to the last moment, and passed away without a struggle. He died, as he had expressed a desire to, on Easter morning. For nearly half a century Colonel Andrews had been identified with the progress and advancement of Texas; he labored especially for the South and Southwest of Texas, and left behind him many enduring monuments of his labors. He was broad minded and large hearted, liberal in his views on all questions, and ever ready to aid all enterprises for the public good[*].

---

[*] The writer was executor of the estate of H. B. Andrews and this article was written from information derived from Andrews' papers and from information from his private secretary. J. J. Stevens. — Vinton L. James.

IX. MAYOR THIELEPAPE AND THE CITIZENS OF SAN ANTONIO

The military appointees of Col. J. J. Reynolds U. S. Army, for mayor of San Antonio on November 8th, 1867, was W. C. H. Thielepape, and for Chief Justice of Bexar County in 1865 was A. Simering, who after the "late unpleasantness" was kept very busy administering the oath of amnesty to prominent citizens of San Antonio of former southern persuasion. Mayor Thielepape, on account of his military official appointment, did not have the unqualified support of the citizens of San Antonio, who had a lingering resentment of anything that reminded them of their late defeat.

Secretary of War Balknap was to arrive in San Antonio for the purpose of selecting a site for a proposed military post. The citizens of San Antonio, through the efforts of Mayor Thielepape, were at last aroused to welcome the Secretary of War with a grand parade and torch light procession to be given at the San Pedro Springs, (the only place large enough at that time to entertain such an assembly). From the corner of Main Avenue and Romana Street to San Pedro Springs was an unbroken mesquite thicket, which extended on both sides of the road, which was lighted by torch lights on high poles placed in the ground. The procession started with the mayor at the head of the parade, but instead of a white way a high wind storm blew up and all the lights went out, which was a great disappointment to everybody. Alex Sweet (the humorist), then the local city reporter of the old San Antonio Herald, wrote up the memorable event as near as I can remember, as follows:

"Mr. Secretary Belknap was waiting seated in the pavilion at San Pedro Springs for the arrival of the mayor, who met him without waiting for an introduction. The secretary, not knowing his honor, politely asked him to be seated, but Mr. Thielepape remained standing, and in a grand eloquent speech informed Mr. Belknap that he was the mayor of San Antonio. Mr. Belknap replied for him to take two seats"; but laying all joking aside, Mayor Thielepape made an excellent official as the following event shows.

In 1852 the City of San Antonio, to raise money to build the old Bat Cave and City Hall on Military Plaza, sold 108 acres of land situated at the head of the San Antonio River to James R. Sweet and others, and the said property afterwards was bought by Geo. W. Brackenridge, the banker, who offered to sell the 108 acres to the City of San Antonio for the following liberal terms: No cash, but the interest at eight per cent (8%) on the principal amounting to $4000.00 per annum, and fifty years following January 22nd, 1872, the principal to mature. The city council, through the influence of the mayor, promptly accepted the proposition. The matter at once became a subject of consuming interest to the citizens of San Antonio, and an opposition rapidly developed to defeat the purchase, but Mayor Thielepape fought with all his might to clinch the bargain, but the opposing faction won the day by bringing great influence to bear on provisional Governor Davis, who, to pour oil on the troubled waters and end the strife, immediately appointed S. G. Newton mayor in place of Thielepape.

Mayor Thielepape was absolutely right in favoring the purchase of the 108 acres at the head of the river. This land was the most beautiful spot in Texas; there were no artesian wells to drain the source, and the flow was four times the present volume, and to think that the city in 1852 swapped that lovely property for the old Bat Cave was a most unfortunate deal. Thielepape had vision: he was progressive and he accepted Brackenridge's liberal offer for payment, and knew the city in coming years would endorse his views.

Thielepape's pride was hurt when the citizens of San Antonio would not sustain or sanction his work, and he, a short time after his dismissal, shook the dust of San Antonio from his feet, and I do not remember of his ever returning to San Antonio.*

---

* Thielepape as Mayor of San Antonio.

X. EARLY GERMAN IMMIGRATION TO TEXAS

Many Notables Dissatisfied With Conditions in Homeland Set Out for New World to Brave the Hardships in Pioneering—Made Friends of Hostile Red Men and Laid Foundations of Prosperous Towns

Under the Spanish rule, the empresarios were allowed large grants of land in Texas, provided they paid the costs of the survey, recording fees, taxes, etc., and that they bring a number of Catholic emigrants within a specified time.

With the independence of Mexico from Spanish rule in 1821, begins the immigration into Texas of the German race.

On April 6, 1830, a decree was passed prohibiting further immigration from the United States by the Mexican congress. This brewed trouble and helped to bring on the war of independence.

Mexican colonization law of the State of Coahuila and Texas in 1825 not only invited immigrants with protection of person and property, but the colonists were to be exempt from taxation for 10 years. The empresarios were given five sites (leagues) and five labors of land for each 100 families brought in. After this law passed, applications for grants became so numerous that in a short time the whole country from the Sabine to the Nueces rivers in Texas was covered by claims of the various empresarios.

West Texas 84 years ago was the undisputed hunting grounds of hostile Indian tribes, who dominated the country and jealously guarded their domain, against every encroachment of civilization. It took strong hearts and arms to enter into this dangerous country. President Sam Houston, who was a friend of the Indians, tried to protect them against unjust invasions of their rights, and time and time again would not allow state troops to infringe on their hunting ground, unless the Indians committed crimes deserving punishment.

Many Germans were forced to flee their native land in Europe to escape military tyranny. The German's love of adventure, the desire for liberty, and for betterment of conditions were the reasons for seeking a new home in Texas. The remedy for over-population was emigration.

The first German settlers in Texas were established in 1823 on lands of Baron von Bastrop, located within 30 miles of the present city of Austin, on the Colorado River. The muster rolls and archives at Austin contain names of many Germans who fought for the independence of Texas.

Frederick Ernst and Charles Fordtran came to Texas in 1834 and established the first German settlement. They called the place "Industry", and it was about 16 miles from Houston. Mrs. Ernst opened a hotel, which became a gathering place for Germans traveling from Galveston and Houston to the interior of Texas.

Robert Kleberg fought in the battle of San Jacinto. He founded Cat Springs in 1835, and enclosed 10 acres of land for a farm. Of all the early German settlers in Texas, Robert Kleberg was one of the most prominent. After the fall of the Alamo, Kleberg and other Germans enlisted and fought for Texas' independence at the battle of San Jacinto.

Washington County in 1845 received Carl F. and George Giesecke, and Wilhelm Apollo Groos, whose three sons later established the Groos Bank in San Antonio. They were all highly educated men.

Most of the emigrants coming to Texas in the early '40's were peasants and mechanics. Many highly educated men came in 1845 and founded Sisterdale. Among these were Dr. Adolf Douay, Dr. Runge, Ed Degener, Julius Dressel and Dr. A. Hertzberg. Dr. Douay was the founder of the first German newspaper in San Antonio in 1854, and he fearlessly advocated abolition of slavery. Ed Degener represented the Fourth Congressional District of Texas in Washington from 1870 to 1874. Degener and Dressel were taken to San Antonio in 1862 as prisoners of war; and the other intellectuals abandoned Sister- dale, which settlement did not survive the Civil War. Sister- dale was named after two mountains overlooking Sister Creek, one of the most beautiful and romantic places in West Texas.

According to the best information now available, there were 10,000 Germans in Texas in 1840 and 20,000 in 1845. On April 20, 1842, 14 German princes and noblemen met at Biebrich on the Rhine, Germany, and formed an association for the purchase of lands in Texas, which they called "The Mainzer Adelsverin". This association promised to defray the expenses of the German emigrants to Texas and to assist them financially until they became self-supporting. Count Castell was appointed general manager and supervisor. Heinrich Fisher and Burkart Mueller, two Texas Germans of Houston, had obtained an immense land concession in West Texas from President Sam Houston on condition that they settle 600 families on the land within 18 months. The grant was situated on the south side of the Colorado River between the Llano and San Saba rivers and extended west to the Rio Grande and south through the Uvalde Canyon to the mouth of the Nueces River. This grant took in over three million acres.

Fisher, who went to Europe, had never seen the land, but he described it as the finest of farming land to Count Castell in Germany. On June 24, 1844, the Adelsverin purchased the grant for $9,000- None of the officers of the Adelsverin knew anything of the cost of living conditions in Texas, consequently the lack of funds to care for the immigrants after their arrival in Texas, brought on an early collapse of the enterprise.

Prince Solms Braunfels was appointed commissioner general, July, 1844, and his first sad experience on his arrival in Texas was to learn that the Fisher and Miller grant had been forfeited by the lapse of time. Later the Texas Legislature extended the time of the grant to Jan. 20, 1845. In November, 1844, 200 immigrants had arrived with all their bulky baggage at Galveston, all anxious to go to their future home. After two months of waiting at Indianola, they began their march to the interior of Texas. By aid of Dr. Lindheimer, Prince Solms was fortunate in finding a haven of rest for his weary band at "Las Fontants" (The Fountains) on the Comal and Guadalupe rivers, where 1,300 acres of land were purchased by him for $800.

On March 14, 1845, the German emigrants arrived at their first settlement in West Texas and named it New Braunfels in honor of Prince Solms Braunfels, who later returned to Germany.

Baron Otfried von Meusebach, a naturalized citizen of Texas and known as John O. Meusebach, came from Nassau, Germany. He was born in 1812, was highly educated at the universities of Bonn and Halle, where he studied law. political economy, and finance, and he died near the town of Loyal Valley between Fredericksburg and Mason on May 29, 1897, at the age of 85 years. He was a courageous man and displayed great tact and skill in making treaties with the Indians.

He won the confidence, respect, and friendship of the red men. Had it not been for his ability and perseverance in avoiding disaster, New Braunfels and Fredericksburg would have perished when the protection promised the emigrants by the noblemen and princes of Germany was shattered. So the bubble burst, leaving the emigrants to their own resources. It proved to be a good thing, however, as they soon established, by hard work, a firm foundation for their families and made New Braunfels and Fredericksburg the garden spots of Texas.

Baron von Meusebach succeeded Prince Solms Braunfels as commissioner general. Meusebach, on examination, found the finances of the association in a hopeless condition, with a debt contracted by Prince Solms of $120,000, and with only $24,000 on hand, hardly sufficient to pay the floating indebtedness. Four thousand emigrants were then on the way to Texas. They had to be cared for after their arrival at Galveston, and to be transported in small craft to Indianola. 100 miles southwest. At the latter place they were to be housed and cared for an indefinite period, and the expenses to be met for sustenance on the road to New Braunfels, all on the meager sum of $6 per person. Any other man under such circumstances would have resigned, but not Meusebach. He immediately proved bis great ability to assist, and finally by herculean efforts and promises, he raised funds sufficient to start the expedition on the road to the interior of Texas.

The winter of 1845-46 was very severe yet, despite this, there arrived at Galveston, 5,247 immigrants in 36 ships, All had heavy, bulky baggage, which had to be transported to New Braunfels by way of Indianola. Meusebach, with hardly any funds on hand, did his best to assist them. Rains fell continuously. The emigrants, poorly housed and nourished at Indianola, contracted fevers and several hundreds died. The suffering was intense. It was with great joy they at last received the news that 100 teams had arrived to convey them to the settlements. The war between the United States and Mexico broke out in May, 1846, and the United States Government commandeered all horses and teams for its own use. This made it impossible for Meusebach to find enough horses to transport the new arrivals inland. Five hundred men of the emigrants enlisted for six months to fight for the United States in the war against Mexico, under the command of Capt. August Buchel, one of the German emigrants.

The emigrants eventually started inland under great handicaps, This move proved disastrous. More than 200 perished and the bleached bones of the dead marked the road of hardship and death. The survivors who reached New Braunfels and Fredericksburg carried germs of a disease that developed into an epidemic, entailing a total loss of nearly a thousand persons. Meusebach was blamed and threatened with bodily harm for the catastrophe, but he met his accusers without fear and placed the blame on the Adelsverein, who had neglected to send sufficient funds to pay the expenses of the emigrants after their arrival in Texas.

In December, 1845, Von Meusebach sent an expedition of 36 men from New Braunfels to the Pedernales, where he had purchased 10,000 acres of land for a settlement. Here the party built a block house. On April 26, 1846. the first group of colonists arrived and named the place Fredericksburg. During all this time Meusebach was almost without funds. He sent urgent appeals to Germany for assistance without avail. At the close of the year none of the emigrants had reached the Fisher and Mueller lands. New Braunfels and Fredericksburg were outside of the grant. Meusebach appealed to President Sam Houston for protection against the hostile Indians, who dominated the country, without success. He also appealed to John James who was the district surveyor. James refused to allow his men to survey the land without a treaty first made with the Indians.

On January, 1847, Von Meusebach, with three wagons and 45 well-armed men headed an expedition to the Comanche territory. where the land of the Fisher and Mueller grant was situated. On Feb. 1, 1847, he crossed the Llano River into the territory of the Indians. A Mexican, by name Lorenzo, who had lived many years with the Comanches, was taken along as guide and interpreter. Meusebach advanced cautiously, always prepared to meet a sudden attack by the Indians, who, although unseen by him, were following and watching Meuse- bacb and his little band. Meusebach exercised great care in selecting night camps. The tents were pitched in the center and were surrounded by the closed wagons. The fires were kept burning all night, with four guards on constant duty. A courier from President Sam Houston arrived with orders for Meusebach and his party to recross the Llano because the Indians were on the warpath. Meusebach determined to proceed and, if possible, make a treaty with the Indians. On the morning of Feb. 5, about where the town of Brady is now situated, eight Comanche Indians were seen riding towards the camp, carrying a white flag. The Mexican, Lorenzo, was sent to meet them. The Indian Chief Ketemaesy solemnly inquired after the chief of the palefaces. Von Meusebach then rode towards them and was asked about his intentions.

"If they had entered the land of the Indians with a friendly purpose, all would be well. If they had come to fight, the Comanche were ready".

Meusebach answered that his people had only friendly designs, that they had come from far across the waters and had built two cities in the neighborhood, where the Indians would be received with the same hospitality which he expected of the Indians.

Ketemaesy said he would inform the other chiefs and would call them to meet in counsel the next full moon. On Feb. 7, the Indian village was reached near the San Saba River. Five hundred Indian warriors, all mounted, were drawn up in a long line in front of the wigwam. Meusebach was required to advance with only a few men. He was met midway by as many Indians. After a friendly greeting and hand-shaking, they fired their rifles into the air as a token of good faith. Meusebach was invited to enter the Indian village with his company as guests, where they remained all day. The expedition remained in the vicinity several days.

On Feb. 10, the Indian scouts led Meusebach further into the wilderness and met Santa Anna, the great war chief of the Comanches, who also inquired of his intentions of invading the territory of the Indians, Meusebach satisfied the chief that his intentions were only friendly, and gave him presents. On Feb. 27. the Indian scouts led the party to a large village, where the great council of peace was to be enacted in which 20 other Indian chiefs participated with Chiefs Santa Anna and Buffalo Hump. They sat down on buffalo robes, and the pipe of peace was smoked. Meusebach made a great speech, saying: "The Germans are industrious and know how to win from the earth many things the Indians like to eat, and they will always have plenty for themselves and their brother Indians, who kill the buffalo and the deer. We will always share our products with you if you choose the path of peace. I do not propose to drive you from your bunting grounds. When the buffalo has gone north and when you cannot kill any more game, then come to us and exchange your hides for the necessities of life".

This ended the council, and a treaty of peace between the German pioneers and the Comanches was agreed upon, which later was ratified at Fredericksburg. The opening up of this vast territory of over 3,000,000 acres of land to cultivation was without doubt the most important German pioneer work in Texas. The State of Texas owes a debt of gratitude to the Germans. The Indians lived up to the treaty as long as Chief Santa Anna lived. He often visited with his party not only Fredericksburg but also the town of New Braunfels where he spent several days at various times. Capt. Jack Hays, the greatest Indian fighter Texas ever produced, said he "never had any trouble with Indians in the territory settled by the Germans, but as soon as he was outside trouble always developed". The Indians had great respect for Von Meusebach, whom they named "El Sol Colorado", "The Flowing Beard".

The survey of the lands on the Llano and San Saba followed the treaty with the Indians. Forty young men in 1847, students of the Universities of Gussen and Heidelburg, Germany, all highly educated and imbued with communistic principles, pictured West Texas as the land for professional men, and formed a society called "The Forty", located the towns of Bettina and Castell on the Llano River. Gustave Schleicher and Dr. F. Herff were the leaders. Theordore Schleuning and others composed the balance of the "Forty". After several years of strenuous pioneer life in the wilderness, in 1850 they left the Llano country for the more congenial and remunerative life in San Antonio. Dr. Herff while on the Llano performed a successful operation on an Indian chief for cataract of the eye and restored his sight. He was rewarded with the present from the chief of a young Mexican girl captive whom Herff cared for and educated and who was afterwards happily married to a good man. Dr. Herff died in San Antonio at the age of 91 years. He was universally beloved by his fellow citizens. He was the most noted physician in Texas, and because of bis many successful surgical operations his reputation became nation-wide and his death was sincerely mourned.

Gustave Schleicher represented San Antonio in the Legislature at Austin, in 1859, was a member of the Texas Senate in 1861, served as major of rangers in the Confederacy and practiced law in San Antonio. In 1875 he was elected to the United States Congress at Washington. He was re-elected in 1876 and 1878. and died in Washington, D. C., Jan. 10, 1879. He was the brainiest man ever sent to Washington from this district and was so regarded by his peers. His death was a great loss, as his intellect and profound wisdom on important state questions had obtained favorable attention over the nation. The writer remembers the Honorable Ed. Degener and Gustave Schleicher, who often visited my father at the old James home on Commerce Street. Degener's home fronted on Travis Park and Schleicher was interested with my father in lands on the Pedernales and San Saba streams. Degener, in the U. S. Congress from 1870 to 1874, was tall, slender, and always well dressed. Schleicher was a very large and fleshy man who cared very little for his personal appearance.

German influence in the development of Texas can hardly be overestimated. Their noble and courageous work in winning wide stretches of land from the Indians should always be remembered. In the field of culture, the Germans started the training of small children in the kindergarten system. The first German Saengerfest in Texas was organized at New Braunfels on March 2, 1853. San Antonio was represented by J. Schmitt, Gustave Schleicher, Alex Sartor, J. Conrad, J. Riotte, with Adolf Doual as leader.

The German song, "Das Deutsche Lied", accompanied the emigrants on their dreary march across the broad Texas prairies, cheered them in their daily toil, and brightened their firesides in the evening.

Castroville was founded by Henry Castro, Sept. 3, 1844, and settled by French Alsatians and German emigrants, John James was the surveyor who plotted the town of Castroville and divided the land among the emigrants. Disposal of the land by lots was begun Oct. 25, 1846. Castro's colony numbered 700 inhabitants after two years' existence.

Olmstead, the author of "Journey Through Texas on Horseback in 1855", says the meals furnished travelers in East Texas, consisted of fat hog meat and cornbread as a regular diet, occasionally varied with butter and eggs, prepared by slave labor. He also writes in glowing terms of the elegant repasts furnished him in New Braunfels, Sisterdale, and Quihi by the German housewives; of not only having wild game meats, butter, eggs, but also all the different varieties of vegetables. Olmstead also in 1855 writes that the condition of life among the Indians in West Texas was absolutely pitiful; they had been driven from the well-watered and productive lands in South Texas where game was abundant to the barren, arid, and mountainous region where they faced starvation.

Under the auspices of the Verein a total of 7,380 emigrants had come to Texas. In 1847-48-49 about 15,000 more Germans bad arrived, and more than 10,000 from 1830 to 1850. This makes a total of 33,000 Germans in Texas in 1850. The Germans composed one-fifth of the total white population in Texas in 1850, and 6,000 lived in Eastern Texas) 10,000 were in Central Texas; 15,000 lived in Western Texas.

Victor Bracht, who came from Dusseldorf, Germany, to Texas in 1845, spoke German, English, French and Italian. He was the author of "Texas im Jabre 1848" ("Texas in the Year 1848"). His enthusiasm for his adopted country knew no bounds. The German government sent him to Texas to look after the interests of the colonists. Bracht came to Texas as an emigrant of the Mainzer Adelsverein in 1846. In an article in Bremen, Germany, as a naturalized citizen of Texas, he said; "I am enjoying all the liberties that God and nature grant to man. I have never suffered want here; in fact, want is unknown in this part of the world.

"Oct. 8, 1846. San Antonio is constantly growing. It has five or six hundred bouses with a population of about three thousand, mostly Mexicans, many Germans and Frenchmen. Trade is extensive. It has been almost two years since I left Germany for this glorious country and every hour and day I learn to love my new home better.

"Aug. 26, 1846. A single peach orchard in San Antonio yielded $1,200 in cash; vegetables fetch better prices, William Elliot lives in clover; he built the finest and largest house in Texas (the Plaza Hotel) on Mayor Plaza, and rented it for $1,400 a year. The question whether a diligent man can make a living in Texas, is ridiculous. A man can earn more in three months than he can during a year in Germany. Game and fish are abundant. A good horse and rifle, these companions can provide many meals in Texas that everyone can afford. Prices of food in San Antonio in 1848 as follows: Fresh beef, 2 to 4 cents a pound; fish, 5 to 6 cents a pound; venison, 1 to 4 cents a pound; lard, 4 to 6 cents a pound; wild turkey, 35 to 50c each.

"February, 1847. I have returned from the San Saba region. The great distance from the sea, prevents me from establishing a home there. I would rather own a single acre in the immediate vicinity of human civilization and culture than own a square mile in that uninhabited and almost inaccessible wilderness,

"March, 1847. The Elliot building on Plaza Mayor now has a rival in the magnificent stone building of the French consul, Gilbeau (on South Flores Street). One of the taverns in San Antonio has two billiard tables and in a room adjoining is a reading room where a German newspaper, "Die Volks Tribune", of St. Louis, is kept. Women pay more attention to dress in San Antonio than they do in New York, or in the large cities of Europe. We have balls and revelries. Men, thank God, are not so particular, they appear in shirt-sleeves or woolen jackets. I made all my visits to San Antonio in leather clothes, which even the fashionable and cultured Mrs. Elliot did take no notice of. New Braunfels has 3,000 and Fredericksburg 1,000 inhabitants. New Braunfels in 1848 was the fourth largest city in Texas, only exceeded by Galveston, Houston and San Antonio".

XI. COMMERCE STREET

Pioneer Business Men Laid the Foundation for Wealth Along Its Way and the Night Life Supplied the City with its Thrills

The writer was born on Commerce Street where he spent his youth. Commerce Street once was called Main Street. The following article on Commerce Street is as the writer remembers it after the Civil War:

The plazas were filled with high weeds and stagnant water after rains. Garbage wagons were insufficient to carry off the trash. Dirt and kitchen refuse were relegated to the back yard, which attracted flies by tens of thousands and rats by thousands.

(The author is indebted for the major part of the above article to the book, German Element in Texas", by Moritz Tiling; also to Olmstead's book, "Journey Through Texas on Horseback in 1855", and to Victor Bracht's "Texas in Jahre 1848.")

Carcasses of cats and dogs and other dead animals were thrown in the river. Shallow wells furnished the water supply, The unpaved streets were quagmires after rains. The sidewalks were made of flat slate rocks. There were no sewers, no waterworks, nor street lights at night. The many livery stables located in the heart of the city were a perpetual menace to health The unsanitary condition could not have been worse,

Main Plaza was used as a parking place for carriages and public hacks.

Crowds of people at night harkened to the harangues of venders of patent medicines, and cure-all-ailments.

The diamond king pulled teeth, accompanied by a loud brass band to drown the painful cries of his patients. Military Plaza was filled with two-wheel Mexican carrettas with wood for sale, hay wagons, and other wagons loaded with wild game. Venison hams sold for 50c and wild turkeys for 25c.

Indian boys fresh from the wilds of West Texas, shot arrows with marvelous accuracy at small coins placed in a forked stick. At night long rows of tables, were presided over by the chili queens, who dispensed Mexican dishes to hungry customers.

The public cantina was ablaze with lights and sounds of dance music. There the pretty senoritas and their partners enjoyed tripping the light fantastic until the wee small hours of the morning.

Jack Harris' Variety Theatre at Commerce and Soledad streets, opened with a bevy of attractive dancing and singing girls, followed later, farther west on Commerce Street, by the Washington, Belle Union, and Grey Mule Theatres.

In the early seventies Commerce Street merchants experienced great prosperity. During the Franco-Prussian War, in 1873, wool sold in San Antonio for 50 cents a pound, and millions of dollars' profit to stockmen were realized from the cattle drives from West Texas to Kansas, which made the money very plentiful and so the merchants and bankers of Commerce Street reaped a harvest.

Commerce Street runs east and west and is the longest business street in the city of San Antonio. The road east connects San Antonio with the coast towns of Lavaca and Indianola, which formerly were the principal ports of entry to Southwest Texas. The west Commerce Street road connected San Antonio with the towns of Uvalde, Eagle Pass, El Paso, and the army border posts.

The first German Club on East Commerce Street was the organization of the San Antonio Schuetzen Verein in 1852, with Reimann Neuman, a gun and locksmith, as president. This Rifle Club was located on the Powder House hill, close to the cemeteries. Among the original members were the following young men, who became prominent in the history of San Antonio: A. Nette, E. Dosch, A, Sartor, Dreiss, Captain Braubach and others. Cakes, beer, and cold lunches supplied the refreshments.

The first, and oldest German paper published in Texas in 1869, was the "Freie Presse fur Texas" by A. Siemering and Pollmer and the printing office was located on the south side of East Commerce Street; afterwards it was edited by Robert Hanschke and Dr. A. Rochs,

In the 70's a wealthy Mexican family, by the name of Garcia, bad their home in a two-story rock house on the south side of East Commerce Street. They enjoyed themselves riding around the city streets in a fine carriage. The family consisted of two sons, Nicolas and Jose, and a beautiful daughter, Zulima, who was acknowledged as the most accomplished pianist in the city. This Mexican family moved in the best social circles,

George Schroeder kept a grocery and horse feed store, and a Mr. A. Hallamuda ran a general merchandise store on the north side of East Commerce Street,

Saint Joseph Cathedral stood on the corner of Commerce and Bonham streets and west of it was the Arbeiters Verein (The Working Men's Club.)

Beginning at the northwest corner of Commerce and Alamo streets, there was a two-story adobe house, in which Mrs. Baer had a confectionery store. This property was owned by the Umshied family, who lived in another two-story house facing Commerce Street. The large lot was enclosed with a rock fence, which extended west to Commerce Street bridge. There was no Losoya Street then, Losoya Street was afterwards opened by a city council ordinance on April 3, 1872. Afterwards Mrs. Baer moved further west on Commerce Street and the firm name became Harnisch & Baer. Raphael Diaz, a "Cuba Libre" man, established and conducted a cigar and tobacco store on this corner for many years. Diaz was expelled from Cuba for political reasons. He donated freely of his wealth towards financing the revolution in Cuba.

Commerce Street bridge, an early public improvement, was built in 1842 and served the city well. It withstood the great flood of March 22, 1865, when the Houston Street bridge and all the other bridges were swept away and seven people in the city lost their lives. One man. Dannenberg. attempted to cross Commerce Street bridge during the flood stage and was swept off and drowned. This old bridge had a warning sign painted in large letters in English, Spanish and German languages: "WALK YOUR HORSES, OR YOU WILL BE FINED."

The plan of the Commerce Street bridge was considered Aug. 5, 1842, and it was ordered that the same be built the following Sept. 4". The minutes of the Council dated Aug. 13, contain the following:

"Whereas certain lots on the east side of the Alamo ditch be sold. The collector, James L. Trueheart, the following amounts were received for lots sold: Sam Maverick, $56; James Robinson. $58; L. Colquhon, $58; W. B, Jacques, $59; and B- Callaghan, $45, making a total of $276, one-half paid in cash, other half in notes ordered by the corporation to be paid Higginbotham, the builder, on account of bridge, and every person having carts shall furnish them one day with yoke of oxen to haul dirt, and every lone man shall, present himself with pick or spade and report to Mr, Callaghan, who shall credit him with the sum of $1.00 for a cart and a pair of oxen and 50 cents for each lone man on their taxes, and all owners of carts to furnish hides, to haul either rubbish or dirt,"

West from Commerce Street bridge was a large vacant lot subject to overflow. Here old Grandpa A. Sartor, in a one- story adobe room, had a watch and clock store. In the rear next to the river was an enclosed space full of old empty beer kegs, which formerly must have been a brewery. A few old buildings extended west to our old home.

The John James two-story house on West Commerce Street was built by Joseph Schmitt in 1847, Before the Civil War the James' entertained many of the U. S. army officers, then stationed in San Antonio, who afterwards became famous. Mrs. James' two younger sisters. Josephine and Fannie Belle Milby, married U.S. army officers. In 1849, Major General Worth, commanding the U. S. forces in Texas, died at the James residence on Commerce Street, during the cholera epidemic. His monument is prominent on Madison Square, New York City.

Then came P. C, Taylor's residence, store and camp yard. Taylor also had a lime kiln near the head of the river. This property was owned by the Callaghan estate. Next came the Kloepper Hotel, a two-story house with a long L-shaped one- story in the rear. Mrs. Kloepper was a widow with two children, Adolph, who afterwards became a printer, and Helena, who is now living and the wife of George C. Saur. Kloepper Hotel afterwards became the first public school in San Antonio. Mr. Martin, a former Presbyterian minister, was the principal. Next came the Presbyterian Church, built in 1846. It was the first Protestant church in San Antonio. The Rev. John McCullough was minister. Staacke had a wagon yard later on this site.

Hugo 8 Schmeltzer's two-story rock store occupied the space where the Sherwin-Williams paint store now is.

Then came the Antonio Menchaca residence at Navarro and Commerce streets, where the beautiful new Groos Bank building stands.

Menchaca was a Spanish San Jacinto Battle veteran; he was most popular and greatly loved, as he gave the Texans great assistance in their fight for freedom from Mexico, Menchaca's front yard was a colorful flower garden; the house, a long one- story building, was set back in the yard. He also had a family of pretty daughters, one of whom married J. B. Lacoste, a Frenchman, who built the first waterworks plant and ice factory in San Antonio.

Navarro Street was then only an alley which led to the river, and to a foot-bridge supported by empty barrels. Across from the Navarro lane, on the West Side, lived Mr. Richter in a one- story front room, with a rear of two stories, the lot extending to the river. Richter ran a barroom. He had a family of several boys and one girl. Two of his sons are still living, the oldest, Ernest, worked all of his life for the Wells Fargo Co. Another brother, William Richter, was a barber who advertised his calling by large bottles of leeches in his office window. Next to Richter's was a vacant lot, part of the time occupied as a beer garden, which also was very popular.

Next came the two-story Hummel Building. The lower east floor was occupied by the Behrends Book Store. Nic Tengg was then his clerk, and afterwards became his successor. Behrends was president and originator of the old German-English school on South Alamo Street. An open driveway separated Behrends' Book Store from Hummel and Mauermann's gun store. Next came Dosch and Rische's Saloon, which for a long time was the elite German saloon in town. Many of the notable characters of San Antonio met here daily and exchanged reminiscences. Old man Viveroux, a frequenter of the saloon who kept a machine shop on Navarro Street, made a steel coffin to be used at his death and kept it on display in his shop.

Next, on a large lot, a long one-story house, set back in the yard, facing east, was the George W, Giddings home, his family, consisting of one boy and several pretty girls. Giddings, in 1857, was the owner of a stage line that operated between San Antonio and El Paso; then George W. Brackenridge's bank, which is still doing business. Then came a number of one-story stores, among which was the famous Ernst Restaurant, which George W. Brackenridge and his many friends and others patronized, and in which they ate Ernst's famous broiled steaks; then Volrath Saddlery, then Mrs. Feile's French Millinery Shop, Bodowskys Barber Shop, Nette Drug Store, Adams and Wicks, government contractors, then Diefenbach Saloon, and Effinger's Jewelry Store.

At the northeast corner of Commerce and St. Mary streets was the store of Wilson Riddle, who married the widow of Harvey Canterbury. Riddle's daughter Sarah, married Robert Eager. Mrs. Sarah Eager, hale and hearty and a great favorite, is living today on South Alamo Street, and is over 90 years of age. She is said to be the first white child born in San Antonio. J, T. Thornton's First Bank was on this corner.

Across St. Mary Street, where D. Sullivan's Bank now is. was A. Moke's retail dry goods store. Jack Labatt killed a man named Alford inside this building. Then Pentenreider's art store, and next was John Twohig's Bank. Mr. Greisenbeck was his assistant. Twohig had a private bridge across the river to his home, which is standing in the rear of the present Pubic Service Company's lot, where he entertained his friends with the choicest food and liquors that money could buy. He was most religious and left his wealth to the Catholic Church. He had an unmarried sister, Miss Kate Twohig, who was very popular, and to her old age entertained lavishly in the Twohig home. Her death was universally regretted.

St. Mary's Street in the late '50's had a temporary foot bridge over the river wide enough for two people to pass. A man, evidently intoxicated, one night fell off the bridge and was drowned. Former City Auditor Charles Hummell, then a lad, bad a trot line stretched across the river below the bridge and the man's dead body was caught on two hooks. Hummel next morning in running his trot line thought he had hooked a big catfish when he felt the great weight on his line, but he was dumbfounded and frightened when he discovered a body coming to the surface. He screamed for assistance, and the body was recovered. A woman, a suicide, jumped off this foot bridge, and a negro man who attempted to save her also drowned.

Next came Samuel Bell's Jewelry store. Samuel Bell, the originator, came from Tennessee in the '50's. He was a master worker in steel and his hand-made knives were real works of art. He had several sons who carried on the large business after his death. During the Civil War the elder Bell's sympathies were with the North, which made him a target for persecution.

Rice's saddlery shop made the finest saddles and harness and did a large business.

Samuel Maverick's residence in 1840 stood at Commerce and Soledad streets. Haas Cl Oppenheimer had a clothing store here at a later date. John McDonald, a former mayor and prominent politician of San Antonio, was killed by Dr. Devine, a druggist, on this corner. Devine was acquitted,

Across the street was the notorious Jack Harris saloon and variety theater. This was the most widely advertised resort in Western Texas. The pretty soubrettes were graceful dancers and good singers, and were popular. They had many admirers among the rich cattlemen and money-spenders who patronized the place. Indeed, many of these girls were not only pretty, but had great personal charms, and the purity of their lives amid their bad surroundings attracted several admirers who fell in love and married them, and today their descendants are among the respected people in San Antonio. Jack Harris was killed by Ben Thompson of Austin in this resort May 11, 1882 King Fisher, Ben Thompson, and Joe Foster were also killed there March 11, 1884.

Next came the "White Elephant," with the gambling emporium upstairs and bar downstairs, conducted by Billy Simms and Sam Berliner. Then came Noyes & Langholtz's saddlery and harness store, where the old Plaza Hotel formerly stood. On the corner of Main Avenue and Main Plaza L. Wolfson had his large dry goods store. Across the street was a long two- story adobe building occupied by Antonio Navarro's real estate office. Navarro was a member of the Santa Fe expedition in 1842 which left Austin and finally reached New Mexico after experiencing every hardship of hunger and thirst, which left them so weak and helpless that the Mexican authorities of New Mexico made them prisoners and subjected them to all the indignities and cruelties imaginable and they were finally compelled to walk two thousand miles as prisoners to Mexico City. Navarro was one of the three Mexican signers of the 1836 Declaration of Texas Independence.

At Flores and Commerce streets was Fritz Schreiner's saloon. Schreiner was about as broad and fat as he was long. He was good natured, very popular, and for many years was an alderman of the city. In the center of the block on the north side of Military Plaza was the largest drug store in San Antonio, conducted by Kalteyer & Son.

Across Flores Street on the north corner was Muegge's feed and grain store.

At the corner of Commerce and Camaron streets was the Catholic Orphan Asylum.

Starting at the southwest corner of Commerce and Alamo streets was a large one-story building, fronting on Alamo Street, occupied by a man named Mills, who was engaged in the drug business. Afterwards A. Driess also carried on a drug store at the same place with his home in the rear. The large lot extended to Commerce Street bridge. Afterwards Driess died, and Simon Fest conducted a beer garden and restaurant in the place, and the first oyster saloon in San Antonio was established here. Across the river, in a house raised on pilings, lived the Widow Wren. She was a laundress and had two sons. Andrew, and Tom, who worked for the hardware firm of Leroux Cf Cosgrove. Across Casino Street was the blacksmith shop of Conrad Beckmann. Alex Sartor's jewelry store and home came next. Afterwards Heusinger conducted a hardware store there, then Tips & Haerman succeeded Heusinger. Then at the corner of Commerce and Presa streets, in a rock one-story building, was Wagner 8 Rummel's wholesale grocery. Across Presa Street was Robin's French bakery in a two-story adobe building; then came Clavin's drug store in a two-story rock building.

Next was a one-story building where a number of young printers, of whom Charles Seabaugh was one, April 3, 1875, started a paper, which was the San Antonia Express. At the cornet of Commerce and Navarro was the Beckmann shoe store. Mr. White afterwards conducted a tin shop at the same place. Across Navarro Street, on the corner, was a long livery stable, owned by Bacon and Lilly, which extended to Market Street. Afterwards Gen. William Steele and CoL T, G. Williams, two retired Confederate officers, had a commission house here. Next door was Mrs. Schmidt's hotel and restaurant. The lot extended to Market Street. Mrs. Schmidt had the reputation of setting the best table in the city. In the center of this large lot was a vine-covered pavilion in which the celebrities and business men of the day sat and chatted the time away, waiting for the dinner bell to call them. Henry Lewis, the brilliant lawyer, Judge George H. Paschal, Stuttering Lane, and others patronized Mrs. Schmidt's restaurant. She had a son named August.

Next came the Tengg book store, then Duerler's ice cream and candy store, then the two-story dry goods store of Zork 8 Griesenbeck Zork's family lived upstairs. Living with them was a pretty young red-headed lady, who was governess of the Zork girls and who married Capt. Karber, who rode a beautiful horse and was grand marshal of San Antonio parades. Karber had a beautiful long black beard and was a handsome man. Then came Barleman's barber shop on the corner. Across the street was the hardware store and tin shop of Leroux 8 Crosgrove. Next was the wholesale dry goods store of Barney and Michael Oppenheimer. D. 8 A. Oppenheimer's store was also in this block. The United States postoffice was opposite A. Nette's store. Norton 8 Deutz hardware store came next; then T. C. Frost's auction house, with Hosack as the auctioneer. Then came Goldfrank and Frank 0 Company, wholesale dry goods.

A. Morris had a dry goods store at Yturri and Commerce streets. After he died, his son, Hosea, continued the business. The Bennett 8 Thornton Bank was on the opposite corner of Yturri Street. Afterwards Lockwood 8 Kampmann conducted a banking business at the same place. Next came Capt. Merritt's fine grocery and liquor store, then George Horner's saloon. Horner had the reputation of dispensing the finest liquor over the bar, and was patronized by the wealthy and successful business men of San Antonio. Then came Gamble's book store.

At the corner of Main Plaza, in the Daunhauer Building, Solomon Deuhts had a gent's emporium. Gen. Santa Anna had his headquarters at this corner during the battle and fall of the Alamo. On the corner where the Frost National Bank stands was the store of Milby 8 Pyron, general merchandise. Elmendorf's hardware store was also on the corner of Military Plaza and West Commerce Street.

In the year of 1850 John James and J. R. Sweet entered into a partnership in the general merchandise business. The store was located on the north side of West Commerce Street. The partnership was dissolved in 1862 when Sweet assumed the rank of colonel of his regiment in the Confederate Army.

In 1866 after the defeat of the South, the writer, then a lad of eight years, saw the triumphant entry of the Union Army as they passed his home on Commerce Street, on their way to their camp at San Pedro Springs. Again on the following 4th of July celebration he saw the same United States troops pass amid the blare of trumpets and the clanking of sabres, the rattling of guns and the deep rumbling of the artillery over the unpaved streets, while the military band played patriotic music. He remembered distinctly seeing old man Samuel Bell riding in an open carriage at the head of the parade, standing upright, waving enthusiastically a large Union flag. His long white beard and hair reached below his shoulders, his cameo like features shone with happiness and joy for Texas' return to the Union. This venerable man standing erect, waving that flag made a picture which left memories not to be effaced. Bell, for waving the Union flag at the beginning of the Civil War, was threatened by the Confederates with hanging. Bell had two sons who fought in the Southern Army, and one son who fought in the Northern Army. The people of Southern persuasion viewed this 1866 4th of July celebration with sullen looks and silence and utter helplessness and bitter disappointment, as they had fought so bard and lost everything and all in vain. There were many good citizens who enjoyed the return of the Stars and Stripes, especially the Germans, many of whom were Northern sympathizers.

Mrs. Yturri was a wealthy Spanish woman, a descendant of the Canary Islanders. She owned all the property fronting on Commerce Street from her residence, at the corner of Yturri Street west to include the corner of Commerce and Main Plaza. She entertained at two different times two Presidents of Texas, Sam Houston and Mirabeau Lamar. Mrs, Maverick in her memories states that this historical event occurred at Mrs. Yturri's home, "which was beautifully decorated with flowers and palms for the occasion, and was also attended by the alcalde of San Antonio, Juan N. Seguin, whose fat wife dancing with President Lamar led the ball."

Mrs. Jacques rented the corner at Commerce and Main Plaza for a restaurant. She invited all the young American men and ladies then living in San Antonio to a grand feast.

Mrs. Maverick, then a young mother of her first born, Sam Maverick, Jr., who is now living, and nearing 100 years of age. and all the party "after the feast paraded along Soledad Street and had such a good time." Mrs. Jacques was very popular and charitable and during the cholera epidemic in 1849 nursed the afflicted. In the cholera epidemic of 1866, she nursed a prominent lawyer, Russell Howard, from whom she contracted the disease and died.

Theodore Schleuning had a grocery store at Commerce and South Alamo streets. W. C. A. Thielepape, who afterwards became mayor of San Antonio in 1867, was his bookkeeper, Thielepape was appointed mayor of San Antonio by Colonel J. J. Reynolds, U. S. Army, on

November 8th, 1867, and served to March 28th, 1870. He was again appointed mayor by Governor E. J. Davis; he served as mayor to November 12th, 1872.

XII. MARKET STREET

In the late forties the prominent merchants in San Antonio were Bryan Callaghan and the firm of Nat Lewis and Groesbeck, who had their stores on the northeast corner of Market Street and Main Plaza directly opposite the old Court House and on a direct line with the north side of Galan Street.*

More interesting and tragic events of the early days of San Antonio have occurred in Market Street than in any other street. The first court house and jail was situated on the northwest corner of Market Street and Main Plaza, and on March 19, 1840, the first great tragedy occurred on this historic spot. The Indian chiefs from the wilds of West Texas came to San Antonio to make a treaty with the civil and military authorities with regard to the deliverance of white captives then held by the Indians in Sabinal Canyon. The result of the pow-wow not being satisfactory either to the white or red men, a fight ensued which resulted in the death of thirty-seven Indians and seven whites.

Market Street was first named Calabosa Street on account of the jail being located on the street, and Commerce Street was called Main Street. I will endeavor to give the history of the owner of each house and lot commencing from the northwest corner of Market Street and Main Plaza and continuing east to the end of the street at

---

* (For some of the incidents of the above article the writer is indebted to William Corner, San Antonio de Bexar, Mrs, Mavericks' memories, Charles Hummel, and to the January number of The Southwestern Historical Quarterly Magazine, and City Council records of San Antonio.)

its intersection with Alamo Street, The first records of the City Council in June, 1842, show that it proposed and carried "that the city jail on Calabosa (Market) Street be repaired, and the mayor was requested to take charge of the key until some arrangement could be effected whereby the county was to furnish a lock with two keys so the city and county authorities could have access to the jail." Due to the lack of openings in the adobe houses and to the great heat in the summer time, residents, for coolness, slept in the streets at night. For protection from Indian attacks cattle hides were suspended from chains across Market Street. This precaution prevented the Indians disturbing the rest of the sleepers by shooting arrows at them. In 1855 Enoch Jones erected on this old Court House site the first three-story building in San Antonio. This building was later occupied (for a long time) by Bennet, Cochran and Minter's grocery and liquor store during the sixties and seventies. The Market House, the architecture of which was classic Grecian, was built by John Fries about 1856. This commodious structure was for many years patronized by residents of San Antonio, who went with baskets on their arms in the early morning hours to purchase meats and vegetables for the day's consumption. The entire Market House was surrounded by an alley which gave the tenants access by wagon to their different stalls. Charles Hummel's gun store and George Horner's saloon fronted on Commerce Street and had access on their rear by this alley. Mr. Bergstrom and his sons had their butcher stand to the right of the Market Street entrance. Jose Panaloza, an influential Mexican politician and butcher, and George Dashiel, afterwards for many years popular District Clerk of Bexar County, also had meat stalls. Mrs. Liar kept a vegetable stand, and Sallie Royal, a giant yellow negress, ran a coffee stand. For some reason Sally incurred the enmity of the Callaghan regime in 1885, and she was ordered to vacate. Antonio Bruni, the market master, was called upon to eject her. He attempted to do this, but Sally resisted. When Bruni threatened to use force, the indignant negress seized him and dragged him by force and threw him bodily into the "fish pond," which was a tank filled with water drained from the Market House roof. It was a cement tank about twenty feet square and about three feet deep, and was used by the market tenants for drinking and cleaning purposes. Sally brought suit against the city for damages, and for years the famous case of "Sally Royal versus the City of San Antonio" was fought in the Bexar County courts with the verdict finally in favor of the City. Sally appealed, and after a great while the Supreme Court of Texas rendered a verdict in favor of Sally and granted her damages to the sum of two thousand dollars. This amount was never paid, and to this day that judgment stands against the City. Before the Supreme Court awarded her damages, Sally died, leaving no heirs to collect the money.

The next in line was the famous Bull Head Saloon. A large painted bull's head was the sign over the door. This saloon was mainly patronized by the sporting element of San Antonio. Here gambling and drinking were freely indulged. East of this saloon was the corner of Yturri and Market streets in which was the rear end of the wealthy Spanish Yturri home, which fronted on Commerce Street. Here President Sam Houston and Mira- beau Lamar, the most famous men of the Republic of Texas, were entertained at different times with a grand ball by the wealthy Yturri family.

Heiligman's Saloon was on the corner across Yturri Street. Next was the rear of Norton and Deutz Hardware Store which fronted on Commerce Street. Goldfrank and Frank also had the rear of their wholesale dry goods establishment on Market Street.

Mr. Braden, proprietor of the Braden Hotel, was an energetic and popular man. who early identified himself with the upbuilding of the city. He was at one time head of the San Antonio Fire Department, and his hotel was one of the earliest and most popular resorts. The Braden Hotel was built according to the architectural style of that period, as was also the Kloepper Hotel, the James home on Commerce Street, and the Jacques boarding house on Soledad Street. This style was of two stories with wide galleries on the front on both floors, and an ell containing rooms for the guests. When Mr. Braden retired from the hotel business, he was succeeded by Mr. John Bosshardt, who continued the management. Bosshardt bad two sons, Frank, who is an attorney at law, and Charles, who is in the employ of the city at the present time.

Next fronting on the alley, Corcoran Street, where the Oppenheimer Bank and office building is now, was Leroux and Cosgrove's hardware store which extended to Market Street. Across the alley was a residence. Then came the rear of the wholesale and retail establishment of Barney and Michael Oppenheimer. Barney Oppenheimer was a very prominent bachelor. At one time he was appointed as general on the Governor's staff, an honorary position. Nic Tengg's store on Commerce Street extended through to Market Street, Next was a residence at one time occupied by General W. B. Knox, a great politician and a former sheriff of Bexar County. Adjoining was the home of Mrs. Schmidt, a widow, who conducted a high class restaurant and boarding house during the sixties. This building fronted on Commerce Street and extended back to Market Street on which it had an entrance, She bad a son named August, who assisted her in the management. On the north corner of Navarro and Market was a livery stable which occupied the site for many years.

Across Navarro Street was the Baetz and Lange blacksmith shop. Further east were several small business houses, and at the corner of Presa and Market streets was the shop of Fisher, the tailor. Across Presa, on the corner, was another tailor shop and the residence of Scheer. Then came the one-story residence of Mr. Bayless, a bookkeeper of the firm of Adams and Wicks, wealthy government contractors. Mrs. Bayless, who had a beautiful daughter named Stella, committed suicide. Adjacent was the lot owned by Conrad Beckmann, whose blacksmith shop fronted on Commerce Street. He had a pretty rock residence at the corner of Market and Casino Street, and his lot extended to the San Antonio River. There was no bridge over the river on Market Street in those days.

Across the river was an adobe one-story building, the "Brewer House", which fronted on South Alamo Street and extended west along Market Street to the river. In this building occurred the death of Bill Hart, who was described by Captain Dobbin, Bexar County sheriff of that day, as "the worst desperado in Texas". Captain Dobbin's account of the killing is as follows: "Bill Hart was killed on May 29, 1857, and along with him his companion Miller and a government teamster named Wood. Fieldstrop, a discharged soldier who had been employed by the vigilance committee of San Antonio to watch Hart and his party, was also killed. When Hart and Miller passed on their way, they were fired upon by Fieldstrop with a shotgun, and Miller was killed. Bill Hart was mortally wounded, his right wrist and left thigh broken besides having eleven buckshot wounds in the region of his kidneys. Nevertheless, he reached the Brewer House, where he took shelter. Fieldstrop, having reloaded his gun, approached the house where Hart had taken shelter to finish him when Woods came out of the door and ordered Fieldstrop off. Fieldstrop fired, killing Woods instantly. Hart then appeared supporting himself with an old shovel shaft and with a pistol in his unwounded left hand. Fieldstrop's gun missed fire. Hart fired, shooting Fieldstrop in the center of the forehead. He then retired in a dying condition into the room. Jim Taylor rushed into the house to finish Hart, who shot Taylor through the right breast. Before dying, however, Taylor killed Hart, This was the first killing in San Antonio by the vigilance committee, five men met their death".

Commencing from the southwest corner of Market Street and Main Plaza, the first house was that of the Montez family, on the site now occupied by the Prudential Hotel. Afterwards the Montez home was used as the business place of Mr. Asa Mitchell, who came to Texas in 1822 and fought for Texas in the Battle of San Jacinto. Later, in 1846, he established himself and his family in San Antonio. Asa Mitchell was a noted character. He was a large land-owner, and at one time owned ten thousand acres of land at the confluence of the Medina and San Antonio rivers. Here he built a large rock residence, which is today the home of his decedents. In the war between the states, he cast his lot with the South and became head of the vigilance committee in San Antonio.

Samuel Bell, who came to San Antonio in 1852, conducted a jewelry store on Main Street. Bell was a northern sympathizer, and when Texas declared for the South, he waved a Union flag in front of his store. The vigilance committee met and decided to bang Bell; but Asa Mitchell declared that if anyone attacked Bell, it would be over his dead body. When the Union troops entered San Antonio in 1866, they arrested Mitchell and we're going to hang him, when Bell interceded and saved his life.

In the eighties the famous Maison Blanche French restaurant was established on Market Street and was well patronized by the epicures of San Antonio, who got their first taste of French cooking here. Further east was the restaurant of Michael Ryan, the father of Joe Ryan, a former city attorney of San Antonio who became famous for his legal attainments and today is one of the supreme court commissioners of the state of Texas.

Korn's confectionery store was next in line. He had two daughters, Hulda and Minnie. Minnie married Celeste Pinge- not, a cattleman; and Hulda married August Cline, a well known United States scout, who became famous in the Indian wars on the western plans of the United States. Cline also served with the noted Kit Carson in the early days of the Indian warfare in New Mexico. He at one time was stationed at Fort Clark, Texas, and became the scout for General Mackenzie during his successful campaigns against the Indians in West Texas. The town of Cline in Uvalde County, where he died in his ninetieth year, was named after him. Cline is buried in the U. S. cemetery in San Antonio, Texas.

On the southwest corner of Market and Yturri streets was the old iron-front building which was the grain and feed store of the popular Jack Labatt, who married a Miss Wier. He had serious trouble with a man named Alford, who was killed by Labaft. Labatt was acquitted by the District Court of Bexar County.

A foot bridge floated by empty barrels crossed the San Antonio River at Yturri Street for an entrance to Wolfram's Garden (formerly Bowen's Island) where a convention hall, beer saloon, and a garden were erected where now stands the beautiful Plaza Hotel. The pavilion was used for dancing, political meetings, and general amusement, and was a popular resort directly in the heart of the city.

The Perch saloon and residence was at the corner, and next in line east was Pereida's jewelry store. Adjoining was the city's fire and engine house. Upstairs in this building was a dancing school. Among the pupils here were the writer and T. C. Frost, who at that time was courting Miss Josephine Houston whom he later married. Next in line was a livery stable, convenient for the guests at Braden's Hotel to stable their horses. Huth's seed store and Eula's cigar store came next, Then came Felder's shoe store. After Felder died, Mrs. Felder, a midwife, advertised her calling.

The Mill Bridge ford was one of the most picturesque places in San Antonio. Here an army of small boys standing almost waist deep in the water were busily engaged in washing buggies and other vehicles for pay. In former days the San Antonio River had never been tapped at its source by artesian wells and consequently its flow was four times its present volume. In fact, it was at that time the most beautiful stream in West Texas, full of all kinds of fish and its banks adorned with beautiful trees.

On the southeast corner of Market and Navarro streets was the old Nat Lewis grist mill run by water power, which furnished flour and cornmeal in the early days of San Antonio. One summer morning many years ago when the writer was a small boy on his way to school, he entered the door of the old Nat Lewis Mill and saw the most horrible sight—a dead man, the miller, lying naked in bed with his head smashed and bloody, the victim of a murder the previous night. Then was Hutzler's residence and brewery, and across the street, where the San Antonio Carnegie Library is now, was the Holmgreen Foundry, called the Alamo Iron Works, that extended to the river. John McMullen, a prominent citizen and large land owner, also lived at one time where the library is now, and it was here that he was murdered. McMullen County was named after him.

To the east was the beautiful rock residence of Martin Campbell, who was the father of Dr. Charles Campbell, the bacteriologist and famous originator of the bat roost theory. Next came the German Casino Association, built for amusement, and a place for recreation where the early settlers from foreign countries could meet and discuss their different views. This was the first beautiful public building in San Antonio which contained an elaborate stage where theatricals and public and private entertainments were enjoyed. For twenty-five years all the grand balls and dances complimenting the visiting celebrities of the army and state were held at the Casino. Some of the early German emigrants were highly educated and cultured people, who left their mother country to escape military service. The first thing they did when they arrived in San Antonio was to establish in 1858 the Casino Club and the German- English School. This school for many years was patronized by the citizens and was very successful until the advent of the city public schools.

Where the City Water Works is now, was the residence of General William Steele, a former United States army officer who was a captain in 1848. He was instrumental in locating and establishing the many United States army posts in Texas for the purpose of protecting the settlers from Indian depredations, Steele allied himself with the South in the Civil War and attained the high rank of general. He was a gallant and very able officer. After the war he located his home on Market Street and became a member of the firm of Steel and Williams. Afterwards he was appointed by the governor as Adjutant General of Texas, and had supervision of the state's different ranger companies. General William Steele had one daughter, Lilly, who never married. She was the principal of the Brooklyn Avenue (Elinor Brackenridge School) for many years before her death. A new elementary school on South New Braunfels Avenue is called the Lilly Steele School in her honor.

Market Street in former days was not only the place where great tragedies took place, but was also the most popular place for business, amusements and festivities in old San Antonio. In a square building with a flat roof which stood on the southwest corner of Yturri and Market Street, directly opposite the Bull Head gambling saloon, where fortunes were won or lost on the turn of a card, was an establishment where the public fandango dance was enjoyed, This fandango was a relic of former Castilian days, and at one time was very popular in San Antonio, Señora Candelaria, the most outstanding female character of San Antonio history, was the presiding genius of the fandango where the beaux and belles of San Antonio romped, played, and danced to the sweet strains of tire orchestra and dined on the delicious dishes prepared by Señora Candelaria's own hand. Drinks were furnished from across the street by the Bull Head Saloon. Many romances sprang up between the pretty senoritas and American youths, which often led to marriage. Sometimes the festivities were marred by serious fights in which the knife or the pistol was the arbiter and in which death often took a hand. Señora Candelaria was born in Laredo, Tex., in 1785; she claimed to have been a survivor of the siege and fall of the Alamo where she nursed Bowie during his last illness and saw him killed. She lived to be over a hundred years old, and her mind was clear to the end. She loved to relate the remarkable events of her past life in San Antonio.

PART FOUR
Western Texas

I. THE STORY OF WEST TEXAS

The annexation of Texas in 1845 brought peace and happiness to the citizens of the republic of Texas, who had become weary of war with Mexico and the incessant worry of protecting their homes from wild Indian raids. The bloody massacres of Texans at the Alamo and Goliad were gruesome reminiscences of the cost of liberty, and Texas history for the past 100 years was written in the blood of her pioneers. There was also a touch of romance, happiness and love mingled with all the horrors of murder and sudden death. The occupation of the frontier of Texas by the United States troops in 1845 was hailed with delight by the citizens of Texas who were now destined to enjoy the tranquility of life that for so long had been an entire stranger.

The entire country west of San Antonio was almost a "terra incognita" before the establishment of the U. S. military posts which stretched along the Rio Grande for nearly 500 miles extending from New Mexico on the north to the Gulf of Mexico on the south. Many of these forts were named in honor of illustrious officers of the Mexican war, as follows: Forts Quitmann, Davis, McKaveth, Duncan, Ringgold, Worth and Brown; there were also Forts Stockton, Lancaster, Ewell, Clark, San Antonio and Fort Mason. After annexation, this beautiful, wild and interesting country became the training ground for many of the illustrious U. S. officers who received their baptismal fire of war and who afterwards commanded the opposing armies of the United States and the Confederacy during the Civil War. Lieut, U. S. Grant, stationed at Corpus Christi with Gen. Taylor's army of advance on Mexico, made a trip to San Antonio and Austin in 1845, and, to repeat his exact words, "there was not a house between Corpus Christi and San Antonio, and San Antonio and Austin. There was not a minute of the time during the entire journey when deer, antelope and wild turkey could not be seen in great numbers," and later he alludes to the immense herd of wild horses encountered by the army on the Nueces River, between Corpus Christi and Brownsville, "that extended right and left as far as the eye could reach." Many of the horses of the U. S. army were recruited from these wild herds, and Grant speaks in glowing terms of their endurance.

The battles of Palo Alto and Resaca de Palma were fought on West Texas soil, and were Lieut. U. S. Grant's first taste of actual war.

In 1849 Col. Albert Sidney Johnston made a topographical survey of the country between Indianola, Texas, and Santa Fe, New Mexico, His report of the country traversed is the first authentic Information on record. Col. Johnston regarded himself as a Texan, and soon his grave at Austin will be adorned by a handsome monument. The money for which was lately appropriated by the Texas legislature.

In 1885 Lieut. J. B. Hood (afterwards commander of the Southern Army of Tennessee) gained a signal victory on Devil's River, near its confluence with the Rio Grande in a bloody battle with a superior force of Comanche Indians, and here he first came to be regarded as a dashing cavalry officer. And it was he who established Camp Wood in the Nueces Canon. Hood fell in love with Texas, invested in property at Camp Verde, and contemplated resigning from the U. S. Army to become a citizen of Texas. He afterwards joined the Confederacy, though a native of Kentucky, giving Texas as his home State.

In 1855 Lieut. Fitzhugh Lee killed an Indian warrior in a hand to hand conflict, near Ft. Mason, Texas.

The matchless Robt. E. Lee was commander of the Department of Texas in 1860.

Gen. Geo, Thomas, the "Rock of Chickamauga" and Gen. James Longstreet were also remembered by many of San Antonio's oldest citizens.

During the early days in West Texas the life of the U. S. officers was occupied not only in training the soldiers in the art of war, scouting and battling with wild Indians, but in hunting and fishing in this sportsman's paradise which afforded them pleasant recreation. At night, when the arched blue dome of heaven's canopy of bright stars shone resplendent in this Southern clime and fanned by the gentle breezes, then the soft, sweet music of the fandango stole languidly through the air, and the dark, lustrous-eyed senoritas tripped the light fantastic with their uniformed partners, their graceful movements blending in perfect harmony with the seductive music of the waltz. It is the same old story the world over. Many happy marriages are recorded between the young U. S. officers and the bewitchingly beautiful dark-eyed senoritas of Spain and Mexico.

San Antonio, in 1845, was only a small town, inhabited mostly by Mexicans, Indians, and foreigners, with only a few Americans. It is in the memory of living citizens when herds of wild horses, antelope, and deer were to be seen ranging on the Alazan Creek, which is at present a populous suburb, adorned with handsome dwellings and business houses. The chain of mountains, extending from New Braunfels on the east through Comal, Bandera, Bexar, Medina, Uvalde, Kinney and to Val Verde counties to where Devil's River mountains crowd on the Rio Grande River on the west, is the dividing line between the plains and mountains of West Texas. The Comal, Guadalupe, San Antonio, Medina. Sabinal, Leona and Nueces rivers have their sources in this continuous chain of mountains, where their crystal waters flow, abounding in cataracts, with a path cut through solid rock and gravel. Many beautiful varieties of fish, which can be clearly seen at a depth of 15 feet, sport in these clear waters. The banks of these mountain streams are overhung with massive vine-clad cliffs; in the valleys, grace- full, tall, nut-bearing and other grand trees adorn the rivers' banks. In the woods black bear, panther, peccary and other wild animals abound, with three different varieties of quail. All the above beautiful streams, with the exception of Devil's River, traverse the immense plains of Southwest Texas, extending from Del Rio, on the Rio Grand River, to Brownsville, Texas, on the Gulf coast.

Formerly this was a treeless prairie, covered entirely with a rank growth of grass almost waist high, that bowed gracefully to the passing breeze, and as far as the horizon's view, it was unbroken as a calm sea, imparting to the beholder the feeling of wonder and delight. These rolling prairies were pasture grounds for immense herds of deer, graceful antelope, wild horses and the uncouth and ponderous buffalo. During the fall and winter, when the grass became crisp and dry, the Indians would start immense prairie fires that would sweep the entire country until stopped by a river or some natural barrier, leaving an appearance of utter desolation.

At night the melancholy cry of prowling lobo and other wolves broke the intense solitude of the prairie.

The transportation of merchandise to the frontier towns and military posts was carried on by means of trains, consisting of many large wagons, called prairie schooners, each holding as much as 6,000 pounds, drawn by numerous small Mexican mules, four in a line, with Mexican drivers, all under one boss, who was held responsible. These caravans crept along slowly over the plains during the day, and at the approach of night the wagons were drawn up in an immense circle, with the mules and the men in the center. This precaution was necessary to guard against night attacks by Indians. Merchandise was conveyed west of San Antonio as far as El Paso, Texas, Chihuahua, Mexico, and Brownsville, Texas.

The mesquite trees were in evidence, but only where civilization existed. Their absence was accounted for by the devastating effects of the Indian prairie fires: yet along the banks of the streams large timber abounded, which furnished the only protection in summer from the fierce rays of the sun and in winter from the cold blasts of the Texas norther.

Thrilling reminiscences of Indian story-telling of theft and murder, kept the ranchmen in constant terror until the advent of the United States troops' occupation brought tranquility and peace.

West of Devil's River a marked change takes place in the face of the country. The surface becomes more rolling and hilly and less covered with trees. Devil's River, on account of its vertical sides, is difficult to approach. The Pecos River is narrow and deep, and exceedingly crooked in its course, with a rapid current. Its waters are turbid and bitter, and its clay banks so steep that for nearly 200 miles an animal can hardly approach the water in safety, with not a tree or bush to mark its course.

The mountains in the vicinity of Ft. Davis do not form a continuous chain, but are made of single conical peaks, intersecting each other so as to form an almost impenetrable barrier.

San Antonio is about 650 feet elevation: Devil's River, 900 feet; Pecos, 1900 feet; Ft. Davis, 5766: then descending west until at El Paso 3536 feet. No wood exists in this rugged country except the scrubby mesquite.

Many colonies from France and Germany flocked to Southwest Texas during the last days of the Republic. At the time of the beginning of the Civil War, this fertile, beautiful and inviting country was prosperous and the people happy and contented. The men were called from their homes to assist the dying struggles of the Confederacy; the farms and ranches were abandoned, and their business entirely neglected. The many thousands of live stock became wild and retreated to the mountains and dense chaparral had taken possession of the plains. After the war these wild herds of cattle were reclaimed by the cowboys, and vast herds of beeves were annually driven overland to Eastern markets in Kansas, which industry was exceedingly remunerative: and here again the cowboy's career, whose wild abandon and recklessness made him an interesting and picturesque character. The range being open for everybody, the vast herds of live stock became inseparably mingled, and during the droughts and inclement weather, cattle would drift hundreds of miles from the home range. Dishonesty in handling these cattle soon caused the cattle business to become entirely demoralized, and every ranchman commenced appropriating from his neighbor to recuperate his losses, which brought the cattle business into bad repute, and the cattle raising on a large scale almost ceased to exist. The sheep industry (in 1873) was then introduced, and the dry climate, great variety of food and the altitude, made Southwest Texas an ideal sheep range, and during the Franco-Prussian War of 1873 wool was sold at 45 cents gold per pound, which gave a great impetus to the business, and in a few years immense flocks of sheep took the place of the cattle, and millions of pounds of wool were annually marketed in San Antonio. Adverse national legislation, by removing the protective import duty on raw products, such as wool, etc., almost caused the entire destruction of this most promising industry of sheep raising for which such a pastoral country as Western Texas was so peculiarly adapted. At the present time ranches and farms are enclosed by fences; there is no more vacant land. The cattle and sheep industry is prosperous, with values in land rapidly advancing. The sheep industry is confined to the rugged hills west of Devil's River: the cattle ranges to the south.

Irrigation is now the agricultural fad. Artesian water can be readily had at reasonable expense, and the land that cost only a nominal sum with the aid of irrigation has accomplished wonders in the production of vegetables, etc.; and being so far south, it has a decided advantage in the early markets over northern produce.

San Antonio is beautifully situated near the headwaters of the San Antonio River. It is the metropolis of Texas, and is the fairest and most interesting and progressive city of its size in the South. It has many miles of broad asphalt streets, which are shaded by beautiful trees. Twenty lovely parks containing 400 acres afford ample breathing place for its inhabitants. Its chain of missions, erected by the Franciscan Fathers hundreds of years ago, are standing relics of a romantic past. Pure artesian water for drinking purposes, splendid sewer system, many hot medicinal artesian wells, fine hotels, all go to make it an up-to-date city in every respect. Who can tell but in a few years West Texas is destined to become the sanitarium for the world.

II. THE COYOTE AND LOBO WOLF PERIL

The history of wolves in West Texas during the past fifty years is worthy of attention. The coyote is the Spanish name for the medium size prairie wolf so common over the western United States. It is possessed of a cunning and sense most extraordinary for a four legged brute. The other wild animals during the last twenty-five years have decreased to such an extent, that the enforcement of the most rigid State laws are now necessary for their preservation.

Such are our present game laws. Paradoxically the coyotes are the only animals that have multiplied during this same period until at the present they not only destroy live stock but have even become a menace to human life.

Full Grown Calves Destroyed

The lobo wolf is a powerful animal of twice the size and strength of the coyote. I can remember when a boy I have often seen lobo wolves on the outskirts of San Antonio and, in fact, at that time the lobo was common everywhere in West Texas. One powerful lobo when aroused by hunger would attack and destroy a full grown calf. Cattle when attacked by lobo wolves would present a solid front of horns by forming a ring with the calves in the inside. I have seen a ranchman in early days hurriedly grab his gun in the dead of night and rush through the mesquite and cacti to the assistance of his panic stricken cattle which were bellowing loudly and desperately fighting the lobo wolves.

When the sheep industry became so remunerative, caused by the splendid market price paid for wool and sheep, the flock- master began to give a great deal of attention to the raising of sheep. The sheep is such a defenseless animal that it is the very symbol of meekness. The wolf is its natural enemy. The flockmaster's first duty in the care of his flock began with the destruction of the wolves on the home range.

A bitter and relentless war against wolves was waged by the sheep men in every county in West Texas. Never in the history of Texas had there been so few wolves as in 1888. A flock of lambs could then be left anywhere on that range with perfect safety, and poultry was never disturbed. Wild game of all kinds, now safe from the depredations of the coyote and lobo, multiplied so rapidly that West Texas became famous as a hunter's paradise, and never before or afterwards has game been so abundant.

Wolves were destroyed by traps or poison. Sheepmen purchased strychnine by the pound and the poison was generally carried in his pocket in a buck-skin pouch, and at every opportunity he scattered poisoned baits over the range.

Baited Meat With Poison

To poison coyotes successfully required a great deal of care, because the coyote is a most suspicious and foxy animal. The usual dose was as much strychnine as would remain on the point of a pocket knife. This dose was enclosed in tissue paper and after an incision was made in a piece of meat the tissue paper was pushed inside. A decoy consisted of the haunch of a sheep or cow and was dragged about sun down at the end of a stake rope and the poisoned baits were scattered along the trail at intervals of every few hundred yards. These baits were placed at the end of a sharpened stick about two feet above the ground.

Every caution was previously taken that one's hand did not touch the meat, for the coyote's least suspicion made him reject the most daintily prepared morsel. If the poison was applied loosely, its bitter taste soon permeated the meat and the coyote would not touch it. The tissue paper would not allow the poison to dissolve until in the wolf's stomach.

In 1885 the tariff was taken off wool, which greatly reduced its price and the sheep business suffered in proportion; so much so, that after a few years, the greatest and most remunerative business that West Texas and San Antonio had ever enjoyed, had languished for the want of national protection and almost everybody interested in sheep was anxious to sell out. The price of wool in the spring of 1882 was 27 cents per pound; a few years after it went down to 15 cents and afterwards to 12 cents. The price of land and the hire of sheep herders in the meantime had increased to such an extent that the raising of sheep became no longer profitable.

Cattle values had now increased and it was not long until the cow had taken the place of the sheep on the range.

After the passing of the sheep man, coyotes immediately began to increase. The cow man paid little attention to wolves and seldom trapped or poisoned them.

In 1885 began the fencing of great pastures of land. Open range in West Texas in a short time became a thing of the past. The sheep industry then passed into the hands of a few men who still had faith in the business and who moved their flocks to cheaper mountainous lands on Devil's and Pecos rivers, and to this day the sheep business is almost confined to that district.

Serious Menace at Uvalde

Twenty-five years ago coyotes were so numerous in the plains country south of the mountainous district in West Texas as to become, not only dangerous to domestic animals of all kinds, but even to human life. Mad coyotes, which formerly were unknown, had become so common that several deaths of individuals had resulted from their bites.

It became absolutely necessary for camping parties in Uvalde County to surround their tents with wire netting as a protection against mad coyotes. Even ranch houses had their galleries enclosed with wire netting. Some parents on the outskirts of the town of Uvalde were afraid to send their children to school without an escort. And during the summer months almost a state of panic existed in some counties.

A mad coyote is a most dangerous animal, as it is perfectly fearless and does not hesitate to attack viciously any person or animal it encounters.

The coyote also feeds upon the young of all kinds of game. They kill fawns, eat quail eggs, kill the wild turkey hen and destroy her nest during setting time, and, in fact, all wild fowls that nest on the ground are liable to be attacked and destroyed by this vicious animal.

That there were very few young deer and young turkeys in West Texas at the time when coyotes were so numerous is a fact. The coyotes watch the mother doe secrete her fawns, and during her absence destroy her young. In the same manner this vicious animal kills young calves. A ranchman of Maverick County informed me that one year he had two hundred calves killed by coyotes.

The situation in West Texas became so unbearable from the great coyote peril that the people applied for relief to our great State of Texas.

III. JAMES DUNN, THE TEXAS RANGER

James Dunn was renowned as one of the most daring Indian fighters of his day. His exploits with wild Indians, and his many narrow escapes from death would make as interesting reading as the adventures of Big Foot Wallace, who was his companion in many exciting encounters with Indians.

James Dunn, while a red-headed, freckled-faced Irish boy, was, in the early 30's, captured on the streets of San Antonio by Indians during one of their raids in the city. The color of his hair, and his tender age probably saved his life, for his captors stopped at the Alazan Creek, where Commerce Street now crosses it, to allow the squaws time to wash the freckles from his face and what they thought was red paint from his head. He was a prisoner among the Indians for some time, but finally escaped and returned to San Antonio. While he was with the savages he became proficient in woodcraft, Indian ways, and the trapping of wild game, which afterwards proved a great assistance to him in the stirring life he was to lead.

The Council House fight in San Antonio occurred on March 19, 1840. when sixty-five Comanche Indians engaged in combat with the authorities in the city, and thirty Indians were killed and the remainder were captured. In this fight James Dunn saved the life of John James, the surveyor, then a young man twenty-one years old, After the battle, Indians in revenge, infested the suburbs of San Antonio and murdered every defenseless person encountered by them and created such terror among the settlers that they were unable to work their farms in the vicinity of the Alamo on the east side of the river, and they suffered hardships for want of food. Corn sold at that time for three dollars per bushel on the streets of San Antonio.

About this time a young man named Jack Hays, then twenty-two years old, appeared on the scene and formed the ranger company which was afterwards destined to become famous and to give quiet and peace to the harassed citizens. The requirements to join Hays' company were: "A man had to have courage, good character, be a good rider and a good shot, and have a horse worth $100." In his first ranger company in 1840, for the Republic of Texas, were Ben and Henry McCulloch, who became renowned generals in the Confederate Army, Big Foot Wallace, Kit Ackland, James Dunn and many others who afterwards became famous.

In July, 1841, Captain Hays with forty rangers was surprised at Bandera Pass by a large body of Comanche Indians, who suddenly raised up from both sides and sent a volley of bullets and arrows into the company. Many horses and men were falling from the sudden ambuscade; but Hays, who had never been defeated, cried out, "Stand boys, we can whip them!" After great effort and almost with defeat staring them in the face one of the rangers succeeded in killing the Comanche chief, and the Indians retreated. Hays had several men killed in this desperate battle, and among the wounded was James Dunn.

Another famous battle in which James Dunn participated was in July, 1844, when Hays' rangers, for the first time armed with the new Colts five shooter revolvers, defeated a large band of Indians in the Nueces Canon. The Indians expected an easy victory on account of their large numbers; but when the rangers on horseback met them at close range and did such deadly work with their pistols, the Indians had the surprise of their lives, and took to the brush, leaving many of their braves dead on the field.

A month after the battle in the Nueces Canyon, in August, 1844, Captain Hays sent four of his best scouts back to the Nueces to see if there were any fresh signs of Indians. The men sent on this dangerous mission so far from the settlement were James Dunn, Kit Ackland, Perry and Carlin. After a hard ride the party arrived at the confluence of the West and East Prongs of the Nueces, twelve miles above where the town of Uvalde now stands. They dismounted and prepared a meal, and after eating dinner Ackland lay down to rest. Perry stood guard, and James Dunn and Carlin after unsaddling their horses, took them down to the river to wash them off and take a swim themselves. When they reached the river, they stripped off their clothing and rode their horses bareback into the stream. A band of Indians was concealed nearby and was intently watching their movements; and as soon as Dunn and Carlin were in the water, the Indians attacked the camp. Perry fell with three wounds, two in the body and one in the face. Ackland was also hit in three places with bullets and arrows, but he did not fall. He put up a desperate fight and shot one Indian. Perry managed to recover somewhat and he and Ackland retreated to the river. Dunn and Carlin took them across the river on their horses, and for the time they were out of reach of the Indians. There were large piles of driftwood left by recent rises in the river, where the wounded men, Perry and Ackland, managed separately to conceal themselves. Dunn and Carlin set out for San Antonio, a distance of one hundred and twenty miles. They rode bareback and were naked; and when they arrived, they were in a most deplorable condition, being badly sunburned from riding so far in the hot August weather without clothing. Strange to say, after a few days Ackland and Perry, on foot, staggered into San Antonio, a few hours apart. After careful nursing by the good women of San Antonio, these men soon recovered.

After Hays' Company disbanded, James Dunn married and started a ranch on Potranco Creek, about fifteen miles west of San Antonio, where he lived for many years and had many exploits in defending his stock from Indian raids. During the Civil War he raised a company and was made captain of it. He was killed in the last battle of the Confederacy at a place called Carricitis, near Brownsville, in a fight between the forces of General Banks of the Union Army and the Confederates. So died James Dunn, a brave man, a forgotten hero, a product of San Antonio, whose body lies buried in an unknown grave far from the beautiful city which to protect in its infancy he gave the best years of his life and suffered hardships and financial adversity, so that in future years the ones who came after could reap the benefits derived from his heroic and unselfish life.

The late Clemente Dunn, who died several years ago at San Antonio, was the son of Captain James Dunn.

Captain Jack Hays and John Twohig were brothers-in-law. Both married sisters in the Calvert family of Seguin, Texas. Captain Hays left San Antonio and went to California after the discovery of gold there in 1849. His reputation as a fighter and a fearless officer of the law had preceded his arrival there, and it is said he became the first sheriff of San Francisco, California. He bore a charmed life, and became a terror to evil doers on the Pacific Coast. Captain Hays lived to a good old age, and died in San Francisco about 1884, respected and loved by all who knew him.

IV. ALONG THE NUECES WITH ROD AND GUN

Every State in the Union has its beautiful spots, where Nature unadorned is adorned the most: some place where one, tired of the artificial pleasures and cares of city life, seeks rest and recreation for his limbs, dwarfed from lack of exercise, and relaxation from brain-weary routine work; some place where the running waters, the beautiful foliage, and the chirping of birds, all seem to say, "Come and stay with us!" Seek some shady spot, and look into the crystal-clear waters of the beautiful Nueces, First you will note the tiny perch and the minnows watching you; then, gathering courage, there comes, slowly gliding, a bass with bright eyes and brightly marked sides; then follow others—until you have quite an abundance of silent, inquisitive companions.

The Nueces River in Southwest Texas is said to be the most beautiful stream in the great Lone Star State. Its source is in the mountains of Edwards County, and for 70 miles it rushes through the wildly beautiful canon which bears its name. Along the sides of the mountain tops the fragrant cedar trees extend in groves for miles; at a greater height, groves of pine trees lend additional grandeur to the scene; while below, in the valley, flows the majestic river, named after the groves of tall pecan trees that line its banks—the Spanish name for "nuts" being nueces. Here the angler can ply his art to his heart's content, for in these waters are fish of many varieties. Along the mountains, the hunter can find the black bear and deer, the wild turkey, and quail of several varieties.

Emerging from the mouth of the canon, the waters of the Nueces, on entering the plains, disappear from the surface. For a distance of 15 miles the river flows underground, filtering through its gravel and sandy bed, only to come gushing forth clearer and more sparkling than ever; and thence flowing on, undisturbed, in its long journey to the Gulf of Mexico. The waters of the Nueces are great in volume and of marked clearness—so clear indeed that a bright object may be seen at a depth of 15 feet. At times the river flows over a rocky bed of glistening white pebbles, its centre being dotted with little islands, on which grow the stately sycamore trees. The willow, live-oak, elm, and pecan line the banks, whose rocky shores admit of no place for mud; and, last but not least, you are free from such pests as mosquitoes, red bugs, and the like. As the stream encounters some rocky formation, it is inspiring to see its waters leap and dance in their mad endeavor to find their own level. Frequently their roar heralds an approach to some beautiful cataract. At the foot of these falls are the deep and shady pools. Here are the places where the bass love to stay—giving ample sport to the happy fisherman attracted hitherward.

The varieties of fish that inhabit the Nueces are the large and small-mouth bass, the crappie, gaspagout (pronounced gasper goo), channel and blue catfish, and other varieties. The most reliable bait for the black bass is the live minnow; but I know of no greater ecstasy than to spend an early morning or late afternoon along the banks with a No. 5 phantom minnow. After a little practice one will discard live bait, and depend simply on the knack of dexterously casting over in some shady corner next to that huge rock. Verily, it is fine to see the short ripple of the waters; then to feel the tug on the line and to take part in the fight for life by His Bass-ship until weary and tired, he is dragged from his beautiful home. The gaspagout, to my mind, puts up a harder fight for its life than the black bass; it is also a beautiful fish and of fine flavor. It only frequents places of considerable depth and will not rise to artificial bait— preferring a live minnow. The crappie will take a spoon or "phantom." I have often caught bass very successfully by discarding sinker and float, as follows: Steal carefully along the shallow water where the fish are feeding, until you see a school of bass and perch of various sizes; show yourself and cast among them, and, in a moment, all are gone. But, stealing quietly along under cover until you are within striking distance, place a live minnow on the hook and cast among them with the bait. It will be readily taken; reel in carefully, and you can take a peep at the rest of his companions as they follow the caught fish to the shore. Pull in quietly and remove the fish; then cast again in the same manner, until you are amply rewarded for your pains. Alligator gars frequent the deep holes and often attain a great size, being sometimes 6 feet in length. The small pike-nose gar cuts the bait from the hook and is very difficult to capture, but the large gar swallows the bait, and then either breaks the line or puts up a great fight—taxing a strong man to land one.

Early one winter's morning I shot a large gobbler from his roost on a pecan tree over the Nueces River, and, in falling, he struck the water, dead. Marking the spot, I left the place in pursuit of others. Returning a short while afterwards to secure my prize, I was amazed to see the dead turkey disappear below the water. Thinking it was an optical illusion, I rubbed my eyes and gazed at a tree —expecting it too, with all its branches, to disappear in the earth. But the tree never moved. The bird reappeared and again took a dive—coming again to the surface near the bank. With the assistance of a long stick, I drew the turkey from the water—only to find it almost devoured. Down in the clear depths I could see a long dark shadow following, and closer examination revealed an alligator gar as long as a man. With disgust and anger I swore vengeance, and left the remains for the gar to complete his feast. I can now understand why wild ducks refuse to feed in waters containing these reptiles.

Every summer I traveled 100 miles to spend my vacation in camping out along the Nueces. How the children enjoyed its pure waters! Bathing was their greatest delight, and even the baby captured the black bass with the rod.

A folding Eureka canvas boat is a great desideratum for trolling, casting, and using artificial bait. During the winter months both large and small game are in season, including the peccary or wild pig.

The Nueces Valley is a vast uncultivated area. The soil consists of sand, lime, and alkali formation. The long summer drouths and the earth's sterility offer no encouragement to the tiller of the soil; consequently large bodies of land are fenced and used only for raising cattle and sheep. This sparsely settled country is too far away from the highways of civilization to become depleted of its game and fish, and bids fair to remain for many years to come the ideal bass and hunting ground of Western Texas.

We have the Mexican dove-colored quail, with its pretty top-knot of white. When frightened these birds chatter like the common guinea fowl, and depend more upon artful dodging in and out among the chaparral for their safety than in flight. They will not lie to the dog. The Messina or black breasted quail is much larger than either the Mexican quail or our bob- white. They are much like the latter variety in color and habits, save that the head feathers have a yellowish tint. Then comes bob white—the prettiest and gamiest bird of them all—

whose cries of "Tunas* ripe!—not quite! not quite!'" can be heard in the summer months from all sides in this Land of the Coyotes, the Cactus, and Mesquite.

Coming on the scene one August afternoon, after a hot and sultry day, just as the sun, setting behind the cliffs, was casting its cooling shadows over the waters lying at their base, I saw at a glance an ideal place to try my luck. The narrow stream was rushing between two large rocks into a broad pool. A flat ledge of rock projected far out into the water, and at its point ran the swift current. On the other side, some 10 feet away, was a large rock similar to the one I was standing on, except that it was an island with about a 20-foot channel between it and the opposite bank. In the afternoon the surface water becomes warm from the sun's rays, but below, at a certain depth, the water is chilly. Discarding my float, I sent the bait (a live minnow) to the bottom next to the high rock opposite me and at a point where the current ends. I was rewarded in a short while by landing two bass of medium size, followed by a 2-pound blue catfish. I was having great sport, to the envy of Sam, my companion, who accompanied me on this fishing jaunt—his first attempt at fishing since he was a boy. (Twenty long years past.) He sat perched on a high rock, disgusted with his luck in waiting for a strike. The water being deep and wide, be found it impossible to join me without swimming. My luck seemed to desert me; my attention became absorbed by the natural beauty and wildness of the scene. The sun was beginning to disappear in the western horizon. A stillness came over everything, except the ripple of the current and the waves beating against the rocky ledges, The silence was disturbed by a mother quail, with her covey of little chicks, preparing

---

* ["Tuna" is the fruit of the prickly pear—a species of cactus,—Ed,]

for approaching night, whistling from the chaparral. Noisily a large crow flies by, flapping his wings and breaking the stillness with a harsh "Caw! caw!" as he alights in the tall reeds growing on the little island. And just then I am recalled from my dreams by the point of my rod kissing the water. There is a slight jerk of the line; the multiplying reel sings out, and the 9-ounce split bamboo rod bends double with the strain. All I can do is to keep the line taut and let him play around. Reeling in, I feel the resistance growing stronger and stronger as the line shortens. I have the fish now just below me in the deep water, next to the ledge I am standing on—when away goes the reel again, singing a strident strain. Sam drops his rod, and, deeply interested, watches the fight from the other side. 'What have you got?" he yells across the river. I reel the fish gently but firmly towards me again, and now, pulling the line straight up, can see the great flat body and large dorsal fin. "A gaspagout, and a big one," I cry out in return. Away goes my fish again. I could no more stop that wild rush for liberty than catch a bullet from the muzzle of a gun. The gaspagout seems to grow stronger and stronger. Will this never end? Three times I have brought him to the surface and again he is gone—this time to the bottom of the pool, sulking and resting. Oh, for a landing net! Wildly I look around me for assistance. Sam could stay at his distance no longer. I hear a splash in the water, and soon see him, rod in hand, emerge from the rock opposite me, dripping wet from head to foot. What a picture for a dignified, successful business man of San Antonio. Oh, if only his wife could have seen him then! "Let me help you," he cries. "Help me? I would die ere I would let any one help me," I reply. Leaving the rock, I run around to the gravel bank on my left— the line playing out as I go. I am taking a desperate chance of losing my prize. If I can bring him to me, he will now have the shallow waters to hamper and exhaust him. The fish answers to the strain of the line, coming slowly towards me but fighting every inch of the way: keeping a taut line, I give him no chance to break away or turn to one side. His body now sways from side to side; his strength is fast ebbing away and the game is nearly up. At last, quivering and gasping, I have my prize helpless in my hands. I weigh him with the pocket scales: exactly 4 pounds. What a beauty he is with his bright scaly sides, hog back, and small aristocratic mouth; in shape not unlike a giant perch. Built for speed and power, he is game to the finish. The gaspagout is a royal fish— he carries his jewels with him in the shape of two pearl-like substances under the skin, one over each eye. Let me say again that the gaspagout puts up a harder fight for its life in these waters than the black bass, and he who lands a large one with rod and reel will never forget his experience.

V. THE DEVIL'S RIVER OF TEXAS

It was my custom, during the summer, to take my family for a couple of weeks on a camping trip. The pleasures of such outings are known only to those who go on such expeditions in similar company. One summer we started from San Antonio for Devil's River, the famous stream of southwestern Texas. We arrived duly at Del Rio, the most beautiful little city between San Antonio, Texas, and Los Angeles, California. Here springs of the finest water and of great volume burst from the ground and flow over a level country some three miles, emptying into the Rio Grande. Del Rio has some 2,000 acres of land subject to irrigation by this spring water. Beautiful orchards, great trees and fields of growing grain meet the tourist's eye. Figs, grapes, and fruits of all kinds are hawked around the depot by half-naked little Mexican boys.

A few miles west of Del Rio, the railroad runs along the right bank of the Rio Grande. The scenery here is truly grand. Just across the broad, swift river are the rugged hillsides of Old Mexico. To the right is a precipitous mountain side, and that part which formerly crowded down to the Rio Grande is cut away for the railroad track. The blue waters of Devil's River, swiftly flowing into the muddy Rio Grande, are next seen; then comes the lonely station of Devil's River. The inhabitants at that time were composed of a bachelor railroad telegraph operator and the dwellers of the railroad section house—laborers, entirely Mexican. A wagon and team awaited us, and after loading in our tents, cots and supplies, we followed on foot to our proposed camping place, some two miles north and below the railroad bridge crossing Devil's River. At the first sight of the river, the children went wild with delight. "Just look at the fish! Oh, what a big one! Did you see that one jump?" etc., etc., were their cries. Imagine a perfectly dear stream of water, two hundred feet wide, flowing with a four-miles-an-hour current and an average depth of three feet, over a solid rock bottom as smooth in some places as an asphalt pavement, in which could be seen many varieties of fish sporting in the clear water. There were many small islands covered with trees and with green grass cropped short and clean, as if by a lawn-mower. On the far bank were gigantic pecan, elm, and willow trees, which shaded the stream for quite a distance; and there was a background of the roughest and wildest mountain country in the world. The picture was complete.

After crossing the river we selected a camp below the railroad pumping house, under the dense shade of tall pecan trees, near the river's bank, where we might receive full benefit of the cool south and east breezes. The children immediately donned their bathing suits and plunged into the cool waters. In the intense enjoyment of the first dip in Devil's River they made the lonely hills echo with their cries of delight. That night, as every night afterwards, we slept in the open air. We only used the tents for protection during rainy days. We found the weather in daytime delightfully cool in the shade of the grand trees of our camp, and at night we always slept under one and sometimes two blankets. We never felt a red bug or a tick, nor saw a centipede during our stay, and in defiance to all vermin, including fabled bandits from Mexico, we pitched our camp not four hundred yards from the identical spot where the aforesaid bandits once captured the railroad pumper and held him for ransom.

Next morning I started with rod, reel, and trolling bait for black bass. I waded, and cast along the sides of lily pads and large rocks that projected into the river. In a couple of hours I secured enough black bass for dinner for the entire camp. How the children did enjoy that meal! I never in my life saw such capacity for storing food, It seemed they would never get enough, and it was nearly the same thing every mealtime afterwards. Bathing and fishing, with frequent journeys to interesting places, made our principal occupations. Every morning and afternoon the children went "swimming."

There are two beautiful species of fish in Devil's River that I have never seen in any other stream. One is a mullet, which closely resembles the salt water species in size and habits. Mullet are very numerous in Devil's River, and travel in schools, and in play they jump clear out of the water as do the salt water mullet. The other is a large perch, marked with black lines. This fish is extremely shy of man and will refuse the most tempting bait, I can account for their presence here only in this way: Devil's River and the Pecos River are the only two rivers in Texas, of any consequence, which empty into the Rio Grande. These fish resemble the salt-water mullet and the sheepshead of the Gulf of Mexico, and must have ascended the Rio Grande

River and entered the clear waters of Devil's River. The water of the Pecos is very muddy and has few varieties of fish. By using common sense I managed to capture a good many of these perch. I selected a very long cane rod, using a short, very light, but strong linen line, with no sinker, and baited with grasshoppers. Cautiously I reached a dead tree lying in the shallow water, and using the tree as a blind, I quietly dropped the bait among a school of these perch. The bait was immediately taken; and in an hour's time I had an even dozen of the beauties, which weighed, altogether, five pounds.

These large perch are the best pan fish I ever ate. It was a beautiful sight to see the mullet leaping in the clear water. One could always depend on seeing each mullet leap sometimes four times in succession, and a man with a shot gun could have fine sport shooting them on the jump. It is faster than trap shooting, and, I am told, is great sport.

Bass fishing on Devil's River is a grand sport on account of the general shallowness and clearness of the water, and the few trees along the river's course. It is a great place for long casts. Last summer, near the headwaters of this river, I made a long cast with a triple-gang troller, around a point of an island that projected into a broad, deep pool, a likely place for bass. I kept myself concealed, but saw quite a commotion in the water around the bait, and reeling in the line I had several strikes in quick succession. Imagine my surprise when instead of landing one bass I succeeded in landing three striped beauties! I returned two to the water and retained the largest. This is truth, though seemingly incredible. I caught at least twenty-five pounds of bass that day with the same bait, but I kept only the largest ones.

There is a species of "rock squirrel" here, gray in color. The males have a black stripe on the muzzle, which extends on to the back of the neck. This animal is smaller than the tree squirrel, and lives entirely among the rocks. It seems to be fairly plentiful, as I killed four one afternoon in a short time. Bob white and the Mexican blue quail are very abundant on the hills, also white-and black-tail deer. This I learned, though in summer 1 never hunt and pay very little attention to game out of season.

One afternoon we went to Castle Canon, an awe-inspiring line of perpendicular limestone cliffs, shaped by erosion into fantastic columns resembling the battlements and turrets of old ruined castles, and towering hundreds of feet in height. The camera does not do justice to the effect produced by this strange natural phenomenon. So many are the notable features of this region that a description of Devil's River is not out of place. Its principal source is Beaver Lake, in Val Verde County. Its entire length is only about sixty-five miles, and it is an intermittent stream from Beaver Lake to Pecan Springs, whence its flow is permanent, and is gradually reinforced all the way down by great springs of clear water until its nominal flow is reached. At its source, the country is rolling as far as Pecan Springs, where it gradually becomes more broken, until at a point twenty-five miles from its source the river runs between two precipitous cliffs, reminding one of The Grand Canon of the Colorado River. The place is called Rough Canon, and here the river is almost inaccessible for fifteen miles. The scenery at this stage of its course is wildly beautiful. A person on the bills, near Rough Canon, would never suspect that at a little distance, entirely concealed, was a beautiful, swift-flowing river, for the course is not marked by any break in the topography; yet, mysteriously concealed by deep cliffs, at a short distance below, there flows this grandly beautiful river in its tidy channel cut through the solid rock.

From Rough Canon to its mouth, the landscape along Devil's River is wild in the extreme. The hillsides are scantily covered with thorny bush life, such as prickly pear, sotol (Lasylerion heteracantha), Lechugulla (agave heteranantha), catclaw (acacia weighti), and scrubby mesquite, with scattered bunches of grass on the rocky land.

Under the Spanish occupation of Texas, the Devil's River was named "Rio San Pedro" because of the broken and rocky character of the country. On account of the many disasters which occurred to the early pioneers in finding a suitable crossing for their teams, the Mexicans always said: "El Rio San Pedro es el diablo" (The San Pedro River is the devil). Thus it afterwards became known as "Devil's River."

One of the clauses in the Mexican treaty of 1884 and 1889 stipulates that the flow of the Rio Grande River at El Paso is not to be diminished by diverting the head waters of the Rio Grande. Irrigation in New Mexico for a number of years past has increased to such an extent that there is at present very little flow in the river at El Paso, thus causing the Mexicans pecuniary loss through lack of water for irrigation purposes. Mexico entered suit against the United States for damages, and to offset the Mexican claims, the United States Government, for several years, has regularly employed engineers to measure the streams flowing into the Rio Grande River. The measurements are taken from cables stretched across the streams, from which the operator propels himself, measuring the flow beneath him at regular intervals. The figures recited below are reliable, as they came directly to me from one of the government engineers. He reports: "The Rio Grande has a cross section area of 1,333 square feet river bottom, and discharges under the cable below the mouth of Devil's River 74,275,200 gallons an hour at normal stage. Devil's River has a cross section area of 352 square feet, and discharges 12,787,200 gallons per hour at normal stage. Devil's River supplies about one-sixth of the total flow of the Rio Grande River. The Pecos flow is sluggish and narrow and does not amount to much. The main tributary of the Rio Grande is the Conchos River in Mexico, which empties into the Rio Grande opposite Presidio, Texas. At least seventy-five percent of the volume of the Rio Grande River is supplied from rivers on the Mexican side, and for nearly six hundred miles on the Texas side, from El Paso to Brownsville, Texas, Devil's River and the Pecos are the only two streams emptying into the Rio Grande, except the Pinto and the Sycamore creeks in Kinney County, and these are intermittent streams."

VI. A FISHING TRIP TO DEVIL'S RIVER

At 9 a.m., one Saturday in June, my wife and I boarded the Southern Pacific passenger train at San Antonio for a fishing trip to Devil's River, some 175 miles west. A lunch, a couple of blankets, a few extra clothes and fishing tackle completed as light an outfit as ever a couple started out with to visit a wild and lonely country. The conductor (a friend of mine), at my request, gave me a note to the telegraph operator at Devil's River, requesting him "to try and secure us accommodations if possible" —stating that any courtesy shown us would be appreciated by him. The inhabitants of the section house and telegraph station constituted the entire population. Should we have failed to secure accommodations, we resolved to catch the first east- bound passenger train and return home.

Wheeling west, at the rate of 30 miles an hour, we soon passed the village of Lacoste. Next came to view the pretty little town of Hondo City, with its brand new cottages, brick stores and ornamental, modern courthouse with many gables. At 50 miles from San Antonio we passed without stop the sleepy old town of D'Hanis, surrounded by its beautiful gardens and rich fields full of growing grain. D'Hanis was settled first on December 25, 1844, by emigrants from the Rhenish Provinces of France, headed by Henri de Castro—a French gentleman with a Spanish name who was the father of the colony. He spent $150,000 of his private fortune and succeeded in placing several thousand thrifty peasants on this grant of land. The hard- ships of pioneer life consisted not alone in tilling the soil and building houses, but in repelling invasions from thieving and murdering bands of plains Indians, and many were the trials these people were subjected to — all of which were endured, and, today, there is no happier and more successful community than De Castro's infant colony. They still retain many of the quaint customs and dress of their European homes. Their dialect, spoken in a sing-song manner, sounds strange to a person who is familiar with the German language. They are law abiding, quiet, and very frugal in their habits. They still cling tenaciously to ancient customs, strenuously resisting any charge, and are horrified at the habits their children have acquired since the advent of the railroad.

Looking north from the car window, a long chain of mountains, some 15 miles away, is visible. The mesquite trees cover the surrounding country and appear like an immense orchard of peach trees, the height and leaves of the two trees being similar in appearance. Entering Uvalde County, the landscape changes from the flat, plains surface to the limestone ridges covered with a growth of mesquite, cat claw and other wild plants. In the spring of the year on the many varieties of cacti, protected by an armature of bristling thorns, appear the daintiest blossoms of the most delicate shades of lily-white and dark purple. In the canons the air is redolent with the sweet odor of the wild laurel blossoms, and in the valley the landscape is carpeted with varieties of wild flowers, painted with all the variegated hues of the rainbow. In the grass the lark is trilling sweetly her few notes, while the versatile mockingbirds are dancing with joy from the tops of the highest trees — happily warbling imitations of all the feathered songsters common to this clime.

Ninety-two miles out from San Antonio the train stops at Uvalde. Uvalde was named after Captain Uvalde, an officer of the Mexican Army before Texas was a Republic. He was famous as an Indian fighter. The town is situated near the head of the Leona River, some two miles south of the railway depot, and is hidden from view by immense live-oak trees—only the standpipe of the Water Works Co. and a church steeple being visible from the train. Uvalde has quite an interesting history. It was settled about the same time as D'Hanis. Its pioneers were mostly from the Southern States and East Texas, Fighting Indians, roping the mustang ponies on the prairies, and raising cattle occupied their attention. The rich mesquite meadowlands here were once alive with game of all kinds; and, threaded as it was by many running streams, it came to be regarded as one of the most picturesque and richest pastoral sections of the great Prairie West. The men all went to the front to fight as Confederate soldiers during the Civil War, and the vast herds of cattle roaming on a thousand hills were utterly neglected. The increase of these cattle, unbranded and unmarked, were called "mavericks." Naturally, after the close of the war, the ranchmen's attention was again directed to their neglected interests.

Such opportunities as existed at that time for the rapid accumulation of a fortune in the stock business will never again be duplicated. Thousands of mavericks were roped on the prairies and in the chaparral; these would then be branded and marked. Each ranchman had his separate brand and mark, which was recorded in the county where he lived.

A man's wealth was estimated by the number of calves he branded during the season. An accurate count of his stock was impossible—the range being open for all to run their cattle on the public domain. There being no market for the increasing herds at home, cattle became a drug on the market. Then came the great awakening. One energetic stockman and his assistants rounded-up a vast herd of beeves and started, during the spring of the year, for the northeast. After innumerable hardships he arrived at his destination and realized handsome profits from the sale of his long-horn steers. Thenceforward, every spring, just as the new grass began peeping from beneath the sod, countless herds of cattle commenced their long journey overland to Kansas. No more inspiring scene could be imagined than the process transpiring in the shaping of these herds for the Kansas Trail.

Early in the morning the caballada* is driven to camp: ropes are drawn between trees, and, where no trees are, a long line of men is to be seen holding the tightly drawn cords. The ponies are then driven into this rope corral, and lassos thrown around their necks; then they are led out, saddled up. and, in less time than it takes to tell it, some forty or more cowboys are riding as fast as possible to the main herd, to relieve the night riders. The cowboy with broad sombrero, loosely hung neckerchief, canvas coat, buckskin gloves, pendant revolver at hip, heavy Spanish type of saddle, and spurs jingling from his high-heeled boots, made such a picture as, once seen, is never forgotten. The cowboys now bring in many separate bunches of cattle — all stopping at a certain distance from the main herd of many thousands of long-horned steers. The cutting out, road branding, and the selecting of all desirable beeves now commences.

Listen! listen to the bedlam which has broken loose on this clear spring morning. Calves bleating for their mothers; a thousand cows answering in motherly solicitude; cowboys shouting in English; Mexican vaqueros yelling forth cautions and imprecations in Spanish at some unruly steer that persists in trying to break away from the herd.

---

* Horse herd (from which in derived our English word "cavalcade.")

The commotion caused by many thousands of tramping and lowing animals, the knocking together of horns, and the shouts of the horsemen fairly shakes the earth and presents as stirring a scene of animal and human life as even Rosa Bonheur could wish to behold. How order could ever come out of such chaos, will always remain a mystery to the layman.

The poor cowboy, with no protection in fierce weather save his slicker and blankets, suffered many hardships. On night guard, the cattle would drift from the bed ground for many miles—due to the sleet beating against them—and the herder would have to stay at his post, guarding the drifting cattle, until morning would find him more dead than alive but still on duty. In good weather it was pleasant but monotonous work. The cattle—which had started from their native heath poor in flesh and emaciated by frequent desperate attempts to escape from the herd—are now, after a couple of weeks on the trail, fast taking on flesh and becoming quiet and docile, sleek and glossy. Every day brings fresh pastures of succulent grasses, with abundant water to slake their thirst. All fear of their stampeding is now past. Lost cattle will follow the trail and eventually overtake the main herd. The usual drive was about 12 miles a day.

Arriving in Kansas, the cattle (now in fine condition) are sold, and the cowboy is released from his contract. Many diversions and temptations now beset him. His earnings, accumulated by months of the hardest toil, are apt to be spent with a lavish hand. Wine and worse things than wine meet him at his journey's end. Pleasure being his only thought, he reposes a foolish confidence in the sincerity of his newly-found friends —only to wake some morning to find himself penniless and abandoned. His money gone, no one has any further use for him. With a sad heart he disposes of his favorite pony and saddle, to secure money to defray his expenses home—where he arrives a miserable, penniless and disappointed man.

The owners of the herds sold in Kansas fared little better than their herders. The funds which poured into their coffers from the sale of the "long horns" made these men, entirely unused to wealth, the greatest of spendthrifts. Nothing that money could buy was too good for them. Drinking, gambling, and dissipation went hand in hand. In one short night at the faro table fortunes were lost that required the work of years to accumulate. Pistols were drawn and fired on the slightest provocation from an adversary. On the border every man carried his life in his hands. He who waited for his antagonist to draw his gun first generally found a coffin for a berth and a graveyard for a resting place. No wonder that Uvalde was then called the "wild and wooly town." It was the scene of many disgraceful and horrible crimes—caused by bad whiskey and the desire to pose as a man killer.

Happily, the cowboy of 25 years ago is a character of the past. The conditions that made him then can never exist again. He was a picturesque but disturbing element for the community in which he lived, and it is better that he is gone. Today. Uvalde is as law abiding as any town in the great State of Texas, and is famed for its excellent society, fine schools, and beautiful churches.

Ten miles further on, the train rumbles over the long iron bridge spanning the Nueces River. No water is in sight below, for the river runs underground—coming to the surface two miles below the bridge. Twelve miles west of the Nueces the train runs along the south side of the Anacachio Mountains that run parallel with the track for a distance of 12 miles. Many are the deer and wild turkey that have fallen to my rifle in these mountains. Six miles south of Cline Station are the Uvalde rock asphalt mines; the fame of which for street-paving purposes will, some day, equal that of the Val de Travers mines in France, At Spofford a waiting train on the branch road is ready to carry the passengers to Eagle Pass, where the iron horse crosses the Rio Grande on its way to the City of Mexico.

Our train makes splendid time along the California route and finally stops at Del Rio—-some 160 miles out from San Antonio and a mile or two from the Rio Grande. The beautiful San Felipe Springs burst from the ground here. The water is used for irrigating purposes and many thousands of fertile acres are cultivated. Luscious fruits of many varieties, as well as grain and vegetables, are grown in the greatest profusion. The town, with its pretty white buildings of rock and brick, glistens in the sunlight, while further south several beautiful orchards are to be seen—making this the prettiest town along the Southern Pacific between San Antonio and Los Angeles.

Leaving Del Rio, two miles further on our train runs along, with the Rio Grande on one side and a perpendicular mountain of limestone on the other. Here almost insurmountable difficulties for track-laying were eventually overcome. The sides of the mountain next to the river were blown out and levelled for a distance of 10 miles and the train creeps slowly through this dangerous place, with great walls of rock hanging 100 feet above and directly over the track, with the great river flowing swiftly along only a few feet away. The Rio Grande is here about 500 feet wide, with a very swift current and is noticeable for the total absence of trees along its banks. Looking south, are seen the tall peaks of the Santa Rosa Mountains in Old Mexico — their outlines showing in the distant horizon like clouds. The San Diego River has its source in these mountains, some 30 miles away, from which it empties into the Rio Grande below Del Rio. The San Diego has a greater flow than any other stream on the border; its fall from its source to its mouth (some 27 miles in length) being 3,000 feet (or 110 feet to the mile). Like all mountain streams in this limestone belt, its path is cut through the solid rock, through which its crystal-dear waters flow, and its course abounds in beautiful cataracts. Fish and game of all varieties native to this Western country abound in countless numbers. 'Tis a virgin soil for the hunter and angler, who will here find opportunities for sport that will surpass his wildest dreams. The Mexican laws prohibit the sale of land to any foreigner within 20 leagues of the border. Foreigners caught on Mexican soil with arms are punished and arms confiscated. Permission must first be obtained from the Mexican local authorities before one is allowed to hunt. Black bass and many other varieties of fish abound in this mountain stream; while bear, deer, wild turkey, and the dove-colored, white-winged pigeon are common and even gentle. The native Mexican seldom owns a gun and cares still less to hunt. In winter wild ducks and geese come in by the thousands. This Mexican country, "La Tierra de Dios y Libertad" (The Land of God and Liberty) is destined to be the future paradise for the sportsmen of our Northwestern and Southern States. Vast herds of Mexican cattle are seen from the train, quietly grazing on the hills across the river. Passing out from this dangerous but beautiful place, we enter a more open country along the river. Gazing out from the car windows next the river, one sees a tiny streak of blue water next to the bank; this streak gradually grows larger and larger, until, the train turning north, one can see the deep, blue waters of Devil's River flowing swiftly into the Rio Grande and dividing its muddy black waters far out into the current of the sunlit boundary line between los Estados Unidos and the Great Republic of the South.

After passing the mouth of Devil's River, a couple of miles further on we arrive at Devil's River Station. As this is only a railroad siding, on our getting off, the train once more proceeds up the canon. With some fear as to the outcome of our reception, I boldly mount the steps to the elevated platform forming the gallery of the telegraph station, and present my note from the conductor to Mr, Straw, who invites us to be seated. Mrs, Straw and two pretty children look on us with amazement. My wife and Mrs. Straw are soon conversing like old acquaintances, and we are informed that, on account of a sick child, Mrs. Straw was on the eve of departing for Del Rio on the next East-bound train, and that if it would be agreeable to us, we could stay with Mr. Straw and be bis guests. Of course we gladly consented.

Mrs. Straw had been gone scarcely an hour when we discover that Mr. Straw is a true disciple of Izaak Walton, and he assures us of some rare sport, but not so much as if we had come a month earlier — before the overflow, which had made the river rise some 50 feet (much higher than had ever before been known).

The stream seemed 100 yards across, running swiftly at the rate of four miles an hour, with an average depth of four feet. Large cottonwood and pecan trees line the eastern bank in detached groves. Unchaining a boat, with Mr. Straw at the oars, we are soon on our way across the river. After Mr. Straw had explained to me the general lay of the land, we recrossed the river — my companion having to attend to his telegraph work at the station.

Then my wife and I gathered together our rods, minnow seine and bucket and were soon afloat — headed for the other side of the stream, where Mr. Straw had shown me a likely place for catching minnows. Getting our rods in order, we made a long cast from behind a bunch of cane growing in the river and caught three fine bass. The sun was beginning to set as I changed to a phantom minnow, and in a short time had caught five more bass. How they did fight, with that swift current to aid them! Night coming on, we departed for our haven of refuge. On Mrs. James' going into the cosy, clean little kitchen, she found a hot fire burning; and, as I had already cleaned our catch before leaving the river, supper was soon cooked and the repast was spread out on the open veranda, where we enjoyed the meal in the twilight, with the open sky above us, as only hungry and tired people can.

Night came on, with threatening black clouds massing in the northern horizon, accompanied at intervals by the ominous sounds of distant thunder, promising a storm later on. We sat out under the stars—spinning yarns on hunting and fishing until tired Nature asserted her rights, and we realized that our bedtime had come. The storm that had been brewing attained its full force about midnight, when we were awakened by volley after volley of thunder, accompanied by a mighty roaring of the wind, which every minute seemed to increase in velocity, until the little building sheltering us rocked like a cradle. The •rain came down in torrents and beat hard against the little house; while the flashes of lightning lit up the rough, precipitous cliffs across Devil's River, making them look grander and more awe-inspiring than ever. For an hour or more the storm lasted; then the rain and wind died away, the stars appeared in the blue sky, and there was nothing to recall the tempest save the drip, drip, drip of the water from the eaves of the roof.

Bright and early next morning, we were away to the river again. Not being able to secure minnows, we hired a Mexican to dig some angle worms under the tall pecan trees. Baiting our hooks with these, we cast into the stream, only to discover that the fish would not bite, and the overhanging limbs of the trees made it impossible to cast with the phantom. I noticed a beautiful species of bream in the clear water. It seemed to be about a half pound in weight; the upper part of the fish was of a perch bronze, while the lower part was almost pink in color. It did not appear to be shy, and would let me place the bait almost in its mouth, only to have it recede out of danger. Changing place did not improve matters. I was very desirous of catching one of these beautiful fish, and tried every conceivable way, but without success.

The other side of the river seemed to offer more success; so I divested myself of my heavy clothes; and, with only my lightest garments on, plunged boldly into the swirling waters. Luckily, I retained my hat and shoes, to protect my head from the sun and my feet from the many sharp rocks. In the middle of the stream I was almost swept from my feet by the depth and violence of the current. But, after much persistent effort, I finally managed to get safely through to the other bank; and, once under the shade of the cliffs, I could swiftly send the lure into all the nooks and corners among the rocks, with no overhanging branches to "snag" my hook, and was soon amply repaid by having a nice string of bass hanging from my side. I found this, to me, novel plan delightful. The bottom of the river bed at this point is solid rock and as smooth as an asphalt pavement; the temperature of the water was just right, and the fish, aided by the swift current, put up a game fight.

There was one cast that I made that day which I shall never forget. I was in up to my armpits, when I plainly saw a bass rise and take my minnow and go under and away with the stream. In reeling in, I was surprised at the marvelous impetuosity and great weight of that fish. After considerable labor (which my awkward position doubly increased), I pulled against the fish with my extended rod—throwing all the strain on the reel—when, to my surprise, I saw there were two bass on the phantom, which the strong current had brought to the surface. From where I stood I could not manage my rod and was compelled to let the line slack—all the while striving to better my position. After much maneuvering, I got into shallow water, where I only succeeded in landing one.

True to her promise, Mrs. James met me with dry clothes, and we proceeded to dinner with a fine string of black bass—all caught with the phantom. After a brief siesta, we once more tried to catch some of those beautiful bream that seemed more elusive than ever. How Mrs. James enjoyed that afternoon's fishing in deep water, catching perch and catfish, while I baited her hook with angle-worms! It was amusing to see the awkward way in which she handled the reel at first, but she soon learned its good points and now she would not think of fishing without one.

On the last day of our stay we concluded not to attempt any fishing, as the train that was to carry us back to San Antonio was due at 11 a.m., and so we sauntered up the track to the railroad bridge, catching some pretty scenes with the kodak. On the surrounding hills I noticed many varieties of plant life. The amole plant is here abundant. It grows to a height of about 2 feet; long, ribbon-like blades fall around it, while one straight shoot rises some 5 feet high in its centre. After the blossoms fall, this shoot or reed becomes a barkless stem, straight and hard; and I am told that in pioneer days the Indians used this wood for their arrows.

The amole (sometimes called the "pita") has a potato-like root, which, when dried and crushed, lathers like soap, and the native Mexicans use it for washing woolen goods, such as blankets and the like, to which it imparts a softness and cleanliness that do not follow the use of our common American soaps. Indeed, to-day a famous toilet soap has the amole plant for its basic principle.

On the hills grows the huajillo plant (or, as the Mexicans pronounce it, the "wah-hee-yah"), attaining to a height of some 3 feet and bearing fern-like leaves. Its fruit is a bean that is not unlike our common snap bean save that it is flat. Our Western ranchers all regard this plant as a valued ally. Sheep and cattle will neglect the richest grass, it is said, to browse on the leaves of the huajillo. Its vitality is as great as that of the prickly pear; rough and cold weather have little effect on it. Sleet is the only thing that will make it leafless. During seasons of prolonged cold the cattle and sheep men watch this plant anxiously, as they know that as long as the sleet does not come, their live stock is safe.

Not far from the station the railroad crosses a rugged canon, 50 feet above Devil's River, and the view from this bridge is a grand one. Looking at the beautiful stream, one wonders how it earned its name of Devil's River, which it has borne ever since 1848. In the spring of that year, Capt. Jack Hays, in command of 70 men, left San Antonio for the purpose of opening a road between El Paso and Chihuahua, Mexico. On arriving at the San Pedro River, near its confluence with the Rio Grande, he tried to cross it without careful preparation and met with a number of serious mishaps. There were a number of Mexicans in his party and they voted that it should be called "El Rio del Diablo" (or Devil's River),

Returning to the station in time to catch the train for San Antonio, we sadly bade adieu to Mr. Shaw, who then and there made us promise to visit him again the coming fall. The train soon carried us home, and thus ended one of the most enjoyable trips afield it was ever my lot to enjoy.

VII. MY FIRST TARPON

One Decoration Day found my wife and me at Port Aransas, Texas, the greatest resort in the United States, or in the world, for angling for the "Silver King." The little village of Port Aransas is situated on the northernmost point of Mustang Island. The principal buildings are the government life saving station and Tarpon Inn. Groups of fishermen's cottages are scattered over an area of thirty acres of land sodded with Bermuda grass, with a few oleander and rose bushes to relieve the eye from the absence of all tree life. To the south and east are hills. White dazzling sand is stacked in little hills with such regularity that in the distance they appear like snowy stacks of forage in some deserted field. To the east are the dark blue waters of the Gulf of Mexico, with their long lines of foam- crested waves rolling shoreward, or breaking with great force against the jetties which extend nearly a mile out into the gulf. To the west are seen the quiet waters of Aransas Bay, and the government light house in the distance. Aransas Pass is the narrow deep channel of water between Mustang and St. Joseph's islands, and is also the deepest channel connecting Aransas Bay with the Gulf of Mexico.

Fish life of all varieties peculiar to the gulf waters frequent this pass. Thousands of jelly fish, called "cabbage heads, ' float near the surface, having the appearance of innocent beautiful crimson mushrooms, but armed with a slimy substance that is very painful to animal life. Mullet you see leaping everywhere.

Thousands upon thousands of fish, from the gigantic porpoise to the tiny ink fish, are constantly going and coming from the gulf and the bay. Numerous pleasure boats are anchored in the cove at the end of Mustang Island, some of them belonging to private individuals from the north and south United States, who periodically visit these waters for sport and recreation. In winter, millions of water fowl frequent the marshes west of Port Aransas, and, in season, the honk of the goose and the quack of the duck are ever in the air.

A few words in explanation of my appearance at Port Aransas. Since my earliest recollection I have been a lover of outdoor life; my vacations during boyhood's happy days having been spent in the wilds of western Texas. The farther away from civilization and the wilder my surroundings, the better did I enjoy myself. If I have any particular hobby in outdoor life, I am not aware in what line it is. In January and February I love wild fowl shooting. As soon as the waters in this south land are free from the chill of winter, I find myself with rod and reel, angling for the black bass and other fresh water game fishes that rise to the phantom or the troll. In October I follow my dog after "Bob White." Sometimes I think November and December are the most pleasant months; for then I tread the brown leaves under foot in the mountain districts of West Texas, in a still hunt for buck deer and wild turkeys. In conclusion I will state: for the last fifty years, I do not remember having passed a single season in which I have not had my share of hunting and angling.

Angling, with me, is ever associated with warm weather, tall shade trees growing along clear silvery mountain streams of swift running waters, where one can see the bass before sending the lure for him to seize. It is an actual fact that a friend of mine living near the head waters of the Nueces River, would select the fish among the many that were visible in the clear waters, for his dinner, and would not be satisfied until he caught the one he wanted. During all my years of angling in fresh water, I have experienced every pleasure that a disciple of Izaak Walton could feel, yet I always have desired that I might have the exciting sport of landing a tarpon, the king of all game fishes.

I had spent one summer near Rockport, Texas, and, though I tried many times, yet I never succeeded in landing a tarpon. Tarpon fishing since then has become a simple problem, A rod, best in single piece, capable of great resistance, yet elastic; an up-to-date tarpon reel and line; and a man to row your skiff are the main requirements for success.

At 8 o'clock in the morning, on Decoration Day, three anglers, one from Omaha, Nebraska, another from Austin, Texas, and I, with three separate boats and rowers, started from the Inn, trolling with about forty feet of line out in the channel toward the gulf. The sea was at high tide, and there was little wind. The gentleman from Omaha was just ahead of me, near the right shore, when he hung a large jack fish, a species of king fish which is considered the greatest puller, for its weight, of all the fishes along this coast, I watched the fight with great interest and admired the skill displayed by the angler in handling this powerful fish. He had supreme confidence in his Green- heart rod and tackle, and with the butt of the rod under his right leg, his left hand just below the center of his rod, and his right hand on the reel handle, he held that strong and fast fish taut, giving him no chance to make line, but brought the fish to the surface after a few minutes, the fish furiously lashing the water around it into a foam. The boatman's gaff ended the fight, and the king fish got his freedom. During the next hour I succeeded in getting a few strikes, and caught a Spanish mackerel, I had been all this time on a constant strain, awaiting the supreme moment when I could jerk the steel hook into the bony mouth of the tarpon.

The Omaha man hooked a tarpon about four feet long, near the gulf end of the jetties, which he handled in the same manner as the jack fish. It was exciting and beautiful to see the tarpon spring clear of the water into the air, his silvery scales glistening in the morning sunlight, with wide open mouth, trying bis best to clear himself of the relentless hook. The angler, by main strength and his splendid tackle, gave the fish little line—too little; I thought—for the tarpon, after ten minutes of hard and fast fighting, at last succeeded in clearing itself of the hook. Things had begun to look exceedingly monotonous to me. I was taking more interest in my surroundings than I was in landing a tarpon. The strokes of the boatman, who was now thoroughly tired, were so slow that I reeled my line in and cut off the sinker, which allowed the bait to float with the current. It was very rought in the gulf, I almost began to feel the effects of sea sickness as the small boat would almost disappear in the trough of the waves.

About 11 o'clock, after I had given up all hopes of success, suddenly I received a great shock, like a shot from a rifle, and against all the resistance that I could immediately give, my reel began to sing, and many feet of line disappeared, I not having the experience of the Omaha man in holding my fish in hand from the start. Before 1 could place the butt of the rod under my leg and right hand firmly against the reel, I suppose 150 feet of line was out. After my first surprise was over, I settled down to business. The fish seemed well hooked, and even though I held the reel as tightly as I possibly could, the line continued to play out, and the fish with all its power made swiftly for the gulf. The boatman, backing with both oars with all his might, followed in the same direction. Then the tarpon with a great leap, sprang fifteen feet in the air. The boatman exclaimed, "He is a big one; try to reel in some line." I reeled hard, again and again;

the reel would make one or two revolutions, but no slack could I take up. It seemed something must give. The reel was regulated so as to let line out after a certain resistance, and I was powerless to stop the fish's lunges. Again the giant fish made a leap into the air, shaking his wide open mouth in his vain efforts to dislodge the hook. Fortunately for us the tarpon now changed its course in an opposite direction, towards the channel; the boatman rowed as swiftly as possible in the same direction. Away we sped through the waters, the fish about 150 feet to the right, going up the channel. During this last change on the program I succeeded in reeling up a good deal of line. The giant fish still fought strongly, sometimes on my right, sometimes on my left. He would have pulled me from the boat had not the boatman with wonderful tact, always at the right moment, shifted the stern of the boat to a position where I could command my fish. For nearly three quarters of an hour, the battle was on. I had now settled down to work and success was simply a matter of endurance on my part. I was recovering from the shock of my first surprise, and felt now I was equal to counteract every new move the fish would make, and had my fish well in hand. The boatman saw I knew my business and never once tried to advise me. He and I were both too much occupied to speak. With a shout of delight I passed the gentleman from Austin; the boatman was making for the shore, the tarpon going quickly in the same direction.

We had gone at least a mile from the place where the tarpon was first hooked, and were slowly nearing the south shore of the gulf. Here we rested. The tarpon was lying near the bottom, slowly moving with the boat. Suddenly he commenced fighting to get under the boat, which was only prevented by a heroic effort of the boatman in pulling away from him. I now, on advice of the boatman, commenced to "pump" him (by giving him several quick upward jerks), which brought the tarpon, within a few feet of the boat; and with a spasmodic effort the giant fish succeeded in half clearing his immense body from the water. He went down again still fighting strongly, and we were forced to follow him. The boatman was afraid of my losing the fish, and remarked that it would be dangerous to try and land him yet. Sometimes the fish for a moment would appear exhausted and float on the surface of the water, yet it always regained its power for another effort a few moments later. I now regained my line and kept the great fish taut within a few feet of me. He again floated on the surface as if completely winded, and his wonderful strength was now fast ebbing away, and suddenly I felt the boat driven shoreward. The boatman sprang into the shallow water and grasped the wire leader, which brought the tarpon's head toward him. The giant fish struggled hard, made its last powerful effort to escape, but the boatman gave it no time, and in a few moments had laid the monster on the sand. Hurriedly I sprang after him, but he needed no assistance. Though a fish of such wonderful vitality and strength in the water, it was the most helpless thing on land I ever saw. It could not even flop, but lay at full length, six feet, on the glistening sand, so exhausted that it was powerless to move.

With my kodak I succeeded in taking a few pictures of the tarpon before returning it again to the water.

VIII. A WINTER'S HUNT IN WESTERN TEXAS

One day in December, Ben A. and I started from the Beasley Ranch in Kinney County, Texas, for a deer hunt to the south, in that tangle of brush and cactus called the Wilderness Lake Country. A pair of stout horses drew the Studebaker spring wagon, in which John, a Seminole Indian, had arranged our camping outfit, etc.—packing everything skillfully together and placing over all a heavy tarpaulin with the ends tied tightly down to the wagon-bed. We travelled ahead of the wagon in an open buggy, drawn by a couple of ponies. Leaving Kinney County and the Anacanthini Mountains behind us, we drove south over the low-lying plains, through a sandy soil, on which the prickly pear, the tall Yucca plant, and mesquite trees grew in great profusion. As is well known, much of the vegetation common to this country fairly bristles with thorns.

Many years ago the State of Texas passed an act for the purpose of encouraging railroad building in Texas—as follows: "For every mile of railroad completed, the State shall donate 16 sections of land; the same to be exempt from taxation for a term of 25 years." In consequence of this liberal law, the vacant lands in Western Texas were located by railroad corporations in solid bodies of large areas. Then, the railroad corporations, refusing to sell at a reasonable figure, the land was leased to stockmen. Zavalla and Maverick counties are almost wholly owned by a corporation, and, on account of the remoteness from civilization, are sparsely settled. Many of the ranchmen hereabouts have to travel from 30 to 40 miles to reach the nearest post-office.

We journeyed on for many miles over a dim road, through tangled oceans of white-brush, mesquite, and cat-claw. There was nothing to vary the scene, save that, after climbing some moderately steep hills, the view before us as far as the rim of the horizon would be one solid mass of mesquite and a jungle of low, thorny plant life. Occasionally a tiny streak or dark line, extending across the chaparral, revealed the leafless elm trees growing on the banks of some creek — giving a faint variety to the scene. The vastness of our surroundings, together with the impressive silence that reigned supreme in this wilderness, might well appall the soul of any stranger to this section, and he would feel the force of Dante's famous line, "He who enters here leaves Hope behind." But to a lover of Nature — fresh from the city's humdrum and the busy haunts of commerce and the noise of street traffic — this quietness and vastness were refreshing in the extreme. Here Nature's simplicity was seldom disturbed by the foot of man. Here no dancing brook sang its morning song, flowing over golden-colored pebbles; here no giant trees obscured the vault of heaven; here were no dark canons with deep recesses, no lofty mountains, towering to the fleecy sky, no valleys carpeted with a profusion of painted flowers; but, instead, here was a vast monotony of endless chaparral, through which the winter wind sighed and moaned. Here the rabbit, quail, turkey, deer, peccary, panther, and other wild animals roamed at will and were seldom disturbed. The rumbling wagon startled a rabbit, which rose on its hind legs — looking at us in bewilderment but showing no signs of fear. A covey of quail, whirring through the air, would alight directly in our path. Once a lonely coyote stopped in the road, looked at us, and then noiselessly disappeared in the brush. Then the industrious woodpecker began hammering away on a dead mes- quite tree: mockingbirds sang their songs, doves cooed, hawks screamed, and the chaparral cock uttered his solitary and sad notes. Though there was no variety to the scenery around us, the wilderness was teeming with animal and bird life, giving to the man who traversed its solitude sweet communion with Nature, whose beauty bad not yet been marred by the icy blasts of Winter.

After travelling 33 miles through sand and over dim, dusty alkali roads, we camped for the night at a waterhole in the midst of this wilderness. A flock of mallards, with a loud "Quack! quack!" took wing at our approach. We selected a spot for our camp under the live-oak trees fringing the water's edge: and John, our cook, soon had the weary horses free from the harness and hobbled, and the steady tinkling of the bell kept time with their grazing. A cheerful fire soon blazed on the ground; and, as Ben and I left camp with our rifles, a glance behind at our camp, with John putting supper on, afforded a most cheerful sight. Separating from Ben, I was soon lost in the chaparral. Many deer and peccary tracks were visible; also some wild cattle, which I recognized by their gaunt bodies, long horns, big heads, small frames, and extreme wildness as Mexican cattle—brought from the other side of the Rio Grande, the wild cattle, catching my scent, would dash, frightened, through the brush—their long horns, striking against the trees, sounding like the popping of many whips. One would hardly expect to find game where the country was so disturbed. Night comes on suddenly in this far Southern clime, and, as it was growing late, I hurriedly retraced my steps in the direction of camp. A patter of feet in the thicket ahead caused me to stop, when a "javalino" (or peccary) strutted from the low brush and stopped directly in my path, not 20 feet away. The peccary, when not molested, is harmless; but I have seen an enraged peccary come out the victor after a furious fight with six large dogs, in which some of the dogs were killed outright and others badly wounded, I stood perfectly still for a few moments, until the animal slowly Walked out of sight around a bush. I now moved cautiously away in another direction; but a loud grunt and a champing of tusks not three yards away from my feet caused my heart to jump to my throat. I realized my danger. I was surrounded by a bunch of javalinos, with not a tree in sight, in which to take refuge. I dared not move in any direction for fear of running over these vicious animals, scattered as they were through the brush. It was almost dark, and I was far away from camp, surrounded by the fiercest little beasts in the world. One large boar walked around me, emitting a sound much like a strutting turkey gobbler in courting season. He eyed me viciously, and at my least movement would wickedly snap his gleaming white tusks together—every bristle on his short back being raised in defiance and anger. Had I fired a bullet through his body, his cries would have brought every peccary within hearing to my position. I stood perfectly still— afraid to make the least movement until the last peccary had disappeared—and in this way I succeeded in getting away from that bunch of wild bogs. The stars were not out in the sky, and I had nothing except the faint tinkling of the horse bell, far away, to guide me to camp—where I arrived only after much difficulty and abounding in painful wounds from thorns and briars encountered in the darkness.

After a hearty supper, we stretched our tired limbs on the ground, with the bright stars for a canopy. The bullbats were circling and whirling through the air above us with the swishing sound of an ascending Roman candle. The whip-poor-will was calling, and, far away in the north, we faintly heard the coyote's laughing cry. Then another coyote answered in the west, others joining in, until the very air was a-quiver with their weird serenade. Our dog rose to his feet, growled, looked out into the darkness, and, with tail tucked between his legs, whined piteously as he crouched against mv body. Later, away in the night, the monkey-faced owl uttered its shrill, tremulous whistle. A horned owl, hooting in the tree directly over our camp, awoke us at daylight.

In the morning I went to the upper end of the laguna, where I expected to find ducks. After waiting some time, I became careless, stretched myself full length on the bank, and fell asleep. Opening my eyes, I discovered a red object trotting towards me out of the brush on the opposite side of the water hole. Closer investigation revealed a large buck coming to water, My hand quickly stole to my shotgun. Extracting the duck loads, I slipped in place two buckshot shells. By this time the deer was knee-deep in the water. As I raised my gun, he threw up his head and looked straight at me—some 60 yards distant.

I would have preferred a side shot, but could not afford to wait, and fired point-blank at his front. The shot seemed to stagger him for an instant; then, with a wild dash, he sprang to the bank. I let drive the other barrel at him, but without effect. I hurried around the pond, but could discover no blood; and, as the hard ground retained no trace of his tracks, I disconsolately returned to camp. I regretted I had not taken my rifle with me.

During our long, lonely ride of the day before, we had not seen a field or a ranch house; and we met only one cowboy and a lone line rider.* We now concluded we would travel due west, with that dim road as our only

---

* [The line rider keeps the pasture fences m repair. Some of these pastures are from 40 to 50 miles in circumference.—Ed.]

guide. The country became more open as we advanced, and we flushed several coveys of bob whites. Ben and I followed with the pointer dog. "Spot" was an excellent retriever, but was almost destitute of scent, and, to my disgust, he would actually run over quail. All at once we heard the dog barking furiously at some object in a stunted mesquite tree. A closer inspection showed it was a large wild cat of the bob-tail species. I sent a load of No. 8's at close range into the cat's body, and with Spot's assistance it was soon quiet "for keeps." Spot continued to bark up the tree, and another half-grown cat showed up. I did not have the heart to kill Pussy, but determined to capture her alive. John had now arrived with the wagon, and I called him to bring me the dog chain and a sack. In the meantime the cat had sprung from the tree to the ground. Spot closed in and took hold. The cat's claws cut him cruelly and he let go—the cat springing into another tree. I put on my heavy buckskin gloves, and, taking off my Upthegrove hunting coat, ordered John to climb the tree and push Pussy out with a stick, and 1 would grab her "when she lit." John flatly refused to comply—saying the cat would jump on him and scratch him to pieces. However, John finally mounted the lower forks of the tree, and, with a long pole, pushed the growling varmint so hard that it dropped to the ground. I fell on the cat, with my coat and gloved hands to protect me, and, after a furious scuffle and much cat choking, I had Pussy at my mercy. John quickly tied a cord securely around her neck, to which he attached the chain, after which we dropped the cat into an empty corn-sack and tied the end. John refused to drive the wagon alone with the wild-cat, and I was compelled to ride with him—leaving Ben to drive the buggy.

After a while we passed through a gate into an open pasture, almost free from brush. The rich meadowland was covered with a heavy coat of grass, and the many creeks we passed were full of water. The cattle we saw were fat, very gentle, and highly improved. We met the owner of this beautiful ranch—a Mr, Gus Black, with whom I was happily acquainted. After pleasant greetings, Mr. Black informed me that there had previously been many deer thereabouts, but that, for some unaccountable reason, they had drifted away, and lately he had seen but few. Mr. Black rode ahead, his men following, as he desired to talk "cattle talk" to me as well as to show us a nice site for our camp. Suddenly, in front of Mr. Black's horse, a bunch of deer (lying near the road) sprang up all around us and quickly disappeared. We determined to camp here, as water was abundant in the creek close by. Mr. Black, on the plea of urgent work, refused our invitation to dinner and left with his Mexican vaquetos. Half an hour later, a mounted Mexican (and they are the finest riders in the world) dashed excitedly into our camp, and informed us that el Senor Black had roped "un venado" (a deer) and wanted us to go out to the scene immediately, which we did—going through the prickly pear as fast as possible, the jaunty vaquero easily leading the way. Coming on the scene, there, actually, was an immense buck, strung out between two vaqueros, whose lassos had been dropped over the lower part of the deer's horns. The tautly drawn ends of the riatas were wound around the pommel of each saddle, and in this way the panting buck was held as in a vise. It required the combined strength of the two ponies pulling in opposite directions to hold the captive animal, and it was the most novel sight of its kind I ever beheld. How I regretted that I had not taken my kodak on this trip! Mr. Black presented me with the deer, and Sir Cervus, plunging, pitching and fighting, was brought triumphantly into camp, and the ends of the ropes securely tied to two trees. Mr, Black and his men had actually ridden upon the deer asleep under a bush. A vaquero was the first to dash after the frightened animal; and, the country being open and his horse very fast, the lasso swiftly settled over the deer's antlers. Mr. Black's rope was next around his horns, and the game was up. We kept the buck a captive for one day, but saw that no power in the universe could ever tame him; and so, as we had plenty of venison, he was given his liberty one bright morning. The afternoon before, Ben had killed a fat doe. He could easily have shot the little yearling that followed her, but his heart was in the right place, and, be it said to his honor he declined to shoot. Next morning the wild-cat was gone. She had slipped her head from the noose and silently stolen away.

The next day we started our outfit from camp in time to reach Muerlo Lake for an afternoon with the ducks. We found wildfowl of many varieties there. Ben and I hunted on opposite sides of the lake—our object being to keep the ducks on the wing. We succeeded in bagging 10—although some 4 or 5 more fell in deep water, where it was impossible to reach them without rubber boots. The remaining ducks went out to the middle of the lake, where nothing except a rifle ball, could reach them. About dark we could see great flocks of ducks flying in from the feeding grounds to sleep on the lake, and we succeeded in killing a few more. All night long we could hear the mallard drake's noisy call.

Next morning the fleecy clouds shifted north—indicating a change in the weather. Thousands of ducks passed overhead, on their way to the feeding grounds. We could distinguish flocks of teal, butterballs, sprigtails, spoonbills, mallard, canvasback, and redheads. In winter the first duck to arrive is the teal; the mallard or greenhead is the last. The ducks on arrival are poor in flesh; but, after a month or so of undisturbed feeding in these inland lakes, they become very fat. I shot a flying mallard one winter which broke open when its heavy body struck the hard ground. It was too fat to eat.

The next night we arrived at the ranch for which we had started, just in time to escape a snow storm that came in the night. Next morning the landscape was beautiful. The snow had drifted in heaps at the foot of the prickly pear and yucca plants — the black-brush and mesquite trees looking out of place in their snowy mantles. It was bitter cold, and a great contrast with the hot weather of the previous day. West Texas is noted for its sudden changes of temperature; yet it is very unusual for snow to fall in winter. Then the sun came out in all its glory, and in a few hours only patches of snow were visible here and there. We concluded that afternoon to hunt some wild turkeys that roosted in a thickly wooded canon three miles east of the ranch. We arrived at the canon a couple of hours before sundown; tied our horses; and then proceeded on foot, with the greatest caution, to a grove of live-oak trees a quarter of a mile farther on. Under the live-oak trees we found evidence of their having roosted there the night previous. I waited under the trees, while Ben went to some other large trees above me. A squirrel discovered me, and it was comical to see how intently the little animal watched me. His curiosity led him to within a few feet of my place of concealment, when a movement of ray cramped limbs would send him scampering away in the greatest confusion. He evidently believed my intentions hostile, for he now commenced a furious barking, which attracted his companions, who also joined in his attack on me. I was fearful that the noise would frighten the turkeys that I knew would soon be in to roost, so I did not move. It was almost dark when the sound of many wings striking against the branches of the trees gave evidence that the squirrels' barking had alarmed the turkeys which were now starting to roost somewhere else. As soon as it was "good dark" I made my way cautiously in my stocking feet to their roost. A wild "Put! put!" and the hurry of many wings through the air, showed I was discovered. One turkey alighted in the tree under which Ben was on guard, and he brought it down in good style. With the departure of the sun it began to grow bitterly cold, and we reluctantly concluded not to follow the frightened turkeys. And thus ended our last winter's hunt in Western Texas.

IX. HUNTING IN THE GUADALUPE MOUNTAINS

One Saturday morning at ten a.m. on Nov. 18th. I boarded the San Antonio and Aransas Pass passenger train at San Antonio bound north through the Guadalupe Valley, for a deer and turkey hunt in the hills between Comfort and Fredericksburg. After 10 miles travel the train left the mesquite flats and the San Antonio Valley behind, and ascended the hilly country covered with live-oak trees. On passing through the Leon Valley the country became more broken, and the picturesque scenery was a pleasant change from the monotonous mesquite and cactus country on the plains of Southwest Texas. The train stopped a few minutes at the town of Boerne. The substantial buildings of stone that dotted the Cibolo Valley glistened in the sunlight against a background of bleak and almost barren hills. Many pretty farm houses and fields were scattered here and there, nestling quietly in the rich valley. The town is the ideal health resort and sanitarium of Western Texas. Its altitude, dryness, and cool atmosphere are especially adapted for the curing of people suffering with lung trouble and malaria.

Leaving Boerne, the ascent is gradual until the approach to the Guadalupe River, which the train crosses and proceeds up the valley to the towns of Waring and Comfort. The Guadalupe Valley was formerly the scene of many bloody conflicts between rival bands of wild Indians, who fought for the supremacy of these beautiful hunting grounds.

During the year 1846, the nucleus of the Fisher and Miller Colony was established near Fredericksburg by German emigrants, whose success afterwards attracted others until their settlements were extended to the surrounding valleys. Whenever the German settled, he became rooted to the soil, and to-day Western Texas owes more to the German nation for the sinew, bone, and brain, that made up the splendid material that accomplished more for the development of West Texas than all the other foreign nations combined. The sturdy Germans were plain, honest people accustomed to hardships and rigid economy, and who afterwards became intensely patriotic in their love for their adopted country. Many of these emigrants, by reason of their superior education, soon tired of the hardships of pioneer life in the wilderness, and sought employment in the neighboring cities; and to-day, the most prominent, respected, and wealthy citizens of San Antonio were members of the Fredericksburg colony of 1846, who not only have established great business houses, but are progressive and most liberal in assisting all enterprises that tend to advance the growth and prosperity of their adopted city and country.

At Comfort I left the train, and after partaking of a hearty dinner, departed on the north bound Fredericksburg stage. The driver, a phlegmatic German, was decidedly averse to conversation; but after partaking of beer and cigars, which I had provided, he condescended to impart some information to me regarding the picturesque country we were passing. The road to Fredericksburg was a gradual rocky ascent until near the famous divide between Fredericksburg and the Guadalupe Valley (which years ago balked the advance of the San Antonio and Aransas Pass Road to Fredericksburg), where the ascent became more precipitous, and after a mile of tedious crawling and straining of four horses, we finally attained the summit, From the top of this hill one gets a splendid view of the surrounding country, and as far as the eye can reach the scene is a vast panorama of natural beauty. I could plainly see the cypress trees on the banks of the fair Guadalupe River ten miles away; the frost-bitten leaves, which reflected the afternoon sun, appeared like a slender bank of pale red ribbon extended through the valley, The white rock farm houses and fields, surrounded by rock fences, in which were great hay stacks, and the chimney's smoke curling upward against the precipitous mountain side reminded me of the rustic scene in Sol Smith Russell's beautiful play "Peaceful Valley."

Northwest, far away rose cloud-like in appearance against a threatening horizon a commanding chain of mountains, Around us the gray rock covered the bare places, and the chain of hills was clothed to its summit with grass and trees. The leaves of the Spanish and pin oak were turned by the.frost to a deep red; the leaves of the shumac to a scarlet; while the live oaks, um touched by the winter's hand, were still a dark green. Altogether the scene had a variety of color that was exceedingly pleasing to the eye.

I left the stage at the top of the hill and proceeded on foot along a path on the mountain ridge where walking was delightful, surrounded, as I was, by the rustling sound of the falling autumn leaves. I descended into the valley, where I found the Spanish oak trees growing along the sides of the hills so dense as to be almost impassable; yet in the valley the land is comparatively open. At four p. m. I arrived at the ranch I was seeking, which was hidden from view by a spur in the valley. The ranch house and barns were shaded by large live oak trees and were painted red with white trimmings, ornamented by tall chimneys laid in cut rock, which glistened in the evening sun and looked very pretty against the rugged mountain background seamed with gulches and traversed by ravines, and covered with trees, the leaves of which were red, scarlet, and green. Southward the narrow valley stretched away for a mile, where a sharp turn of a hill abruptly closed the scene. The houses, built on an incline, were terraced and surrounded by substantial rock fences; and everything was arranged most conveniently for both man and beast. It certainly was the prettiest and most complete ranch I ever saw.

After dinner the next day, in company with Pablo, a Mexican vaquero, we shouldered our rifles and went west on foot to hunt deer among the hills some two miles distant. Pablo was in the act of opening a gate, when I observed a bunch of turkeys running up the road some sixty yards in advance. I rested my rifle on a wire fence and deliberately aimed at the rear gobbler, but to my surprise discovered by the snap that there was no cartridge in the barrel. The last of the turkeys had then disappeared around a bush; and when Pablo opened the gate I ran ahead in time to get several shots at a running turkey, but without effect. All had disappeared except one hen, that stopped to yelp about one hundred yards away in the center of the road. I fired, shooting her through the neck. Pablo also succeeded in shooting several times, but missed. The turkeys had taken wing, and were sailing away over the trees in all directions. I told Pablo to continue after deer, and I would try and get another turkey, I returned to the place where the turkeys were first flushed, but made no attempt at concealment, except to lie quietly on the ground under the shade of a Spanish oak and await events. Badly scattered turkeys when not too much hunted will always come together where first frightened. Their yelping now commenced on all sides, and after a while everything was quiet, I had almost given up hopes of seeing more turkeys, when I was suddenly aroused from my lethargy by a sharp "put-put," and casting my eyes in the direction of the sound I saw five gobblers with heads together observing me not twenty yards away. I quietly raised my rifle and fired, killing the largest one in the bunch, when the remainder took wing and scattered in all directions. I did not care to kill any more turkeys, but hung the two birds on a tree near the road for Pablo to bring. On his returning about dark, he found the entire bunch of turkeys roosting in the trees not two hundred yards from the place where I killed their two companions. On my return to the ranch, I found that Pablo had succeeded in killing a fat buck, which be afterwards brought in with a wagon.

Next morning, as the rays of light began to gild the eastern horizon, I had finished breakfast; and sun-up found me on top of the highest ridge, where I arrived almost breathless, after a tedious walk up the stiff long hill. Deer always seek the highest point to greet the rising sun and bask in its warm rays. After a mile of cautious hunting I saw deer tracks in the cow path to my right, and proceeded cautiously along an open path around a ridge. Suddenly I heard a clatter of hoofs on the stony ground; and looking about a hundred yards ahead, I plainly saw two large pair of deer horns moving rapidly over the bunches of low shin oak. The first buck crossed an opening, saw me, and turned before I could fire; the second followed the first; and as he appeared in view, I fired as he made the turn, and I could plainly hear the thud of the soft-nosed bullet as it struck him, but he disappeared from sight. I found great difficulty in trailing on account of the hard ground, and the red leaves which showed no trace of a track or blood. I then proceeded around the hill in the direction in which the deer had disappeared, when suddenly before I could say "Jack Robinson," the wounded deer, hearing my advance, sprang over some bushes and was lost to view in a thicket. I took the trail, which showed a little blood, but I now determined to return to the ranch for a dog, as it was getting late.

After much delay I secured the company of a neighboring ranchman, his son, his two dogs, one a cross between a bull and a shepherd, named "Beaver," the other a full blooded shepherd called "Cherry." I secured my kodak, and mounting our horses, we left hurriedly for the scene of the wounded deer. When we arrived at the place, Beaver immediately took the trail, but lost it. Finally he ran down the hill-side into the valley, where he and Cherry again appeared at their wit's end. We then scattered to assist the dogs, when I observed Beaver running up the steep incline near me. I followed as fast as my horse could carry me up the steep, rocky hill, after the dogs, which were now going straight ahead; and a few minutes later I caught sight of the wounded buck breaking from cover, followed closely by Beaver and Cherry. I waited breathlessly a few moments to locate the fleeing animals, but not a sound broke the stillness except a scuffling in the distance. I arrived on the scene in time to see Beaver catch the buck by his nose and throw him on his knees and hold him fast while Cherry had him by the neck. Not a sound escaped the dogs, so fiercely were they occupied in the death struggle. I sprang to the ground with my kodak ready, and took several pictures of the deer and dogs. The wounded deer succeeded in shaking off its assailants and going a few yards, when he was again pulled to the ground. My hunting knife soon ended the buck's career. The 30-30 bullet had passed through the flesh of one ham below the skin and entered the other squarely in the center, smashing the bone in a frightful manner. This was one of the largest and oldest bucks I have ever killed, and after gutting, it required the united efforts of three of us to place it on a horse.

The following day was beautiful, and not caring to shoot any more game, I spent the time rambling through the woods on the tops of the mountains; the land of which is level and not over 200 yards in breadth, and covered with many varieties of oak trees.

In the late afternoon as I was quietly walking along, I suddenly saw a doe feeding under the trees 75 yards away. I sat down and watched her many minutes. I could see a startled look in her large expressive eyes as she raised her pretty head to discover the scented danger. She stepped so lightly with her sinewy, elastic, and tapering limbs as to become a living picture of wild grace and beauty, with the spirit of the wood around her. What a sin for a cruel bullet to end a life so inoffensive, whose only crime was that she lived. I remembered the deer and turkeys still hanging at the ranch, and allowed her to go unmolested.

The time having arrived for my departure, with many regrets I left this interesting country where my outing had been so pleasant.

X. HUNTING DEER BY STARLIGHT

In the winter of '98, in company with a friend. Sam, and my son John, 12 years old, who had accompanied me on previous hunting and fishing trips, I left San Antonio on the Southern Pacific train Westward bound for a deer hunt in the foothills of the Anacachio mountains. Pulling in at a ranch 12 miles from the railroad, we stayed overnight and arranged for our hunt.

We engaged Juan Garcia, a Mexican, to care for the horses and to cook. He was acquainted with the country, was a fine shot, and a successful hunter. Next morning our wagon and team appeared; and, after packing in our outfit, we left the ranch to camp wherever we found good hunting. A drought had extended through the summer, with no prospects yet for rain. The grass that remained was dry, and the wind scattered its blades in every direction. Cattle, gaunt and dim eyed wandered hopelessly in quest of food and water. Hungry calves on tottering legs were bumping their mothers in vain for milk. Emaciated animals fed on the lower leaves of the prickly pear, where the thorns were fewest, whose sappy substance furnished both food and water; they also browsed on the huajillo, (wa- heo), whose fern-like leaves afforded more substance than the prickly pear.

Few bob whites were seen, but there were many coveys of blue quails, which when flushed would fly a few hundred yards, then alighting, would run rapidly away. It required quick work to secure a shot at this wary bird, but we got enough for supper and breakfast. Meeting an old acquaintance, I learned where the deer were ranging. On account of the drought, game, where not molested, lurked in the vicinity of water. He told us that at his Western windmill among the hills many deer watered, and were damaging the dirt bank of the reservoir by climbing along its sides and tearing the earth away. Arriving at the tank, we looked for signs. There were many deer and coyote tracks in the mud about the trough, which was supplied by a pipe from the reservoir. A float and valve kept the trough full, but leakage kept the ground marshy with water standing in places around the trough.

We made camp i of a mile farther west, so as not to disturb deer coming for water. Sam and I shouldered our 30-30's and, taking different directions, went in quest of deer. John, my son, had obtained at the ranch an old fashioned, brass mounted, rim fire .44 caliber Winchester carbine that must have been in use 20 years. Cautioning him to follow the meanderings of the creek, and by no means let it out of sight, and to return to camp on the same road, Sam and I quickly disappeared in the chaparral.

The wind had died and everything was so quiet that walking was noisy either on the crip leaves or on rocky ridges. After a few hours' diligent hunting I returned to camp before dark, having seen only coyotes, rabbits, and blue quail. Not caring to disturb the quail, I had not fired a shot. I found John sitting by the fire, with a woebegone countenance.

"O, papa!" he exclaimed, "there are lots of deer here."

Then he gave way to tears and could only sob, Juan laughingly told me in broken English that John had gotten into a bunch of deer. Presently John related his experience. He came unexpectedly on several deer lying in a motte of timber. Their curiosity aroused by the quietness of his approach and his diminutive size, they had not tried to escape. John had shot a big buck staring at him, not 20 feet away. It seemed to fall, but remembering my advice not to approach a wounded buck, he had dropped the gun and climbed a tree, while the deer disappeared in the brush. On his way to camp he had three shots at a doe, but failed even to wound her.

His disappointment was too much for him, and he could only find relief in tears and abuse of the old gun. After a hearty supper of broiled quail, baker's bread, Jersey butter, and a cup of hot coffee, we discussed the deer problem. There were plenty of deer in the thick chaparral. They fed all through the bright, starlight nights, sleeping concealed in the thickets all day. The stillness and our own noisy tread revealed our approach long before we came in view; and as the deer had only to step aside in the thick brush and remain quiet, it was impossible to locate them.

After supper Juan suggested that if one of us would conceal himself near the trough and remain quiet the deer would come in for water during the night. Not caring to risk the uncertainty of a rifle shot at night we decided to use a shot gun, of which we had two miserable excuses; one a No. 20 Belgian make,

costing new only $10; the other, a made-over musket changed in the breech to chamber a No. 12 shot gun shell. Finding only one buckshot shell No. 12 and 2 B. B. shells for the No. 20 among our ammunition, Sam selected the musket, and taking a blanket, left for the trough. I do not remember how long he was gone. I was awakened by his plea, "Let me get under the cover." He said he had shot a big doe that had come for water. It was so badly wounded that he had caught it by the tail as it was entering the brush, but it had turned on him so fiercely that he concluded to wait till morning to locate it. Next morning we sent Juan after the wounded deer. He trailed it through dusty paths and over bare hills and found a dangerously wounded 10 prong buck. He killed it, and returned for the wagon to bring in the carcass. On seeing the large buck Sam congratulated himself on not hanging on to the tail hold.

The next morning and evening we walked many miles, but saw no deer. The next night I took my station at the trough with the No. 20 shot gun and 2 shells. I have hunted deer every year since I was a boy 15 years old, but this was my first experience at potting game. I had come a long way for game, and after walking many miles over rough and broken country in vain, I felt justified after exhausting all honorable means, in resorting to this cowardly system of hunting. It was cold, lonely, and disagreeable, sitting against a briar bush through the night, straining my eyes in the starlight.

A coyote came close and snarled at me; I made a motion in his direction; he left and never came back. The coyotes' unearthly howling and the owls' hooting kept me company during my watch. All at once I saw silhouetted against the starry sky, an object which seemed to have risen from the earth. A strange sensation took possession of me; every fiber in my body tingled with the joy of confronting the game which I had traveled so far and striven so hard to find.

I fired and heard the game in the brush, but remembering Sam's experience, quietly resumed my watch. After an hour a deer's head appeared, directly over the trough, not 15 feet from me; it as silently withdrew. In a few moments I saw it again walking toward me, though it made not the least noise. It seemed like hunting ghosts. Stopping in the mire in front of me, it slowly raised its head suspiciously in my direction. Covering its neck- I fired, killing a fat, young buck. I dragged it from the mud, gutted it. left my handkerchief suspended from the bush as a guard against coyotes, and left it for the night. Next morning we found the first deer I shot, not far way, dead.

Loading our wagon with our outfit and three dear, we hunted ahead of it for quail, as that was to be our last day out. We had great sport. Blue quails seldom fly, and will not lie for a dog, but are artful dodgers and fast sprinters in the chaparral. We shot them flying, running, one at a time, and we did not kill more than 3 out of every covey we flushed; in the evening we counted more than 80. Rabbits were plentiful, but we did not shoot any.

XI. HUNTING IN WESTERN TEXAS

Western Texas in winter looks cold and forbidding with its grey clad hills and dark line of leafless trees in the valleys; but in this southland, Nature soon tires of the dreariness of Winter's barren hue, and begins early in the year to clothe the landscape with many delights. The graceful elm trees are the first to don their pale green dresses—conspicuous and beautiful amidst their desolate surroundings. It is spring time. The golden, crisp leaves lie under foot, and overhead, against a leaden sky, V-shaped flocks of geese are flying northward. Buttercups nod a Good Morning to one from between the grass tufts; the wild laurel almost oppresses you with its bluish, sweet-scented blossoms; from the fragrant white cat-claw buds bees are sipping sweetness; the stately yucca surprises you with its mass of cream-colored blossoms, protected on all sides by bayonet-like leaves. Standing on the hills, they appear at a distance like white sentinels on duty, proclaiming to the world that Spring has at last arrived in Western Texas. There is an abundance of birdlife:—including doves, red birds, the golden faced woodpecker, and that sweetest songster of Dixie, the mocking bird. The rattlesnake, awakened from its long winter stupor, delights in basking in the sunshine, and is more active and dangerous now than at any other time. Bob white's cheery whistle is heard over the land, as his thoughts now gently turn to love and matrimony.

During the damp and early days of spring, the scent of wild animals is easily followed by the hounds, and their deepmouthed baying makes hill and valley echo and re-echo as. they follow the trail of some of the hereditary enemies of their race.

Hunting with hounds in Western Texas supplies to the ranchman an element of sport that never becomes monotonous. No two hounds have the same voice; their hunting qualities are as varied as the different traits of people; and a good pack must combine fleetness, scent, endurance, and courage. It is only after long experience that one is able to distinguish by the cry the position of each dog and reasonably foretell what animal is being pursued. The wild-cat will lead the dogs through the thickest chaparral, and unless closely pressed, will run in an immense circle. The fox will exhaust every trick to throw the dogs off the trail before it will abandon its favorite haunts; and, as a last resort, will take to the hills, where I have viewed many beautiful and exciting runs — with every dog in pursuit and baying loudly in chorus after the cunning animal.

My neighbor, William Beasley (whose long white beard and the grey hairs of three score years and ten give him a venerable appearance), in the excitement of the chase becomes a boy again; and it is difficult for me to keep up with him as he rides rapidly through the thickets and pear thorns, yelling encouragement to the dogs.

During the early spring months when work with the cattle is slack, we have many pleasant hunts together. His approach to the ranch was always heralded far away by the glad bark of his dogs, which were met far down the valley by my dogs, in anticipation of the coming hunt. When the dogs saw us saddling our horses and donning our leggings and canvas coats, they would commence the most unearthly howling, and quiet was only restored when, with a wave of the hand, we sent the dogs forward — we following leisurely. The many dogs soon spread out over the country, scenting for game. Our hunts are exciting and attended with many thrilling episodes, especially after a run of many miles after some wily old wild-cat that has long succeeded in evading capture. Oftentimes we could have easily shot our quarry, but preferred letting the hounds have the sport of running him down. Sometimes a cat will double on his tracks for quite a distance and then spring high into a tree, run along limb after limb among the closely growing timber, and, finally, hide in the forks of a tree. The entire pack of dogs would be utterly foiled when they arrived at the abrupt termination of the trail, until some "foxy" old hound, wise in such tricks, by long scrutiny of the different trees would finally discover his feline majesty; and by a glad bark, which all the dogs repeat, would cause the cat to jump into the undergrowth, with all the dogs in full cry behind him.

Along the south side of the Anacachio Mountains, in Kinney County, the ragged canons emerge and form a beautiful level meadow of many hundred acres in extent, which is skirted by immense live oak trees in scattered clumps here and there. In the center of this picturesque place is a dense thicket of thorny vegetation —forming an impenetrable barrier both to horse and man— which bears the local name of "Christmas Mott." The place has its tradition, too, to the effect that, many years ago, an old settler, who was passing this weird spot late one Christmas Eve, plainly saw by the brilliant starlight a most startling apparition. All the wild animals that roamed the hills and valleys were here congregated in countless numbers and all were down on their knees, as if in devout prayer. It is said that the old settler stood appalled— afraid to make the least movement. After watching them for a while, he reverently withdrew and resumed his journey. But, ever afterwards, this beautiful place has been known as Christmas Mott.

One spring afternoon, after a slight rain, Mr. Beasley and I arrived at this picturesque spot. We fully expected to start a panther that was known to resort here, and in a short while the hounds were on his trail in full cry, Our progress was slow on account of the dense briar growth and the hounds were soon half a mile in advance. We left the thicket, and looking north over the broad meadows skirting the timber, we plainly saw a dark object emerge from the thicket and rapidly disappear into the mesquite timber. Mr. Beasley shouted "Bear!" Spurring our horses forward, we soon arrived at the particular spot where the varmint, with the hounds in close pursuit, had disappeared. It was evident, from the baying of the dogs, that the quarry had turned and was not coming in our direction. Soon a large javalino appeared just ahead of the dogs, which overtook him within a few feet. One hound dog took hold of the enraged peccary, which whirled, and, with lightning-like rapidity, gashed the dog terribly in the side—laying the quivering flesh wide open. I realized the danger to the dogs, and, as opportunity offered, rode quickly to the javalino, and, with my disengaged hand, placed my small-bore rifle almost against the wild hog's neck, fired, and killed it instantly.

We did not care to have our dogs killed by the javalinos, and concluded to return instantly to the ranch; but, on our road home, the pack again jumped some animal in the fringe of timber, and, baying in grand chorus, disappeared in rapid pursuit. We were compelled to go around the clumps (or "bosques") on account of the brush, and the sound of the dogs' voices was soon far, far away. One mile quickly passed, than another, but the dogs seemed to be going faster and faster. Suddenly the trailing ceased; and the dogs' glad bark informed us that the animal, whatever it was, was at last at bay. Imagine our disgust and horror to see an immense wild boar. With foam-champing tusks, ears flat on neck, and every bristle quivering with defiance, the old hero stood his ground—the dogs rushing in and as hurriedly retreating from his furious onslaughts. Knowing the danger of those four-inch curved tusks, we attempted to call the pack off, but it was of no use. The snapping of the boar's jaws sounded like the clapping of many hands. Lily, the bravest of the pack, emerged from the melee with one shoulder ripped wide open. A six-months old puppy of hers, rushing to his mother's assistance, was hurled bodily into a clump of chaparral I now dismounted, and approached as near as possible, determined to kill the beast. My first shot only wounded him— causing him to stagger and the dogs to attack with renewed fierceness. But Richard was himself again in a minute, and three more dogs were quickly put hors de combat. As a Mexican vaquero from a nearby ranch put it, it was "una guerra al cuchillo" —a war to the knife. Only two dogs were now able to stand up to him, and I had been waiting for a chance to send in a second bullet. I followed it with a third—this last taking him through the head back of the left ear. He kept his feet for a few seconds, swaying from side to side, and then fell over —stone dead. I secured the boar's hide and had it tanned as a souvenir of the fight—a fight which I hope never to see repeated.

After we had treated the dogs' wounds, we each carried a wounded dog in front on our saddle. The wounded puppy we put in a sack, swung him on to a saddle-horn, and sadly journeyed towards home. The setting sun was casting long shadows ere we arrived at the ranch, and, looking behind us toward the distant hills, we could dimly make out the figures of five of the pack limping homeward. It required many days of nursing before they recovered, and we vowed hereafter to teach our dogs to let wild boars alone.

XII. TEXAS

The Land

A wild beautiful country
Is Texas —
A land of infinite variety and possibilities;
Vast prairies stretch away — spacious, free, trackless-
As far as eye can see.
Grasses, knee-high, restless as the Billows on the ocean.
Quiver and ripple in the strong Breeze;
Hugh cliffs.
Castellated
By Titan hands Through ages
Of Time,
Rise straight
And sheer.
Deep canyons.
Cut by swift Rivers, rise
Like massive Walls in Giant cities.
Rushing, leaping, foaming
Waters roar
Over rocky
Ledges and
Spread complaining.
Breaking themselves
Into bits on rocks Below;
Then flow, broad and wide.
Through cypress lined banks,
Crystalline clear, filled with
Silver hordes of finny folk.
Forests, deep and dark, of moss hung
Live oaks, sycamore, cottonwoods, and elms
Darken the land.
And over to the east and south the great Gulf

Roars its challenge on winter nights
And dashes madly against the unresisting
Shore;
But curls lovingly, hungrily, as she
Washes — washes
The golden sands caressingly on Summer eves, on moonlight
Flooded shores.
Earth, rich in accumulated properties
Gathered and hoarded through the ages.
Is waiting — waiting — waiting for the
Master Hand to unlock
Her treasures.

Animal life too —
The graceful deer and antelope,
The wily coyote who howls on lonely
Hills;
The lobo wolves, fierce, tameless,
Ravening;
The buffalo, the shaggy headed monarch.
Roamed at will — all waiting, waiting,
Watching furtively for
The Master Hunter.

And birds wait too —
Doves, cooing mournfully, comfortless;
Quail, top-knotted, quick-darting,
Whirring,
Running with swift skimming
Movements
Over the dry plains;
Great-eyed owls, hoo-hooing with eerie
Cry and with great golden-yellow eyes
Staring blindly from the trees;
The mocking bird, singing his heart out

To his mate On moonlight nights;
The redbird, flashing scarlet light
From bush to tree.

And reptiles covertly await—
The rattlesnake, sliding, stealthily gliding
Through the brush with sinuous
Movement, rattling warningly, menacingly;
The lizard, sunning himself movelessly
On a stone like an old Mayan image;
Tarantulas, velvet black, with upright
Legs raised—threateningly, ready to spring;
All these—and more—denizens and lords
Long undisturbed, inhabit the land—
The waiting land of Texas.

The People

And after thousands of years they came—
The people,
Red in color like the red earth of the Eastlands,
Sinewy, strong, lithe as the bobcat and
Stealthy as the puma.
Silent people, friendly, not hostile;
Yet fierce and savage when
Opposed or oppressed.
Then
A new people came—
Strong, fierce men from
Over the sea.
The Spaniard seeking for gold, relentlessly
Pressing onward, accompanied by
The Padres—Franciscans, Dominicans—
Pausing to build missions, enduringly Built, Missions
Of rude strength to resist the invader,
Yet with the graceful beauty of
Rose carved windows.

Men of vision, men of God, were these Padres,
Doing what they could to heal the
Wounds made by
The avaricious warriors.
The French too, came to the waiting land.
A gallant, courtly people. Graceful, quick,
Seeking a mighty River's source.
A stockade built,
An enmity incurred.
A new frontier
Destroyed before begun.
Then
Hardy white men — Anglo-Saxons —
Stubbornly pressing southward with
Dreams of wealth untold and
Freedom wrested from the land
By hard labor.
Persistent, bearing all hardship,
Facing death daily,
Fighting nobly, sometimes hopelessly,
But ever winning slowly,
Success at last and Freedom
And Victory — these Men and women of Texas.

The Land and the People

And the waiting Land
Tried each one hardly,
Yielding only to the Master Hand.
Slowly she yielded up her treasures,
Her thick flowing black gold, her silver horde.
Her ripening fields, her snowy
Cotton,
Her flocks and herds.
All these she gave — accepted, welcomed
The Master Hand — the Pioneer.
And still she secrets within her depths,

Her valleys and hills
Untold wealth to be yielded up in
Time to the strong, the persistent.
The Conqueror.
And the Land has become one with the People
And the People one with the Land.

Agnes L. James

www.ingramcontent.com/pod-product-compliance
Lightning Source LLC
LaVergne TN
LVHW032004070526
838202LV00058B/6284